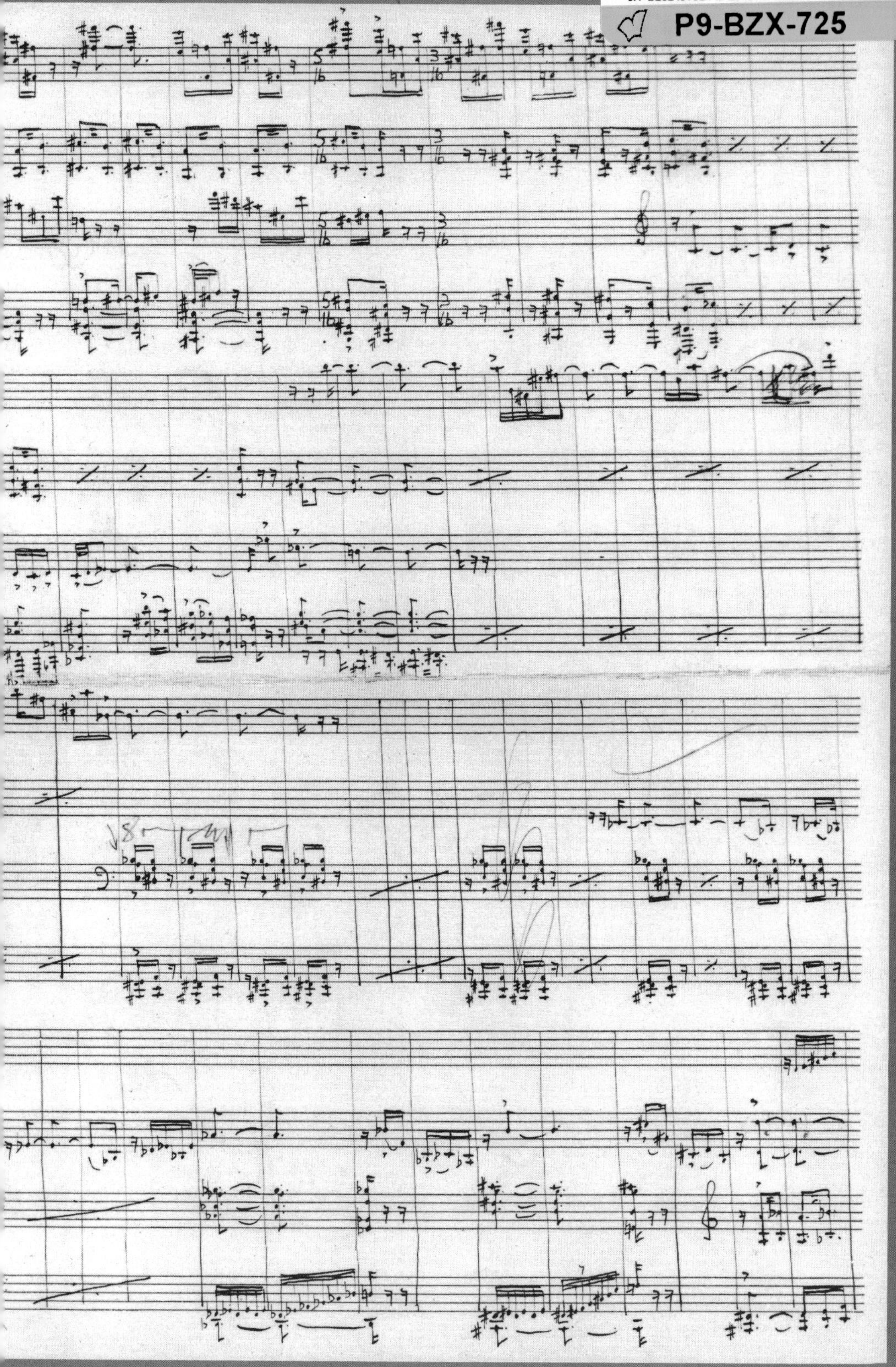

WILLIAM WALTON

WILLIAM WALTON

Behind the Façade

SUSANA WALTON

Oxford   New York

OXFORD UNIVERSITY PRESS

1988

Oxford University Press, Walton Street, Oxford OX2 6DP

Oxford New York Toronto
Delhi Bombay Calcutta Madras Karachi
Petaling Jaya Singapore Hong Kong Tokyo
Nairobi Dar es Salaam Cape Town
Melbourne Auckland

and associated companies in
Beirut Berlin Ibadan Nicosia

Oxford is a trade mark of Oxford University Press

Published in the United States by
Oxford University Press, New York

British Library Cataloguing in Publication Data
Walton, Susana
William Walton: behind the façade.
1. Walton, William, 1902–1983
2. Composers—Great Britain—.
Biography
I. Title
780'.92'4   ML410.W292
ISBN 0–19–315156–1

Library of Congress Cataloging-in-Publication Data
Walton, Susana
William Walton: behind the Façade.
"Missing manuscripts".
Includes index.
1. Walton, William, 1902–1983. 2. Composers—
England—Biography. I. Title.
ML410.W292W3   1988   780'.92'4 [B]   87–24054
ISBN 0–19–315156–1

Set by Latimer Trend & Company Ltd.
Printed in Great Britain by
Butler & Tanner Ltd, Frome, Somerset

Acknowledgements

I GRATEFULLY acknowledge the assistance of the following: Brian de Breffny, for a lifetime of friendship, a colossal memory reviving scenes of our younger days in Forio, and most particularly for his generosity and kindness in extensively editing my corrected draft; Maureen Murray, for giving her valuable time to cut down to a realistic size my first, almost illegible draft; Dr Stewart Craggs, for indefatigable research and for making it possible for William to acquire his letters to Siegfried Sassoon; Diana Foss Sparks and Christopher Foss, for the invaluable early portrait of William, by making available to me his letters to and from their parents, Dora and Hubert Foss.

Of the many others who responded to my requests for information, I thank especially Mrs Grisha Piatigorsky, Lady Camrose, the Dowager Viscountess Wimborne, HRH Princess Ludwig of Hesse and the Rhine, Lord Olivier, Sir Yehudi and Lady Menuhin, Jack Buckley, Griselda Kentner, Dallas Bower, Colin Graham, Angus Morrison, Dorle Soria, John Ward, Neil Tierney, Peter Quennell, Helga Keller, Dr Jean Shanks (Princess Yuri Galitzine), Rosemary Ryan, who typed the final text, Lord Goodman, who extended a protective umbrella over my endeavour, and Mrs Ethel Boosey.

S.W.

Contents

Illustrations

The two pages of music manuscript on the endpapers are part of the material Walton discarded from the original version of the slow movement of his First Symphony (reproduced by kind permission of Angus Morrison).

Illustrations

Illustrations

William with André Previn, Rome 1974 (*photograph: George Mott*)

William at work, La Mortella 1978 (*photograph: Christopher Warde-Jones*)

Susana photographed by Cecil Beaton (*Sotheby's*)

BETWEEN PAGES 178 AND 179

Susana and William photographed by Cecil Beaton (*Sotheby's*)

The garden and home of La Mortella

William and Sacheverell Sitwell, March 1981 (*London Weekend Television*)

William and Mstislav Rostropovich (*photograph: Christina Burton*)

Memorial stone in Westminster Abbey (*photograph: Malcolm Crowthers*)

The tailpiece on page 238 is from a bookplate designed by Gino Severini

1

Courtship and Marriage in Buenos Aires

I T was October 1948. I had been working for the British Council in Buenos Aires since the beginning of the year, when the office received notification from the Council's London headquarters that Dr William Walton was coming as a delegate to an important international meeting of the Performing Right Society, and that we should take especial care of him. I had no idea who he was, and did not realize that I had recently heard his music in the film of *Henry V* shown at the Council.

My first duty was to organize a press conference in our music centre to introduce the forty-six-year-old composer to the Press, and, believing that Dr Walton might be amused to meet someone outside the music world, I asked Bebita Llambi-Campbell de Ferreyra, a young married friend from Córdoba, to come.

I hoped Bebita would provide the female companionship that a European visitor to Buenos Aires would appreciate. She was older than me and very sophisticated, and had taken Lawrence Durrell under her wing when he was teaching English at the University of Córdoba, sent there by the British Council. Bebita had been his confidante when he incurred the displeasure of the provincial university's hierarchy, and eventually she was to inspire him in the creation of his composite character Justine.

The president of the Performing Right Society, Leslie Boosey, was also Benjamin Britten's publisher, and couldn't resist the temptation to be present at the press conference. Boosey, who was shorter than Dr Walton, stood in front of him, answered most of the questions, and generally usurped the occasion. However, this only amused Walton, because, I learned later, it

I

had been the efforts of Leslie Boosey that had made it worth while for serious composers and their publishers to belong to the Performing Right Society. Publishers had previously been more interested in selling music than in collecting royalties, exactly the opposite of what obtains today. William was to explain to me how grateful he was to Leslie Boosey, because he had made it possible for composers to make a living from their music.

After several dreary questions, such as 'Who is the best-known contemporary composer in Britain?', to which Boosey wickedly replied, 'Why, Benjamin Britten, of course,' William was suddenly asked, 'Dr Walton, what do you think of Argentine women?' William's interest in the opposite sex was confirmed when, with only a moment's hesitation, and looking directly at me, he said, 'I think so highly of Argentine women that I intend to . . . meet lots of them.' He told me later that he had been about to say 'I intend to marry one', but thought that that would have caused too much of a stir, as he had only just arrived in the city and had not yet been introduced to me. However, without my noticing it, he had singled me out, and since the beginning of the interview he had been watching me from above Leslie Boosey's head. Years later he was to say that he had thought I was an orphan, but could see that I had possibilities. The orphan look was no doubt compounded by my wearing a copy of the latest Dior 'New Look', a grey woollen dress demurely buttoned from neck to hem with tiny pearl buttons and showing a red and white checked underskirt under a widely flared skirt. I thought this post-war creation was very becoming.

That evening William had determined to arrive before anyone else at the Plaza Hotel, where I had organized a dinner for the British delegates. Alas, the taxi-driver took him on a round trip of the seamier side of town, and he was exasperated to find that he was the last guest to arrive. But, determined not to be thwarted, he suggested after dinner going on to a night-club. I pleaded that I had had a long day in the office, whereupon he suddenly said, 'You will be very surprised, Miss Gil, to hear that I am going to marry you!' 'Don't be ridiculous, Dr Walton,' I spluttered, but he was clearly undeterred.

The following morning he appeared at my office and asked

my boss to allow me to guide him on a shopping expedition. His first question was, 'Have you thought of what I said last night?' I said, 'Of course not, I assumed you were a little drunk.'

Each morning for two weeks William came to my office to go shopping, and each morning for two weeks he asked me if I would marry him. I continued to laugh it off and say no thank you. Poor Mr Montague, my boss, was getting a tiny bit impatient with these daily 'shopping expeditions', and tried to suggest another lady in the office as his guide, but William wouldn't hear of it. We must have walked for miles, up and down the Florida Street shopping area, but only once did we buy anything—a pair of nylon stockings for one of his girl-friends in England, but I lost them within the hour. While we walked, William couldn't resist pulling my leg, saying such things as that the only reason he had accepted the invitation to attend this conference was because he had understood Buenos Aires was the centre of the white slave traffic, and that now he couldn't believe that he had come to the right city.

One morning William was late for our shopping expedition. He explained that he had been summoned with the other delegates by Evita Perón to be at her office at the Ministry of Labour at nine o'clock. However, when they arrived, Evita was not there. Her office was bare, he said, except for an enormous desk and an armchair. After waiting for two hours William got bored, sat at her desk, and inspected all the drawers. Then he further shocked the rest of the delegation by falling asleep with his feet on her desk. Yet another hour went by before she finally appeared, escorted by two burly henchmen who were doped to the eyebrows. She said a few words, looked at no one, and then left. William was very struck by this well-dressed, beautiful, blonde young woman who wielded such power. In the corridors the British delegates saw the hoard of petitioners waiting in line, hoping for some favour from the President's wife. These people believed that a mere glimpse of her or a chance to touch her sleeve would resolve their problems. What the British delegates didn't know was that Evita's secretaries took the name of each applicant and suggested to each how best to please Señora Perón so that she would not forget their request. The supplicants would be informed that Evita venerated, above all other saints, the miraculous Virgin of Luján, so, to be sure of persuading Evita Perón to acknowledge a plea, a petitioner would be told to send her a gold medal of appropriate weight. In this way Evita collected fourteen kilograms of gold medals each day. These medals were duly melted down and sent as ingots to her private account in a Swiss bank. Evita's trusted courier, a young woman friend from her days as an entertainer, who had become her secretary, once tried to keep one of these consignments for herself. It was common knowledge that Evita's secret agents had eventually traced her in Brazil and shot her dead.

One evening, William took me to a ball in Hurlingham, the English-style country club on the outskirts of Buenos Aires, where 'natives' could not then become members. On the return journey, he chased me all the way down an empty train until I found a guard and a ticket controller, by whom I sat. They were my chaperons. William was determined to kiss me, and I was equally determined that he should not. I believe he had never met such reticence before.

The conference was held in Buenos Aires to try to get Argentina to sign the Berne Convention. At the time books were translated and music was played on the radio in Argentina, regardless of copyright dues. William had been invited for his prominence as an artist, and not for his expertise in copyright law, so it was suggested to him that he need not attend *all* the meetings. Hence he had time for the shopping expeditions. President Perón himself presided over the opening ceremony. His speech was cheered by chants of PEE-RÓN, PEE-RÓN, PEE-RÓN. When Leslie Boosey, chairman of the conference, replied in his best French, William could not resist getting to his feet and cheering loudly BOO-SÉY, BOO-SÉY, BOO-SÉY. Perón may have taken exception to this, because, before long, BOO-SÉY was adopted as the opposition's cry.

Retelling this episode of his life to friends in London, William would say with a broad smile, 'I really hadn't wanted to go to Buenos Aires at all. Leslie Boosey persuaded me to go, I suppose to try and cheer me up after Alice's death.'* The other members

---

* Hon. Alice Katherine Sibell Grosvenor, youngest daughter of 2nd Baron Ebury, m. Ivor Guest, 1st Viscount Wimborne. She was William's constant companion in the last years of her life.

of the delegation, including Eric Coates and A. P. Herbert, had all travelled together on a ship from London. William made it a condition to go on his own, as he was having a recuperating holiday in Capri at the time. He took an Italian steamer from Genoa. The British were allowed only £5 for overseas travel in those days, but he had been given an extra allowance for health reasons. The shock of Alice's death had brought on a serious attack of jaundice, and he had just been released from hospital. Michael Ayrton, who had accompanied him to Capri, had, with the help of his mother, who was a Member of Parliament, managed to get an extra foreign currency allowance for both of them.

When he boarded the steamer he was distressed to find that it was full of Germans, possibly escaping from Europe, who seemed to be extremely well off. He took against the passengers, and spoke to only two people during the crossing; one was the barman, and the other was a young lawyer, Rafael Squirru, who, after studying law in Scotland, was returning home.

Rafael remembers how he and William met on the ship and became friends. A fancy-dress dance was being held to celebrate crossing the Equator. William went dressed as an Italian sailor, having borrowed a uniform, including the jaunty cap, from one of the crew. Rafael chose to be an absent-minded gentleman, impeccable in a black tie and dinner-jacket, but without his trousers. The Latin-American mothers, on seeing him, sent their nubile daughters off to their cabins. This farcical incident amused William, who engaged Rafael in conversation, complimenting him on his saucy idea. Of course he was quite decent, as he wore bathing trunks under his jacket; but his bare legs were enough to shock the sensibilities of these 'mammas'.

The coincidence was that Rafael happened to be a good friend of mine; he was a talented painter, as well as a lawyer. At that time he was facing the predicament of having fallen in love with an Anglo-Argentine beauty, Mary Dodds, whose parents wouldn't hear of a 'native' marrying their daughter. His chance meeting with William on board made him an ally who later encouraged and approved of our wish to get married, and he subsequently stood as a witness for William at our wedding. Three months later Rafael married Mary Dodds, overcoming her parents' protests. They are still happily together in Buenos Aires, where Rafael, who founded the Museum of Modern Art, is considered Argentina's leading art critic.

Leslie Boosey and A. P. Herbert were owed money by the Argentine Performing Right Society from funds frozen during the War. William asked them for a loan, promising to repay it in London. Even so he was very short of money, and giving me lunch after our morning shopping expeditions left him almost bankrupt. He complained that I ate huge amounts of food. Argentines were in the habit of eating a lot of meat. The smell permeating the city at midday was of roasting beef, as this odour would emanate from every kitchen. The many building sites where workers cooked beef on improvised grills added to William's disgust, because the severely rationed British were allowed only the equivalent of one of our meals for an entire month's ration!

My family owned an *estancia*, a medium-sized country estate only fifty miles outside Buenos Aires. I drove William out to visit this place on the first weekend of his stay. At least he would get properly fed, I thought. I can imagine his consternation when confronted by my family and friends all wearing large knives tucked into the wide belts which held up their baggy trousers, called 'bombachas'. He later realized that we used the knives to slice off our favourite juicy morsel from the lamb roasting on the spit. This would be one of our *estancia*-bred Romney Marsh sheep, which often won prizes at the yearly cattle show in Buenos Aires known as 'La Rural', where the best livestock bred in the country would compete.

Our man Edelmiro was an expert on how to cook an *asado* and on how to prepare the concoction to souse it with, using a recipe he kept secret. He also looked and dressed the part. He wore the usual gaucho gear, baggy pants tucked into short, accordion-pleated, leather boots; but his belt was superb, heavily encrusted with silver coins embellishing a wide strip of leather with a handsome silver front buckle held by chains. This belt held an impressive knife with a heavily embossed hilt. He wore a slouchy battered hat over his thick curly black hair, and was proud of his handsome moustache. Round his neck he tied a red cotton handkerchief. He was born on the property, son of

6

Italian parents, and my father had moved his family from a mud-baked hut with a tin roof, known locally as a *rancho de adobe*, into a nice little house with running water and electricity that he had built for them. Edelmiro rode a white shaggy-haired pony; he was bow-legged, which made him very short, as if his legs had been moulded by the belly of his horse.

William thus found himself in the midst of an alien group of meat-eaters and knife-flourishers, all seated on colourful woollen *ponchos* on the grass, washing down what he thought were vast amounts of meat with rough red wine, which he did not enjoy. I overheard him telling my mother, in a show of bravado to hide his discomfort, that bachelors were discriminated against in England, since they were not allowed to claim the allowances for dependants that married men could. As William was forty-six, my mother replied, 'Surely you are old enough by now to have solved that little problem.' 'Oh yes,' he answered, 'I have every intention of doing so, and you will be very surprised to know with whom.' My mother was visibly taken aback, and could hardly wait for the weekend to be over so as to warn me not to lead this poor Englishman up the garden path. She had concluded that he had fallen in love with me.

I suppose that Mama was expecting that according to the normal course of events, before long I would be successfully courted and led to the altar by some suitable young man from our own circle. She may not, however, have nurtured very high hopes for my matrimonial chances because I remember as a child overhearing her say to her friend, 'Well, Susana is ugly, poor little thing, but she is very endearing.'

Back in Buenos Aires I was debating what to do. William was certainly handsome; he was also very different from my Argentine boy-friends. They often bored me with the arrogance of their macho ego and, compared to him, seemed quite uncouth, especially the ones who dressed their hair with *gomina*, a sort of glue that transformed it into what looked like a shiny black, compact helmet. But by nature I was fiercely independent, and wondered what life would be like married to this determined whimsical creature about whose work and life I knew so little. There was also the difference in age—almost twenty-five years. Moreover, he was a foreigner. Would I like living in Europe? I thought, I must do something terribly clever; I will ask God; God must decide. I went into the Victorian church near to our house in town, and said, 'Now, God, what about my marrying William? If you make a beautiful bird fly into this church *now*, it will mean you do not want me to marry William. If no bird appears, I will know I must marry William.' Of course, no bird appeared in that dark, black church; my mind was made up.

The conference came to an end, and William was due to return to England. On our last shopping expedition he was silent on the subject of marriage. When I enquired about this change of tactics, he said that, since I had not agreed to marry him, he would never ask me again, but would return to London and probably marry one of the girls there who were waiting for his return. I panicked and blurted out, 'Please ask me just once more, just try.' He did, with a playful grin, because his ruse had worked. Suddenly we were in each other's arms. It was our first kiss, and I was just twenty-two.

My parents were horrified. William was expected to ask officially for my hand in marriage. My father was a very able lawyer; he asked William to come and see him in his office, instead of talking to him at home. William found himself at an even greater disadvantage since it rained heavily on the way, and he arrived drenched. My father attacked first; he stressed how much younger I was, reflected that I might have been carried away by the novelty of being courted by a well-known European artist, and that I could have no idea of the discomfort of living in post-war England, where everything was still rationed. He even added as a deterrent that I would be given no dowry.

To each of these objections William replied, amid sneezes, 'yes, possibly, maybe'. But at the same time he made it quite clear that he could keep a wife and did not expect a dowry. Nevertheless, when my father suggested that the wisest course would be for William to return alone on the next ship to England, and that he would bring me there to see for myself what life was like, he heard himself saying, 'Well, perhaps you are right.'

When he telephoned to tell me of this dénouement, I was taken aback, and anxiously asked if he still wanted to marry me. He replied, 'Yes,' but sounded miserable; so I resolved to handle my father myself. His objection turned out to be that, since we had intended to marry immediately and leave for England, this haste would be construed to mean that I was 'in trouble', and that this would cause a scandal. To pacify my father, we offered to wait a couple of months before marrying.

My two brothers were no help; they begged William to run while he had the chance, telling him that I was bossy, quick-tempered, and ignorant about music, all of which would make his life impossibly trying. I know next to nothing about music to this day. I tried to remedy this by joining a choir in Buenos Aires, but after two sessions they begged me to leave, because all the singers were reeling with laughter at the peculiar sounds I produced. I then resolved to try to learn by correspondence when I got to London. 'One musician in the family is enough,' was all William would say, adding, '*Not* knowing anything about music is your only virtue.'

My father was worried because I would be leaving the country, and he would not be able to keep an eye on this son-in-law. He had written to the conductor Ernest Ansermet, through mutual friends, hoping to find out something, anything, against William; but the reply was: 'If a daughter of mine intended to marry Walton, I would be proud and overjoyed.'

I discovered years later that at the same time a campaign against our wedding had been mounted in London. Many of William's friends, among them Malcolm Sargent and Walter Legge, had been telephoned by Leslie Boosey on his return to London, begging them to save William from 'ruining his life' by marrying a typist at the British Council. One of that coterie is reported to have said, 'By God, William is going to marry a native.'

I also did not know at the time that when William was not with me he was whiling away the hours with an old flame who happened to be staying in the same hotel. She was a blonde, Anglo-Russian former ballerina, a half-sister of the film star George Sanders. She had recently married a Venetian nobleman, who was conveniently away at the time. Alicia di Robilant told William that he should conform to custom and give his fiancée an engagement ring. Since William could not afford to buy one, she offered him hers for the purpose, perhaps because she was insidiously jealous and hoped this might cause trouble. When William gallantly presented the ring to me, I tried to hide my shock at its ugliness. It was a huge, very pale aquamarine in a monstrous setting. I suggested that William take it back to the shop and change it for something less ostentatious. Of course, then he had to disclose its provenance. As Alicia had expected, I was furious. William explained that I should not be vexed, that it was very good for him to distract his mind with Alicia while conducting a chaste engagement with me, as it relieved his tension. I had to admit some sense in this arrangement.

If my father, who had been writing all over the world to unearth something disparaging about William, had only interrogated the concierge of the hotel where William and Alicia were staying, he would have heard an earful. Of course, as a well-brought-up maiden, I never went near the hotel, so that when the concierge who had witnessed William's liaison read in the newspaper the announcement of William's engagement to a young Argentine society lady, he was utterly bewildered.

Alicia's husband returned, and one evening we all went out to a night-club. Andy di Robilant was much taller than me, and, when I danced the conga with him, my lipstick smeared the breast of his white dinner-jacket. When we returned to our table, Alicia noticed this and hissed at William, 'What did I tell you?' She had been warning William that a young bride like me would take off with the first attractive man she met upon reaching Europe. William got into a jealous rage, and dragged me home, accusing me of unseemly behaviour. I laughed, but resented Alicia's sly trouble-making. Although I was not supposed to be jealous, William most certainly was.

When in town we often went out to dance in the evening. William danced the tango with enormous panache, which greatly surprised me. He also astonished me by saying that he enjoyed the oppressive heat of this month of December, which I hated. Having to try on winter clothes for my trousseau made the heat seem even worse.

Now, however, William's ordeal started, the two months of waiting before we could finally get away. He came every evening to dine at home. My father could hardly bring himself to speak to him, and sat in the farthest corner of the sitting-room immersed in reading newspapers. He seemed concerned to know only which clubs William belonged to. My aunts expostulated about the folly of marrying a man so much older, enquired what was a composer, anyway, and how did he earn a living? Mama wept copious tears whenever she set eyes on him, and cried out, 'Que barbaridad!' best translated as 'What a dreadful business!' William suffered his unpopularity with equanimity, but was very pleased when he met our cook, Margarita, who, in an effort to scare off my suitor, had up to then produced disgusting meals. She now discovered that he had blue eyes, and became an admirer and an ally. She transformed mere food into a feast.

After the conference had come to an end, William had no more free accommodation. For the next two months he was lent a flat by Victoria Ocampo, above the printing press of her magazine *Sur*. Victoria Ocampo was well known for her generosity to writers from all over the world, whom she befriended and sustained during periods of stress. She and her sister Silvina were the first to hear of our engagement, even before my parents had been told, because we happened to be dining at their house that day.

Meanwhile, having agreed, for the sake of propriety, to stay on for those two months, William was sent by the British Council on a tour all over the country, to Córdoba, to Tucumán in the north (where he landed in a field thickly covered in locusts), and to Uruguay, where he conducted performances of his own music.

When William returned to Buenos Aires we went to the Colón Theatre, where Erich Kleiber was the conductor and artistic director of the opera. The citizens of Buenos Aires were very proud of having a splendid opera-house, built in the nineteenth century after the design of the San Carlo in Naples. William was very impressed by its having seven floors built underground, where the same-sized stage was reproduced, so that opera and ballet could be rehearsed simultaneously. In this vast complex it was possible to have done everything necessary for a production, from scene design and building to wig-making. The store of costumes, meticulously kept, included those from productions in which Caruso and Melba had sung, and one worn by Eva

Turner when she sang Leonora in *Fidelio*. She, like William, was born in Oldham and, together with Claudia Muzio, was the only foreign singer to be designated 'prima donna assoluta' in Argentina's temple of opera. Léonide Massine's wife was working on *L'Histoire du soldat*, and we saw Leopold Stokowski conduct with a spotlight on his hands, which were sheathed in tight, white, kid gloves.

William disliked being alone at weekends, so I reluctantly gave up my weekly game of golf. My brothers, Harry and Gonzalo, broke in polo ponies on our *estancia*. These lovely, vivacious, small animals were our pets, trotting to the gate of the paddock when my brothers whistled. When I took William to the *estancia* at a weekend, Harry and Gonzalo proudly offered William their ponies to ride. He pretended to be very keen, but, once the pony was saddled, refused to mount, protesting that he had never seen such a huge beast!

Wily William, learning that I was still a virgin, and never at a loss for a solution, bought me a little book with very nifty illustrations so that I could gain some knowledge. At the last minute, just before the wedding, we were stricken with panic. William's passport had got lost in the Paraguayan Embassy, while waiting for a visa. A sudden revolution in Asunción had put an end to a proposed journey there with Sir Eugene Millington-Drake as guide.

Finally, on 13 December 1948, we were married in the civil court. All was well, and we left happily to change before a family lunch to be held at the Jockey Club. While waiting for William I opened a small white booklet given to me by the judge at the Registry Office. On the cover, in golden letters, I read its name: *El Libro de la Familia* (The Family Book). It had instructions for young couples. One of the paragraphs read: 'If three months, have gone by and you notice nothing different in yourself, you ought to consult a doctor.'

I found these instructions so hilarious that I read them aloud to William. He was aghast. 'Does this mean you want to have children?' he asked. 'Because if you do, I am prepared to divorce you now. I have no intention of having children.' True, we had never spoken about having children; I just assumed that most couples produced offspring. It took me some time to calm

William, and to assure him that I was not interested either way, and that, of course, we would do just as he wanted.

It crossed my mind that, if this was so important to him, he ought to have mentioned it before. After all, he was marrying a South-American Roman Catholic, who, he might have presumed, would normally expect to have children. He was so upset by this incident that it made him physically sick and we were rather late arriving at the Jockey Club—a men's club following the English model, where ladies are allowed only in the restaurant, the hall, and one sitting-room. It then occupied a spacious mansion in the most fashionable street. The grand staircase was built of green, translucent agate. My father had given my coming-out ball there. I will never forget the delight of that party: two orchestras played; high pedestals held urns full of fresh spring flowers on either side of the grand flight of steps which led to the octagonal hall where we received the guests, small round tables with centre-pieces of scented flowers were set up for a late-night supper in the dining-room, and we danced till the early hours, when cups of hot chocolate were served to speed us home. The walls in the dining-room were hung with six beautiful tapestries, one of which hid a balcony for the orchestra, carved out of the long side wall.

Mama did not regard a civil wedding as a 'proper' marriage. The only one that counted, in her view, was a church ceremony. So next day she took me to a surgeon to have my tonsils out, as this would, in her words, 'keep me out of trouble'. The church ceremony was delayed until 20 January, because of the difficulty of getting my documents from the police in my married name. When this second announcement in the papers was read by William's friends in England, they assumed he had married twice—different girls, of course.

Preparations for the church ceremony were bizarre. William borrowed a morning suit from broad-minded Andy di Robilant, but he refused to buy wedding-rings, explaining that Englishmen did not wear them. I bought rings for both of us at a second-hand jewellers, and had our initials and the date engraved. I couldn't imagine what the priest would do without rings to bless. We then called at the small church of San Martín de Tours, where we had decided to marry, to book the church and to show William's certificate of baptism and so on. The priest made William pay ten pesos, and asked him to sign a declaration saying that he agreed to our children being brought up in the Roman Catholic faith. He could not grant us a dispensation to marry without this document, since William was a member of the Church of England. It was lucky that the priest didn't understand English, because William was his most irreverent self, muttering that the chap was mad to think that he intended to have children. This was just another absurdity that irked him; after all, he had already told Mama that he was prepared to become a Catholic in order to marry, if this was deemed necessary. We arranged for the ceremony to take place at nine o'clock at night, hoping that it would be cooler at that time.

I bought a white, *plissé*, chiffon ball dress with a glass-beaded embroidered bodice, and for the church ceremony had the dressmaker sew on a new top with sleeves which could be quickly changed back later to the original. My hair was then jet black and very curly, and a short veil was pinned to it by three flat, white, pearl-embroidered flowers. Mama engaged a home film-maker so that she would be able to remind herself of this occasion, as she then believed firmly that she would never see me again.

The small church was crammed. My natural reaction upon entering on Dad's arm was to stop, kiss, greet, and say hello to all the friends and family congregated there. My father just couldn't proceed along the aisle because of all this kissing, all of which made William, waiting at the altar in his borrowed morning suit, even more nervous. As for me, I could hardly stop laughing because between the ferns and the white agapanthus adorning the altar I could see the dark heads of little men with their cine-cameras. John Hind, the music officer of the British Council, had gathered a choir together, and he himself played the organ. As we walked out down the aisle, he played William's *Crown Imperial*, but William declared it unrecognizable.

The reception for two thousand and the supper for four hundred guests in the illuminated garden of our house after the church ceremony were an even more abysmal trial for William. He spent much of the time tugging at his wedding-ring, trying to slip it off. He complained that I was kissed by everybody, and that nobody kissed him. He also complained that, while people in Europe were dying of hunger, the savages here were pelting us with good rice.

The only Spanish phrase that William learned before leaving Argentina, and never forgot, was the one with which my mother had greeted him every evening when he came to dine: 'Que barbaridad!', an expression he used loudly and frequently at the wedding reception. It did not endear him to my father. In fact, my father continued his hostility for years. When William was knighted in 1951, he couldn't resist writing to my father to say that he had accepted the honour only to make me 'a lady'. My father sent back a furious telegram: 'My daughter was a lady years before you ever met her.'

To show his disapproval of our wedding, my father didn't give William a present, and the money he had put aside for my *dot* he spent on the reception and supper after the church ceremony. He bought enough champagne to regale himself with for years to come.

On a recent visit to Argentina I met an elderly English lady who has lived in Buenos Aires, teaching English literature, for years. She was a great admirer of William's, and still remembers that glamorous reception. She has even treasured a handful of the rice with which we were pelted. This dear lady told me that she had never seen such a lively and lovely bride, and had wondered whether I would ever reach the altar amid my greetings. Further, she remembered the details of the chiffon *plissé* wedding dress.

Some years after our wedding the conductor Malcolm Sargent, on a concert tour of South America, heard in Buenos Aires about our extravagant wedding reception. On his return to London Malcolm was quick to tell the musical upper crust that William's wife was not an impoverished little secretary. He came to supper especially to tell me that, although he had loved me from the moment he had met me and, of course, did not care whether I was a countess or a clerk, he was absolutely delighted to have discovered that I was the daughter of a distinguished lawyer, who hob-nobbed with ambassadors and the like. William and I could only smile.

William's father had died some years before; as for his mother, she showed her approval of his marriage only in a very general sort of way. On hearing from William of his impending wedding, she promptly sent a telegram from Oldham to Buenos Aires congratulating him on marrying the pretty girl whose looks she had admired in a photograph he had sent her from Capri. Of course, that wasn't me! I learned later that the girl in question was a young Swedish painter whom William had met before Alice died. He had invited her to Capri, and, after a tearful, loving farewell at Genoa when he embarked for Argentina, she had written to him every day. On arriving in Buenos Aires, William was so overwhelmed to find a stack of twenty-two letters from her waiting for him that in panic he threw them away, unopened. I'm afraid he treated her in a rather cavalier fashion, but she forgave his behaviour and remained a friend. I met her years later in London.

The ship in which we were to travel back to England was delayed because of taking on cargo. During that week we stayed in a cheap hotel in the downtown red-light district, because the money loaned to William by the Performing Right Society was running out fast. Poor Mama was greatly alarmed by the unsuitable place we had elected to stay in, and was even more agitated when she heard that William refused to have children. She said I was certain to become hysterical without children to care for, and she berated William and insisted on the folly of such a decision. William, unperturbed, gallantly offered to help Mama produce a child by him if she was so very keen to add to the family. Mama was a year younger than William, and still of child-bearing age. Instead of being shocked by his proposition, she merely replied, 'And what would Enrique say?' Enrique, of course, was my father.

Despite the ordeals he had been through, William declared that he liked Buenos Aires very much, and would love to return for a visit; but during the thirty-five years of our marriage we never had a chance to return to Argentina together. From the moment I boarded the ship for Europe I was cut off completely from friends and kept in touch only with my parents and my two brothers.

By contrast with the close ties which bind South-American

families, William's relations with his immediate family seemed very offhand. He told me how pleased he had been to find a job for his younger brother, Alec, in Canada, in a branch of the Bank of Montreal, through the good offices of the father of Georgia Doble* who was a director of the bank. When, after the War, serving in the Canadian army, Alec had wanted to stay in London to work in some musical capacity, William had convinced him that he should return to his job at the bank. Alec's passion for music remained a hobby; he became a director of the Bank of Canada and a tireless supporter and fund-raiser for the Vancouver Symphony and Ballet. He and I became great friends.

William also found a job for his sister Nora in New Zealand as the private secretary to the governor-general. When she intended to return to London after four years of duty, he prevailed upon her to remain and marry one of her boy-friends there. She too followed his advice. The oldest brother, Noel, continued to live in Oldham, where he followed in the steps of their father as an organist and music teacher. William's widowed mother lived with Noel and his family.

William could not resist pulling my leg by saying that he had married only because he hated to eat alone, adding that I had the extra advantage of a family far removed. Little did he know what keen travellers my parents were. Their first visit, to see for themselves how we lived, came only a few months after our marriage. They arrived in the autumn of 1949, stayed in the Dorchester, and paid us an unannounced visit. I believe they were not greatly impressed by our house, but were thrilled to be present at the Albert Hall to hear a promenade concert dedicated to William's music, at which he conducted the First Symphony and *Belshazzar's Feast*. At least, they were astonished and pleased by the tremendous ovation.

* Daughter of Arthur Doble of Montreal, and subsequently the wife of Sir Sacheverell Sitwell, 6th Baronet.

2

My Early Life in Argentina

I WAS born Susana Valeria Rosa Maria Gil Passo, and made a wilful unannounced appearance on 30 August 1926 at five o'clock in the morning. My mother tells how she woke up dreaming that she was swimming, and how it took her a few minutes to realize why she felt neck-deep in water; a small dark head had popped out and was waiting to be coped with. Mama was resourceful and clear-thinking. She sent my father off to telephone the midwife, and to ask her own mother to come immediately. Meanwhile, she put on a pair of rubber gloves that were ready on a tray by the bedside, and proceeded to pull me out, taping and cutting the umbilical cord herself, and placing me by her side under the bed covers until more expert help arrived.

My maternal grandmother soon appeared. Mama had been the first of her children to marry, and she was overjoyed with this, her second grandchild. Alas, I was covered from head to foot in long dark hair, whereupon my resourceful grandmother solved the problem by wiping me all over with a wad of cotton wool. Surprisingly, this removed the offending hair; then, for a year, no hair grew. So, from the start, I was a shock, and then a hairless wonder.

My mother's family name was Passo. They were early colonial settlers from Spain, and had a coat of arms of the sort that the French call 'armes parlantes'—that is to say, the shield depicted a play on the name itself. The motto, 'O que mal passo', might be translated 'Oh, what a dangerous step.' William found this singularly appropriate, and liked to think of himself as the knight in armour on the Passo arms galloping towards a broken bridge, regardless of the breach.

My Passo ancestors belonged to that exclusive band of hot-

Wedding photograph of William's parents, Charles Walton and Louisa Maria Turner, 10 August 1898, at the Macfadyen Memorial Congregational Church, Chorlton-cum-Hardy, Lancashire

Charles Noel Walton and his younger brother William about 1906

93 Werneth Hall Road, Oldham, Lancashire, where William was born on 29 March 1902, is the house on the right

Letter from William to his mother from Christ Church, Oxford, dated 23 October 1918

in my rooms. I am taking both organ and piano lessons from Mr Ley now, as Mr Allchin is too busy with the military.

The 'flu' is getting quite the rage round here, I dont know what it is like at home. Mr Marshall one of the choirmen got it and died last night.

I went to the Musical Club last night.

Christ Church
Oxford

Oct 23rd —

Dear Mother

Thanks for your letter and the £1. I have been and am and shall be very busy. The Dean has made all arrangements about sheets etc. And I can go to him for money when I am without.

I have a most lovely Bechstein upright

William in the 1920's

To Willie Walton
from
Kit Wood
Dec. 1925

Portrait of William by his friend Christopher Wood, December 1925

headed young men who defied the colonial government. One of them served on the triumvirate council called 'La Junta', created in 1810. Since Napoleon had deposed King Ferdinard VII of Spain and had set his own brother, Joseph, in his place, the Junta had been formed to govern, as it were, in the name of the king in exile. Subsequently, Ferdinand retrieved his throne, but the Junta still managed to keep the country free from Spanish rule.

My mother's father, Juan José Passo, was a researcher who devoted his life to studying congenital inherited diseases. His mother, Clotilde Alais, who was half French, was the most lively and beautiful old lady, with smooth unwrinkled skin and a shock of silver-white hair. Mother of twelve sons, she remains a legend in our family because of her imaginative cooking. She wrote a cookery book that has been passed down reverently from one generation to the next.

Her unmarried sister who lived with her had weird powers. In the early part of the nineteenth century most men wore top hats; upon entering the house, my grandfather and his brothers would throw their top hats into the air, so that their auntie could stop the hats in mid-air and direct them by sheer will-power to the hatstand.

My mother and her three sisters later decided that they were the spiritual heirs to this power, and they held seances for years. The most lovely one of these four sisters experienced the wonder of materialization. She was fond of gesticulating with her hands while talking, and after a seance would often find them suddenly full of flowers, fresh flowers that were not to be found in the house. One night they were all gripped by the effects of a violent force; one of the sisters was carried to the opposite corner of the room while still seated on her chair, accompanied by a terrifying bang. They concluded that, if the force that had produced the bang had been directed specifically against any one of them, it would most likely have annihilated her. After their frightening experience they wisely stopped having these seances.

Mama's maternal grandfather, José Maria Rosa, would proudly declare that he was a descendant of Salvator Rosa, the family having originally emigrated from Genoa. He was an extremely able lawyer, made a fortune, and served as Finance Minister in two successive governments. Some of his offspring were eccentric, and some distinguished—not at all what one would call a stable family. One night on returning from his club, he was shot at by his eighteen-year-old daughter. This was Mama's godmother, her Aunt Mimi. My great-grandfather's reaction was merely to shut the door of the house and leave for Europe. Poor Aunt Mimi was eventually interned in an institution, where she lingered on for years and years.

Mama and her brothers and sisters had a black nanny named Trinidad, daughter of a liberated family slave. When the family travelled to Europe, an official from the Customs office would visit the house and issue a permit for whatever was thought useful for taking on a long trip, including the cow necessary to provide fresh milk on board for the children.

My great-grandfather on my father's side, Don Enrique Gil y Bañales, was a government official, a sort of spy, sent out to South America from Spain to report on the activities of the restless colonials. As a Carlist appointee, he, unfortunately, could not return to Spain when Ferdinand VII was reinstated on the throne, so he settled in Uruguay with his young family. His son, Natalio Gil, was my grandfather. Apparently his children found him a very difficult parent, subject to terrible rages. He used to ridicule my father, his eldest son, declaring that he was not clever and would be unable to finish his studies. He made a bet with my father, offering to pay for a trip to Europe if he took his law degree before the age of twenty. My father won the trip to Europe by the time he reached eighteen.

He never forgot visiting his Spanish cousins in Logroño; they still lived in the family house in the town of Nalda, on the Ebro river. There he was shown a poster offering a reward for the head of his grandfather, dead or alive. My father was named after him, and inherited a parchment deed given to an earlier ancestor by King Philip V in 1738, testifying to the 'purity of their blood' and embellished with a coat of arms.

The eldest of ten children, my father became a brilliant lecturer and lawyer. He studied at the University of La Plata's Faculty of Law and Social Sciences. The family lived in a rambling Victorian mansion surrounded by a formal garden with fountains and stables, and my father used to ride to lectures on horseback. After the trip to Europe my father continued his studies at the University of Pennsylvania in 1911, Berlin in 1912, and Harvard in 1915. He then opened important law offices in both Buenos Aires and New York, with partners Aldao and Del Valle.

It was fortunate that my father was successful so young, thus enabling him to help his younger brothers and sisters to complete their education, because my grandfather had spent all his money on frequent trips to Europe, from where he would return with fine clothes, English carriages, elaborate toys, and life-size walking dolls for the children, failing, at the same time, to provide for his family's real needs, such as food or shoes. He died in poverty, after a life of extravagance and travel. My father's generosity to his family extended to his paying off the mortgage on the family house, and even to taking his elder sister to Europe and buying her trousseau. He spent several years in the United States championing the cause of the Pan American Union, publishing books on this subject, lecturing, and attending conferences to forward this ideal.

Coming, as he did, from a first-generation immigrant family, though a good Castilian one, he was bound to feel socially inferior by comparison with Mama's patrician clan. My two brothers and I were known as Gil Passo Rosa, thus giving prominence to my mother's family; the surname Gil alone would not have been socially acceptable. My parents married in 1924 in Buenos Aires after a whirlwind courtship. My father claimed that his children would inherit from Mama's eccentric kin 'the bad blood' of the family, and thought we were certain to grow up idiots. We soon learned to tease him mercilessly over this, and to make fun of his terror of our supposedly native blood and idiocy. We would prance bare-foot, confirming, in his view, our 'Indian' blood; and we would swing our arms and hands awkwardly to give him clear proof of our 'inherited idiocy'. The result of this was that he engaged a governess, Miss Roll, to teach us to speak English before we learned Spanish, convinced that these morons would never be able to learn a foreign language. Both my mother and my gentle grandmother had to learn English to communicate with the three of us. We

learned our native language only in school, to the amazement of
the other children, who could not understand why we spoke
only English when we had never been abroad. This gave us a
sense of isolation which was further increased by Miss Roll not
allowing us to bring home other children we met at the State
school; because she did not approve of their backgrounds, she
deemed them unsuitable playmates.

I grew up longing for the summer holidays, which I could
share with my cousins in Atlantida on the Uruguayan coast, one
of the many extraordinary beaches that one finds along that
coast. Crossing overnight on board a romantic Victorian steamer
with shiny wood panelling, converted gas lamps, and ringing
brass bells was an exciting adventure. I can still smell the bacon-
and-egg dish we were allowed for supper as a treat by stern Miss
Roll, and remember the competition between my brothers, Harry
and Gonzalo, about which of them would sleep in the upper
berth.

We would disembark at the port of Montevideo, after crossing the 150-kilometre-wide River Plate, where the bus driver,
who had been alerted to our arrival, would come all the way
down to the Customs shed to collect us, our bicycles, and the
maids; then he would good-humouredly take Mama to shop for
brooms and other necessities for running a holiday home before
driving the sixty kilometres down the coast to Atlantida.

This resort had been started and promoted by a group of
doctors, who had planted thousands of pines and eucalyptuses
on the sandy dunes. It seemed like a private club, with most
owners of houses well known to each other. The golf club was
an enchanting log cabin, with a difficult course laid through
ravines and sandbanks designed to catch the player out. We had
a small sailing boat, and had only to descend through a pine-
clad cliff to the long long beach where Miss Roll made us walk
for miles each day.

We used to spend two months by the sea, and then the next
two months on our *estancia*, while the long hot summer lingered
on. I embroidered, read, and tried to avoid meddlesome Miss
Roll. There Mama taught me to drive our station-wagon when I
was only nine years old, because, she said, she was tired of
having to collect guests arriving at the railway station twelve

kilometres away. I was so short that my nose only just came above the steering wheel, so I sat on a cushion. I am sure our guests were alarmed at being met by a child chauffeur; in fact, some looked quite terrified. The roads, rough earth tracks, had very little traffic on them, because most of our neighbours rode on horseback or went to the village in a *sulky*, a light carriage. I became an expert driver on those mud tracks, so there was little danger of having an accident.

On reaching the age of ten I explained to Mama that I could not make friends at the State school, because Miss Roll would not allow us to invite children home. Mama then agreed to allow me to attend a fashionable, expensive school run by Spanish nuns, whose order rejoices in the name of 'Las Esclavas de Jesus' (The Slaves of Jesus).

Shy of my bright new friends, I elected to do commercial studies, and took a diploma in accountancy, instead of following the usual Bachelor of Arts course. I wanted to excel on my own, and to avoid direct competition. I worked very hard, and made it a point of honour to pass exams with the highest marks. I next took a degree as a public translator in English, and sat for exams in the Faculty for Foreign Languages at the University of Córdoba. The University of Buenos Aires expected students to attend the lectures at the Faculty for Foreign Languages, while the University of Córdoba allowed students who had been prepared privately to sit for exams. My parents preferred that I should continue my studies with the nuns; this was the reason for travelling to the city of Córdoba.

On one of these visits I met Bebita Llambi-Campbell, who had married into the patrician Ferreyra family and lived in the family French-style mansion in the centre of that delightful colonial town. When Mama and I were asked to dine with old Señora Ferreyra, her married son, Bebita, and her married daughter and son-in-law, we found the long dining-table set for thirty people. The food was superb and was served on ornate dishes, which suggested that a large party of guests had been expected; but, apart from the five family members, Mama and I were the only guests. I could see the sisters-in-law congratulating each other across the table for the sumptuous meal, each believing the other one had ordered it. Before the dessert was served, a very worried man called with a delivery van to retrieve the meal, which had been intended for a wedding at a nearby address. We were all reduced to tears of laughter.

My first job was teaching English at the Argentine–American Cultural Institute. This pleased my father, but displeased my then boy-friend, whose family considered my taking any job a scandal. I taught evening classes in which all the students were much older than myself, so I wore a little hat with a veil to make myself look more mature.

I developed the tradition of cooking inherited from my great-grandmother Clotilde Alais by organizing a cooking class with the aid of a teacher at the house of one of Mama's cousins, Marta Rosa. Her genial father, José Maria Rosa, was delighted to be host to our mutual friends, who congregated in increasing numbers for these Tuesday lunches. We had to stop this agreeable entertainment when the guest list exceeded thirty-two. We had become too popular.

Trips abroad were exciting. My father and I once ventured on a motor trip to the northern provinces of Salta and Jujuy, and then flew on to La Paz in Bolivia, the highest capital city in the world built in a natural basin at 3,636 metres. After I had recovered from three feverish days in bed, stricken by altitude sickness, known to unhappy visitors as *soroche* or Monje's sickness (a splitting headache which made even moving to the window of the hotel bedroom a slow and painful business), we motored in a hired car with two drivers to Lake Titicaca, cradle of the ancient pre-Colombian civilization from which the Incas sprang. To reach this inland sea of almost 1,000 kilometres width at a height of 3,810 metres (the highest navigable water in the world), we had to drive through mountain passes to the bleak and windswept *altiplano*, much of it over 4,000 metres above sea-level. (On a recent trip to Cuzco, which is 3,500 metres high, I cured the altitude sickness by the simple expedient of breathing oxygen provided by the kind hotel staff and collecting twigs of wild mint and anis to smell while exploring the archaeological sights.)

I was struck by how primitive La Paz was. After selling their goods in the market-place, the Indian women would squat, one in front of each other, on the pavement outside the hotel,

delousing each other's hair. They wore bowler hats over coloured handkerchiefs which were tied under their chins, and very
wide skirts with the newest one worn over the older ones. These
voluminous skirts contrasted with their slender dark ankles and
feet. To see them dancing was a curious sight: they rotated
slowly, following each other round a circle, stamping the
ground, and lifting a great cloud of dust. They were probably
drunk on *chicha*, a liquor distilled from corn. The high-pitched
sound of the *chena* (a sort of flute) was their musical accompaniment. From the window of my hotel bedroom I witnessed a
horrid spectacle, and was amazed to see that nobody showed
the slightest alarm when out from the bar opposite stepped a
woman and two men, one of whom suddenly shot the other
dead. The contrast between this behaviour and the hospitality
offered us by the rich tin-mine-owners who were clients of my
father was extreme. With them, the food was served on ornate
silver dishes, while a buxom lady in evening dress sang French
songs during supper. We then drove from the *altiplano* above La
Paz down incredibly steep, winding roads to the minor sources
of the great Amazon river, a trip of only a few hours, which took
us from the cold plateau to a lush valley of orchids in bloom and
tropical forests.

Another visit abroad took place in 1946, when I flew to the
United States, accompanying my father, who had been invited
to lecture there. To fly to and from the States was then a three-
day marathon, as aeroplanes were not able to fly by night. The
overnight stop at Manaos, on the Amazon river, was fascinating. It was only a clearing in the jungle beside a derelict town
with a grand opera-house, a relic of the days of the rubber boom.
We braved a tropical downpour to examine the theatre, where
we found a packed audience of Indians watching a play. The
hotel was disgusting. My bed had rusty tins full of water under
its iron legs, to stop the thousands of cockroaches from climbing
up. I followed the pilot's advice and wrapped the mattress in
newspaper so as to prevent the bedbugs from getting at me
through the sheets.

The next stop was the United States. We landed in Miami,
where I found the creole quarters more attractive than the strip of
hotels and beach. Then followed the gift to me of the Golden

Key to Southern Hospitality by the mayor of Louisville, Kentucky, where I delivered my first lecture ever, to the ladies of the local women's club. We then went to Detroit, where we were shown a Ford car being put together from its first screw, in what seemed like minutes. I left my father in New York and went to stay for a few days at Vassar College in Poughkeepsie, on the river Hudson, where I had been asked to give a talk. We met again in New York, and the excitement of seeing this city for the first time, of walking on Broadway, of being taken to its then famous musicals *The Song of Norway*, *Showboat*, and *Bloomer Girl*, of staying in the grand Ritz Carlton Hotel, and of an almost-forbidden trip to Harlem and Chinatown became treasured memories of the naive nineteen-year-old that I then was.

Meanwhile the political climate in Argentina was deteriorating, as Perón and his wife Evita took increasing control. Indeed, my father was actually put in prison by Perón for publishing a financial newspaper which refused to support Perón's more outrageous claims. 'My enemies say that the peso is losing its value against the dollar,' Perón said. 'Now I ask you, which of you has ever seen a dollar? What we need is a plentiful supply of pesos.' 'Bravo,' yelled the crowd, 'PEE-RÓN, PEE-RÓN, PEE-RÓN.' The newspaper was soon closed down, and my father was released from prison. Thinking it safer to go into hiding, he did not return home. One night he warned us that he had heard that the Perónista gangs were planning an attack on our house.

Perón had filled the city of Buenos Aires with *descamisados*. These were mostly poor people from the northern provinces, brought down to the capital by train to ensure that a roaring crowd would hail him whenever he delivered an address from the balcony of the Casa Rosada (the Argentine White House). They were not allowed to return to the north subsequently but were organized into gangs, which Perón made use of to frighten the opposition. The worst form of intimidation was to attack the homes of well-known people. The *descamisados* would assemble in the street and start painting slogans on the fronts of houses, throwing stones, and breaking window-panes. Finally, they would break in if they could, and end by burning the place down. This Perón would later do, with devastating effect, to the

Jockey Club's mansion in town, in retaliation, it was rumoured, for the society ladies having refused to meet his wife, Evita. The building was burned down together with its valuable collection of pictures and its library.

My maternal grandfather wore a revolver when driving to his country place, and would delight us children by showing us how fast he could draw his revolver from under his left armpit, should a thief stop him on his way. The roads out of town were often mere mud tracks, so driving was slow and could be dangerous. My father thought it wise to teach us how to use firearms while we were still very young, because the house on our *estancia* was miles away from any other house. Because my father was forewarned, when our turn came, we were all armed with revolvers. Indeed, my mother had been given a small, elegant, pearl-handled revolver as one of her wedding presents.

We were now instructed as to how to prepare Molotov cocktails to scare the mob away, should they be daring enough to climb up to the first-floor balconies. We peered out nervously through the slats of the iron shutters protecting the ground-floor windows, watching the slogans being painted amid ineffectual stone-throwing and chanting of slogans. But then some trucks arrived with ladders, which could have meant trouble. We raced up to the flat roof terrace and threw down the prepared Molotov cocktails. Luckily no one was hurt, and they had the desired effect of frightening off the mob.

Mama called a painter next day to paint over the slogans, but instructed him to leave a VIVA PERÓN written on the pavement in front of our door, where we had to walk over it to enter or leave. This was soon painted over, surreptitiously, by a Perón sympathizer.

My only European visit before my marriage followed soon after this adventure. A relation of Mama's, Admiral Stewart, and his wife took me under their wing on a trip to Italy on the first passenger ship to leave Buenos Aires for Genoa after the Second World War. Admiral Stewart was director of the Cosulich Lines, which owned the ship called *Argentina*. The excitement of reaching Genoa and setting foot on European soil was short-lived. The Stewarts had to return on urgent business, and my telegraphic pleas to my father to allow me to continue my trip and join cousins in Paris got only the reply 'Return immediately with those to whom I have entrusted you.'

Life in Buenos Aires was very comfortable, despite growing political unrest. We were not rich but the house was always ready to receive visitors. I remember that ample supplies of food were always on hand, and friends were in the habit of dropping in unexpectedly. The large family clan and the close relationships between my aunts and cousins made it fun to call upon them, and amusement was ready to hand seeing them create problems or solve them.

My decision to find full-time employment caused considerable consternation. In Buenos Aires young girls were still supposed to be accompanied by a chaperon when going out in the evening. The idea of working in an office with people 'one didn't know' was unthinkable. My father, who was always careful with money, not to say downright stingy, tried to bribe me into giving up my planned employment. When I contemptuously refused his money, he was heard to remark that he had bred a snake.

I had applied to become social secretary to the Representative of the British Council, Mr Arthur Montague. At the interview he enquired who I was? I replied cheekily that he could look me up in *Who's Who*, and added that, if he hadn't already done so, why was I being interviewed for the job? Nevertheless, he did employ me, but was later outraged to discover that I spent my salary playing golf. The salary was, in fact, so low that I supplemented it by answering an advertisement from a doctor requesting donors of blood from which he made plasma. Every Saturday I would hurry from the office before midday to get to his consulting room, and there, for the princely sum of ten pesos, I sold what looked like a lot of my precious blood. My brothers were most indignant when they heard of this commercial transaction, as they prided themselves on giving their blood to the hospitals for nothing. In 1948 the Argentine economy started to suffer from inflation. This taught me the wisdom of investing my salary on pay-day in gold coins, which I would gradually sell over the next weeks as need dictated.

At first, to get to the British Council's office, I would take a small fast bus called a *collectivo*. Such buses are still nowadays painted in garish colours, with a lot of shiny chrome, and are adorned with violet-coloured lights. They dash in and out of traffic at great speed, throwing the passengers about. I tried without success to get Mr Montague to collect me on his way to the office. Finally, I bought an adorable bright yellow Ford A31 coupé that I loved, despite its nasty habit of belching smoke when I forgot to replenish the radiator.

So when William came to Buenos Aires in 1948, I was working at the Council and continued to do so until shortly before our wedding.

3

Newly Weds

FOLLOWING our marriage we boarded a *Blue Star* liner for our trip to England. It took twenty-three days, stopping *en route* in Santos, Rio, and Tenerife to unload cargo. This gave us the opportunity of visiting these places.

One way round the £5 foreign currency allowance for British residents travelling abroad was to take a round trip on a British liner, as 'on board' was sterling area, and passengers could spend freely. However, rationing was still in force in Britain, and shipowners were restricted from spending foreign currency for their supplies. Moreover, the chef's repertoire was of the dreariest order. Recalling my earlier abortive trip to Genoa on the SS *Argentina*, I was expecting succulent fare, and now I was more than disappointed. The food was quite unpalatable. Even the ice-cream was made from powdered eggs and powdered milk. I complained so often that William felt obliged to apologize for me to the steward, explaining that I was an Argentine; in fact, the only protests came from the passengers who had boarded in Brazil and from me. The ones on the return trip probably thought that quantity was preferable to quality. Of course, they were emerging from years of wartime restrictions.

Most of the passengers were as dreary as the food. In their English way the ladies in their daytime Dickens and Jones divided skirts and aertex shirts and, worse, their evening dresses which looked more like loose armchair covers of chintz cretonne, were as prissy as those Argentine ladies who had frowned on Rafael Squirru's bare legs. Their prim attitudes provoked the worst in William, and he displayed his particular brand of mischief on several occasions. For instance, he decided to give the other passengers something to talk about. Taking advantage of the paper-thin partitions between the cabins, we enacted the following scene every night: he would beat the floorboards with a leather belt, while I let out great cries of agony. As a result, at breakfast the next morning, all heads would turn around to fix us with disapproving glances as we came in. Despite repeated performances, they did not realize that it was a joke. When a party took place to celebrate crossing the Equator, no one dared to talk to me or to ask me to dance. Moreover, the captain felt aggrieved by William claiming that he could not play the piano.

When we reached Rio, I wrote home to say all was well. William slipped a note into the envelope saying how sorry he was that I had caught a cold because of walking about the cabin with only my pearl necklace on. This elicited a furious telegram from my father to me. His fit of anger greatly amused William. Unrepentant, he declared it was a good job he had not seen my legs—'piano legs', as he described them—until after the engagement, when it was too late to retreat; he had married only because he had given his word and was a gentleman! On other occasions he would say how fortunate it was that I found the food on board so indifferent, as this would give me the chance to lose some weight on the long voyage to England, because he could not bring himself to introduce such a fat wife to his friends in London; were I not to lose weight, he would have to lock me up until I looked more presentable. This banter did not distress me, as I could retort in good fun that around his waist he had allowed two Michelin tyres of fat to grow which were nothing to brag about.

I watched my first cricket game on this trip: the crew against the passengers. The captain of the passengers' team decided that William would be of little use, so he left him to be the last man. To everyone's surprise, it was William who won the game for his side, because the crew team was not able to bowl him out. He loved a game of cricket and told me how easy it had been to stay in. William's prowess caused the ladies to congratulate me; they had been nice enough to try to explain the game to me, but to this day it remains baffling.

Most of the time I had the use of the swimming-pool to myself, which was just as well, because it was quite small. After Rio none of the passengers bathed, despite the very fine weather.

Two days before landing at Tilbury William explained he did

not wish to live in London and have a good time; instead we were going to find a place in the Bay of Naples. This idea appealed to me. Naples brought to mind sun and song. I wondered, though, why he had extolled the virtues of his house in London, his housekeeper, and his car, if we were to live abroad.

Our arrival at Tilbury was an ignominious disaster. Customs impounded all my luggage. The British Consul-General in Buenos Aires had thought it was a good idea to have a list ready of all the presents I was bringing with me. I had been told that, changing residence, one would be allowed to bring all one's effects. Not a bit of it. Presents were frowned upon, especially when they included such goodies as sacks and sacks of sugar and tinned hams. I learned that the Socialist government had decreed that everyone should have the same to eat. It took ages to get my possessions into the country without having to pay duty, but I did. I had won my first victory on European soil.

The ship berthed on 15 February. Our arrival was a great relief to the London Symphony Orchestra, since William had to conduct it in his music at the Albert Hall the following Tuesday. The concert was shared with Ralph Vaughan Williams, who conducted the second half. The orchestra later gave a luncheon at the De Vere Hotel to celebrate our marriage and safe arrival.

We finally reached Lowndes Cottage without my luggage. William had proudly spoken to me of this house in London's Belgravia, recently bequeathed to him by Alice Wimborne, to whom he had been devoted for the past fifteen years. He told me that she had been the most important woman in his life, and that, as with me, he had known on their first encounter that he had met the right person with whom to share his life. He impressed on me what a faithful lover he had been, remaining true to Alice for so long despite her being rather older. This was not entirely truthful.

William's secretary, together with Jane Clark* (with whom William had had a passionate affair), had furnished the house with William's pictures and small pieces of furniture from the

---

* Wife of Sir Kenneth Clark, director of the National Gallery, later Lord Clark.

cottage he had owned in Hollyberry Lane, Hampstead. They had bought a splendid double bed on the black market; our rationing points would never have allowed us to buy even sufficient bedding. William offered to take me in his arms across the threshold in the traditional manner, but then he said I was still too fat, and dropped me on the floor with a great thump.

The housekeeper looked me over disdainfully. She had been a nurse, and had come into William's life to nurse him through the attack of jaundice brought about by Alice's death. Then she had simply stayed on to take care of her bachelor patient. She did not approve of him returning a married man. She was also a bad cook, and at mealtimes we would shift the food around on our plates so as not to offend her and then go straight round to Sloane Square to a restaurant for a decent meal. We soon found a Swiss girl called Frieda, with brilliant blue eyes and golden hair, who moved in with her Spanish boy-friend Ramon to replace the tiresome housekeeper.

A taxi came once a week from the Argentine Embassy with a five-kilogram piece of Argentine beef, a heaven-sent wedding present from the Argentine Beef Company. The house had a large kitchen, a housekeeper's flat on the mews side, an elegant staircase, and a hall, dining-room, and sitting-room on the main floor. Alice had improved the rooms by installing old mahogany doors and carved white marble mantelpieces. Our bedroom was very large for such a small house, and, surprise, surprise, the bathroom had a bidet, rare in an English house. The roof terrace was on the landing opposite the bedroom, and I filled it with tubs of plants. That first spring proved to be lovely, and we often used to dine on the terrace.

Only William's music room was a disappointment—so dark that even during the day he could work only with the electric light on. But William had his own dressing-room and bathroom; we felt like the King and the Queen.

When my suitcases and wedding presents were released from Customs and brought to Lowndes Cottage, I sold a large collection of plated dishes from Argentina that the family had given us, as I did not relish having to polish a lot of silver. I also flogged the appalling engagement ring which had been Alicia di Robilant's. I got £5 for it. William found an outlet for a huge number of crocodile handbags that most of my friends had thought a fitting present for someone about to travel abroad. When his lady friends came to tea or drinks to inspect the bride, he would say, 'Su, please find the bag I bought for . . .' I would run upstairs and select the most suitable, in my view, for the lady in question. (Jane Clark got green snake!)

Soon after we arrived in London, we were invited to a party at the American Embassy to celebrate the first visit to Britain of an American orchestra since the War, the Philadelphia Symphony Orchestra, conducted by Eugene Ormandy. I wore my lovely wedding-dress, now turned into a scintillating evening gown, and a tiara of green enamel laurel leaves and pearl berries lent me by Lady Joan Zuckerman,* the wife of William's old friend Solly Zuckerman. King George and Queen Elizabeth were present. As they came down the long gallery lined with guests, I tried to edge to the front row, while William kept pulling me back. Even so, the Queen noticed William; he had told me that she was a Walton fan. She sailed towards us, her head held upright, not haughtily, but like the elegant bannered mast of a ship, her blue eyes smiling, as well as her mouth. She wore a very wide ball dress, the skirt billowing out in soft yellows, glittering with embroidery and jewellery. I was thrilled to be introduced. She further surprised me by knowing that we had just got married, and asked very kindly if I liked my new country. She said she hoped I was not finding it too difficult to manage a house because of post-war restrictions. I couldn't believe that it was me living through this exciting moment. I was captivated.

Jane Clark gave a party to introduce me to William's friends. It was an ordeal. The kindness of the gesture was quickly dispelled by the trauma of the event. Kenneth, who was the kindest of hosts, was away, and I did not meet him until later. Christabel Aberconway† came to collect us. I knew from William what a generous and valuable friend she had been to him in his youth. On the way to Hampstead she said what a pity it was that I had not been to a hairdresser. My Italian hairdresser in Buenos Aires had kept my hair short and very curly

---

* Daughter of the 2nd Marquess of Reading, née Lady Joan Rufus Isaacs.
† Wife of the 2nd Baron Aberconway, née Christabel Mary Melville Macnaghton.

but I had not yet found one in London who had the knack of handling it as well. I realized it looked wild and fluffed out, but I consoled myself by thinking that Christabel's hair was not beautifully combed either. Anyway, my discomfort was dispelled by her adding, 'My dear, of all the women you will meet tonight, I will probably be the only one that William has not been to bed with. Such a pity.' As William had gleefully told me about all his girl-friends, I could laugh happily at this dotty conversation, and anyway William had already told me how he and Christabel had once been at the point of crossing the bounds of propriety while staying as guests of the Sitwells at Renishaw. The fun was brought to a halt by the unexpected appearance of Osbert. Their ardour cooled at once, and such was their alarm that they never tried again. Of course they remained forever the dearest of friends.

Nevertheless, I was baffled by William telling me not to follow him round like Mary's little lamb. On arrival he was taken over by hoards of friends, so I hardly saw him again until we were about to leave, and I felt abandoned. It was difficult for me to distinguish between Henry Moore the sculptor and Garrett Moore,* the managing director of *The Financial Times*, and even to remember who 'Fred' was (Ashton) and who 'Margot' was (Fonteyn). 'Larry' and 'Vivien', at least, were clear in my mind. They, together with Gaby Pascal, the film producer of *Pygmalion*, kept me company. The Clark's home, Upper Terrace House, was full of beautiful objects and pictures. The camellia bushes that bordered the path from the gate to the house were dusted with snow, which made the evening very special, as I had never seen snow before.

I had chosen to wear a black evening dress, which I thought the height of fashion; it would also, I hoped, make me look older and more mature, as I was younger than William's friends. Larry Olivier told me years later how sorry he was that I was put through that ordeal wearing such an ugly dress. He has never forgotten the occasion, and resented Jane going round exclaiming how 'awful' William's young bride was.

When another great friend of William's, Walter Legge,

---

* Viscount Moore, subsequently (1957) 11th Earl of Drogheda.

returned from the Continent, we met over dinner. He was then the supremo of classical music recordings in Europe, and fortunately admired William's music. A friendly rival, Arnold Bax, used to say, 'It was enough for William to fart for Legge to record it.' I gathered that recordings were all-important if composers were to become known and their work was to be heard. William enjoyed Walter's gossip of the musical world: the follies of famous conductors, what new voices and what new music were attracting attention, and especially what Herbert von Karajan was up to, a man William greatly admired after hearing him conduct an exciting performance of *Belshazzar's Feast* a few years before. I found Walter excessively friendly; he indulged in fierce hugs and slobbering kisses on the neck. Walter looked rather German to me, and told endless stories against the Jews, none of which amused me. I wondered whether I was too prudish.

I soon saw what a lot I had to learn! For instance, I had never seen anyone drunk before. We were invited to a reception at the flat of Erwin and Sophie Stein for their daughter Marion, who had become engaged to marry Lord Harewood, the King's nephew. Erwin Stein, a musicologist of repute who had had to leave Germany, had found in Boosey and Hawkes a publisher eager to make use of his knowledge. The popular press delighted in the Cinderella-type story of a beautiful dark girl of modest means and half-Jewish extraction about to marry into the royal family. William, less romantically, claimed that Marion Stein and George Harewood were both admirers of Benjamin Britten's music and were marrying each other because of this bond.

At the Steins' party William started to flirt with the beautiful wife of the pianist Franz Osborne. His attentions to June Osborne caused him not to notice that his glass was being constantly replenished with what must have been home-made gin. William drove the Bentley home at great speed and somewhat erratically, crossing red lights and narrowly missing lamp-posts. He told Frieda he was not hungry. While I dined alone, I heard a great thud coming from the sitting-room. On investigating, I could not, at first, see William, but discovered him, hidden from view, flat on the floor behind the settee. He said that he was paralysed and could not move his limbs, and explained, as if he thought it true, that he had been poisoned by the Steins—an obscure plot, no doubt, to forward Ben Britten's career! I waited till midnight and, when he still could not move, called our doctor, Amando Child. He was very cross with William for getting drunk, and chided him that at his age he ought to have known better.

For George Harewood and Marion Stein's wedding I went to the beauty salon in Harrods, so that I would look my best. I was late returning home, and William had panicked and called the police, thinking I had got lost. The police had amusingly reassured him, saying that wives had the habit of reappearing, and that in this particular case I was certain to turn up since, in their view, everybody in London would have liked to be at this wedding, and we were lucky enough to have been asked.

The King and Queen were present. We found the wedding hilarious, since the Princess Royal looked extremely tall by contrast with Erwin Stein. When Ben Britten, who had composed the wedding anthem, and Peter Pears, who had sung it, appeared dressed as choirboys in white surplices over red cassocks, we burst into giggles and were silenced only by a severe reprimand from John Piper and his wife in the next pew.

During those first months it was difficult not to reveal to William's friends just how ill-informed I was. One evening, dining with friends, William told a story about a friend who had been sent to a sanatorium in Switzerland to recover from tuberculosis contracted during the War while working in the damp cellars of one of the ministries. It appeared that all the female patients had fallen in love with their doctor, while the doctor had shown a particular partiality to one of the young ladies under his care. Another of the patients had become so jealous that she had put a pin through his French letters. At this point I interrupted William to ask why the lady had done this only to his 'French' letters, since the sanatorium housed many different nationalities. Our friends thought it was intended as a joke, and we all had a good laugh. It was not. I was just thoroughly ignorant.

Sadly, my ignorance had unfortunate consequences. In spite of William's little book of anatomical drawings, and of having fitted myself out with an adorable rubber cap, which I thought looked like a larger version of a Coca-Cola stopper, I soon became pregnant. William, as he had warned me on our wedding-day, refused to have the child. I dashed to our doctor, who couldn't or wouldn't help me, and anyway wasn't allowed to because abortion was illegal in those days in England. I was appalled by the fix in which I now found myself. Instead of it being an occasion for rejoicing, I was worried sick, not knowing what to do, and I resented being made to feel like a criminal. But I had either to abide by William's decision or return to Buenos Aires. I wept and fretted, but stuck to William. Through friends of friends we were given an address in the huge complex of the Chelsea Cloisters. We made an appointment and went there together to see the doctor, but William was told to leave, as I would be escorted home.

To be left alone was terrifying enough, but worse was to come. I was escorted to different flats on different floors. In one I had to leave £80 on a ledge; in another I was shown a kitchen table and met a nameless man in a doctor's mask and gown. I started to tremble violently, with the result that he couldn't perform the operation. After a severe talking-to, I managed to control my anguish and go through with it. Of course, nobody accompanied me home. I was put into a taxi, and had hardly reached the house and my bed before I had a severe haemorrhage. I had a week of high fever, but I forced myself to stop crying, because I saw that it made William look very black. I had only myself to blame. I had agreed not to have children, although I had not realized it would mean taking this awful step. I felt quite sorry for myself, and longed to be comforted. I am sure William felt embarrassed, even guilty. It made him look like a monster. But I did not feel it wise to test further the great love that had impelled him to marry me, so I never mentioned this unhappy experience again.

This episode in our lives must have scarred William equally; a couple of years later, after dinner at Lowndes Cottage with Malcolm Sargent, I sat on the carpet and read aloud a passage from *Kama Sutra* which appealed to William's sense of humour. It was a discourse on the pleasures of making love under water. William added his account of the Emperor Tiberius, who delighted in swimming in the clear Capri waters surrounded by lascivious urchins. Malcolm took a rather severe view of this 'nonsense', and started to abuse William for having married a young woman while not allowing her to have children. William immediately flew into a rage and ejected both Malcolm and me from the house. Malcolm went home, leaving me seated on the steps outside our front door until William's anger had abated and he allowed me in again. It was all most unreasonable, since I had not uttered a word while Malcolm and William were debating the pros and cons of having a family.

4

From Oldham to Oxford

AFTER much pleading, I was taken to Oldham, in the industrial north-west of England, to meet William's family. On the journey north William told me how strong anti-papist feeling remained in parts of England, and that his mother would naturally worry as I was a Roman Catholic and we had married in a Catholic church. She adored William, and just as naturally he disliked being worshipped. Further, William's brother Noel, his sister-in-law Enid, and their two children Michael and Elizabeth (who were probably older than me) were all musicians; and he was sure they would all be disconcerted to discover that he had an unmusical bride. He mentioned that Enid, a Christian Scientist, had taken upon herself, with generous good humour, the task of looking after her mother-in-law.

We filled the car with delicious offerings for William's mother and a bottle of whisky for Noel, and eventually arrived in Oldham. It was a tricky encounter. Maybe she was shy too, but his mother's only question to me was, 'Has the Pope got him?' William's nephew and niece enquired what sort of education I had had. They did not comment on my lack of musical knowledge, and I found their reserve rather a relief. My family had left William in no doubt as to how unpopular he was, while I was left in blissful ignorance as to their opinion of their Uncle Willie's young wife. We arrived in time for high tea; William explained that this was the meal which took the place of both tea and dinner rolled into one.

Visits to Oldham to see his mother forcibly brought back to William how lucky his life had been, how free. This desire to feel free had developed in William, I believe, at a very early age. It partly had to do with money, or rather lack of it, and partly with the unavoidable obligation he felt to work as a composer, which meant escaping his family background. He was born on 29 March 1902 in Oldham in Lancashire, in the north-west of England; he told me that hardly anyone would guess it now from his accent. He was the second of four children.

In his young days Oldham was a pleasant place. His father, Charles Walton, had been a singing teacher and a choirmaster. In fact, he had been one of the first students at the Royal Manchester College of Music when it opened in 1893 with Sir Charles Hallé as its first principal. William's father had probably settled in Oldham because in those days it was very difficult to make a living as a singer (he was a bass-baritone). He had needed a job, which he found in Platt's Ironworks in Oldham. William would often remark that his father was a very good singer and, had he been alive after broadcasting started, he would have been very well known indeed. As it was, he was well known in his district. He gave a recital about once a year, with a local pianist called Willy Lawton. He was also choirmaster of St John's Church, in the district of Oldham. So William's upbringing was very Anglican and, because of his father, he was made to sing in the choir, which he didn't enjoy. He is supposed to have been able to sing before he could read, so when he was little he had not minded singing in the choir; but when he grew up, his father would rap him on the knuckles with his ring whenever he made a mistake, which he rather objected to. The father was very severe, had a violent temper, and was a keen disciplinarian.

William's mother was also a singer; she was a contralto and it was while singing at recitals, at Chorlton-cum-Hardy, that the parents had met. An uncle lived there and William remembered it as a very pleasant part of the world; he had been sent to stay with this uncle when his younger brother, Alec, was born. Mrs Walton's maiden name was Turner. Her family were quite well known as upholsterers and furniture makers, and her father was an excise man in Hull. The tradition in the Turner family is that they were commissioned by Albert, Prince Consort, to make some furniture for Buckingham Palace.

The house William was born in, 93 Werneth Hall Road, was small, one of a row of cottages by a coppice. The look rather respectable but, until recently, had outside loos. His first school was a kindergarten about twenty yards up the road run by a Miss Wilson. He liked this school and remembered meeting there a girl called Eileen Slight. The thought of her always made him giggle as he wondered if she'd still be around. He seems to have been high-spirited and restless from an early age. He delighted in telling me how he had built a wooden platform on four wheels, and how he used to sit his younger sister Nora on it, and push it off from the top of the hill behind the house. He had to run down the hill very fast to catch his 'sledge' before it hit the road to Manchester and the traffic at the foot of the hill.

Because his father couldn't afford to send the second son to the local grammar school, William was sent to a board school. It was not a boarding school, only a board school, and William found it very rough. He resented having the girls separated from the boys by an iron grill. He thought his father had decided to bring him down a peg or two, that he probably deserved. But one day the parents saw in the *Manchester City News* an advertisement about probationer choristers being needed at Christ Church, Oxford. William was nine and, though a bit old for a chorister, they decided to take him for the audition. In fact, they almost didn't go at all; the father had been to the pub the night before and failed to return, so Mrs Walton had to borrow money for the trip from the neighbours. She was finally lent it by the local greengrocer.

The journey from Oldham to Oxford was a long one, about four or five hours, and William had never been on a long train journey before. He was frightfully sick, but, worse, they arrived so late that the singing trial was already over. However, his formidable mother persuaded Dr Thomas Strong, who was then the Dean of Christ Church, and the organist, Henry Ley, to listen to her child. He was asked to sing a piece by Marcello known as 'O Lord, Our Governor' and then was told to sing the middle note of five, a thing he had never done before. He sailed through this little test, and was chosen. He joined the Christ Church Cathedral choir school, where he stayed for six years. Of course he was homesick at first and because of his broad Lancashire accent was bullied by the other boys until he spoke like them, 'properly' as they thought. The school boys got up at seven, had breakfast, then a lesson, and at ten had a choir practice and another one in the afternoon. They also sang at two services a day. Quite a tough discipline. William would often say that their education was almost nil and this was the reason for his supposedly not being able to read or write. It probably was a pretty poor education as, when the First World War came, anyone of age who might have been a schoolmaster was in the army. He would often express the opinion that his musical education consisted of nothing but ploughing through the English anthems. Not quite true, as they had tried to teach him to play the piano, but had not succeeded because of his clumsy hands.

The dean had determined that William should be trained as an organist to help him earn a living, but, perhaps fortunately, he showed no aptitude for musical instruments. He also tried to learn how to play the violin, but because he could not organize his fingers properly he found this excruciating torture. On the other hand he was good at sports, ran the hundred yards, did well in football, and, because he was so small, was allowed to cox the boat of the college. He once ran it aground at the curve of the river and it amused him to tell how he was admonished from the shore over the megaphone: 'Cox, you've buggered that boat' came over loud and clear.

William remembered Oxford as the most beautiful place he had ever seen; Christ Church itself, the quadrangle, and Tom Tower were his lovely new world. To avoid having to return to Oldham when his voice broke, he decided to make himself interesting in the only way he knew, so he set pen to paper and started to write music. And because of his composing he managed to stay on at the choir school. Years later Dean Strong, who was by then Bishop of Oxford, recalled in a letter to Hubert Foss his impression of William at the time (Foss was by then William's publisher):

One Sunday when Walton was in the choir, he brought with him a large bundle of music paper covered with his compositions; he was about fifteen. He asked if he might leave them for me to look at, and then dumped them on the table in my hall. It so happened that the examinations for music degrees were going on just then, and [Sir Hubert] Parry was staying with me. He picked up W[alton]'s MSS and was interested. I remember him saying, 'There's a lot in this chap. You must keep your eye on him.'

Actually William had started to scribble pieces for the choristers to sing at around the age of eleven. He wrote some organ pieces, which, according to him, were pretty awful. He also tried his hand at a couple of four-part songs in the style of Parry and Stanford on which he had been brought up, but found them not very interesting. He wrote 'Tell me where is Fancy bred' and 'Where the Bee sucks', he even tried a set of variations for violin and piano on a theme by Bach, but he threw it away.

William's first introduction to modern music had come early, when Dean Strong had asked the boys to come to him for confirmation classes after the Service on Sunday mornings and had played Schoenberg's six little piano pieces to them, lasting half a second each. William said they had all had a good giggle and had not been impressed. The first orchestral piece he heard was *Tannhäuser*, conducted by Sir Henry Wood, which he found a most impressive noise. The first opera he had managed to hear was Rimsky-Korsakov's *Coq d'or*.

William's father had taken him to the Hallé concerts in Manchester where he had heard Sir Thomas Beecham conduct this work in the 1916 season. *Coq d'or* absolutely transformed William's attitude towards musical life. For years he quoted it in some place or another.

With the First World War in full swing, the first of William's serious money problems began. His father lost all his singing pupils and became completely broke; it was a wonder that they survived. Since he could not pay even the very small fees, something like £8 a year, he was going to take William away from school. William's mother, who looked very frail but was a most determined character, stopped him from doing so, and the dean, sooner than lose this promising young talent, told the parents he would pay the sum out of a trust fund. William believed he had probably done so out of his own pocket. William stayed on to the great age of sixteen, under the general supervision of Hugh Allen, who was at that time organist of New College, although he later became Professor of Music and, later still, director of the Royal College of Music in London.

And then, as the War was still on and undergraduates were sparse, in October 1918 he went straight into Christ Church as an undergraduate. So from being a very old chorister he became a very young undergraduate; he liked to think himself the youngest undergraduate since the reign of Henry VIII, although this was not entirely true.

William joined the Bach Choir, which had very few people in it. Otherwise most of his time in Oxford was spent in the Radcliffe Camera where he found a marvellous music library, the Ellis Library of Music. Ellis had been killed in the early part of the War, and had left his collection of scores to the University. Through studying these scores William mastered his technique of orchestration.

But he didn't work very hard as an undergraduate, proof of which is that he only passed parts one and two of the Bachelor of Music degree. When he failed the composition paper, his examiners were Hugh Allen and Vaughan Williams. He liked to say that he had failed to pass 'responsions' three times because of his lack of a proper education. Responsions involved four subjects, including Greek and mathematics. If he passed in Greek, he would fail in algebra, and this went on for months. Finally it was decided he'd better leave, but he had to be sent down twice!

I'm sure that this lack of a proper education sharpened William's awareness of his special talents. Since childhood he had been uncommonly lucky, a special person: he had been able to sing before he could read; he had been accepted at Oxford against all the odds. He felt impelled to write music, and found he could do so. But this knowledge that his destiny was to make good use of his special talent placed him under a terrible obligation. As I later learned from experience, his life was to be a constant struggle.

Meanwhile one event of his undergraduate years which was to have an immediate influence on his life was William's meeting with the Sitwell family.

5

The Sitwells

IT was not long after our arrival in London that William's long-time patron Osbert Sitwell* invited us to luncheon at his house, 2 Carlyle Square. I knew, of course, that this was the house in which William had stayed for a long time as a guest and protégé of the Sitwells, and that this was where Edith Sitwell and William had worked together on their most famous collaboration, *Façade*. The drawing-room I was now entering was where *Façade* had originally been performed, in January 1922. I longed to see William's room in the attic, but no one suggested showing it to me. We were ushered into the first-floor sitting-room by the housekeeper, Miss Noble, who had looked after William when he had been in residence all those years ago; she seemed very fond of him, and overjoyed to welcome him again. I had never before seen walls covered with pictures hung so close together, side by side and as high as one could see. On the tables and the mantelpiece were many objects of blue glass, Bristol glass, William informed me. I also remember a spun glass ship under a dome and a *petit-point* tapestry embroidered in bright colours and depicting a young woman, whom I presumed was Queen Victoria, hanging prominently on one wall.

Osbert and his friend David Horner (known to the family as Blossom) greeted us. Osbert's slightly bulbous eyes sparkled with life whenever something amused him. Osbert and David presented us with an elegant table with an inlaid marble top as a wedding present, and with a Victorian settee which I took to the Royal School of Needlework to have a cover designed for me to embroider in *petit point*.

Osbert and David seemed to me to be the first of William's

---

* 5th Baronet (1892–1969), eldest son of Sir George Sitwell (1860–1943), and brother of Sacheverell, later 6th Baronet, and of Edith.

friends to be genuinely pleased that we had married. The irony was that I did not know until years later that William had not spoken to the Sitwells for years. He had never mentioned to me this hiatus in their friendship, and they all behaved as if they had seen each other only yesterday.

The dining-room where we had lunch was a very curious feature of the house. It appeared to have been an addition at the foot of the garden, as we had to walk down a long dark corridor in order to reach it. This rectangular room, with a wall of French doors opening on to the garden, had been made to look like a luxurious grotto, with gilt dolphins entwined, holding their tails in the air as supports for side-tables. The chairs were made of black ebony, encrusted with sheets of mother of pearl, which formed the backs into shells. The walls shimmered, covered in a greeny-gold material that gave the visual effect of an undersea cave.

William had first met Osbert's younger brother, Sachie, soon after the end of the First World War. Undergraduates had started to come up to Oxford and Sachie Sitwell and Raymond Mortimer were at Balliol; Sachie was four or five years older than William. When I met Sacheverell, Sachie to all who knew him, I was delighted. Tall, scholarly, kind, and humorous, he always seemed to me to be above such things as their family quarrels. It was Sachie, after all, who had 'discovered' William. He was impressed by the shape of his head, and decided William had a very clever-shaped head, rather like the great John Wesley.

Sachie, according to William, had not attended a single lecture the whole of the time he spent at Oxford. He was in a rebellious mood, and had become extremely left-wing. He had often declared his admiration for Trotsky, only because Trotsky had promised to take the Russians out of the War. This he was most concerned about, since 60 per cent of his friends had been killed in the War. William would repeatedly stress to me how tragic it had been for the country to have a whole generation of young talent blotted out. It had been a blood-bath. Therefore, Sachie was interested in meeting anybody talented and he discovered that William was supposed to be the most talented undergraduate in Oxford. William was then young and inarticulate; he was pale, very thin, and looked delicate and quite unwordly. He told me that he had been fed so little during those War years that he had started to grow in height only after the age of sixteen. Sachie used to ask William out to luncheon, despite the food shortage and what Sachie termed the fearful nastiness of it.

He had found in William a good listener as, partly through nerves and partly through shyness, he was mainly silent. He then asked his older brother Osbert to come to Oxford to meet William, to hear him play part of a piano quartet he had written. William couldn't play the piano, so it was very much on trust that Osbert accepted Sachie's view that William had great talent. At the time Osbert was busy championing another composer, Bernard van Dieren. According to William, the Sitwell brothers were not at all musical, but they knew if they liked what they were listening to.

Osbert and Sachie shared a house in Chelsea at that time, and they asked William to stay during the long vacation. Sachie and William went to as many concerts as they had time for; they heard Cortot play and they became admirers of Busoni. Together they attended every one of his recitals.

William's father, worried about his being in London while still a minor, came to fetch him home. As luck would have it, William had gone out that night with a girl-friend and was nowhere to be found. So the father looked up Sitwell in the telephone directory, and got hold of Osbert's aunt, who was a most charming old lady; she managed to pacify him. He thought everything must be all right, since Osbert and Sachie even promised to go and see him in Oldham and seemed so interested in his son. Their country house, Renishaw in Derbyshire, was not that far from Oldham.

Then in the spring of 1920, while William was still at Oxford, the Sitwells asked him to go with them on a trip. His own family had never been abroad and he liked retelling what this journey had been like. How uncomfortable trains were in those days when there were no sleepers—they had had to share a carriage with two priests. How it had poured with rain all the way through France up to Modane, making him think, 'Great God! Oldham again!' Then the train went into a tunnel, and when it came out on the Italian side they found the most marvellous sun. He never recovered from this moment of revelation, the shock of seeing such brilliant light. They slowly wound their way down to Amalfi, where the Sitwells had stayed before.

William and I would often stay in Amalfi in the years to come, sometimes to visit Osbert and Edith who were staying there for a holiday, or simply to bask in the beauty of the place. It is an old Roman town below the Bay of Naples, with a climate renowned for its mildness; because of its southern aspect, the sun warms it even in winter. In those early years the Sitwells and their friends made a habit of visiting Amalfi every winter. It provided a peaceful setting for work, and it was also very inexpensive.

They stayed in the Albergo Cappuccini, once a monastery, perched on the side of a cliff. It was then owned by the aristocratic Don Alfredo Vozzi. He occupied a cell in the middle of the hotel, while the other monks' cells were allotted to the guests. All the cells had a stunning view of the sea.

William was given the use of a small upright piano in a back laundry room which was put at his disposal. When he had started to compose, he had not used a piano and deplored giving in to everyone telling him that it was a great mistake not to use a piano, as he ought to 'hear' what he wrote. He had perfect pitch and had no need of a piano, but in the end he started to use it. He liked to say that it was this difficulty of playing the piano that stopped him from writing as much as other composers; he didn't like the sound of it, and it was too much trouble. The piano in Lowndes Cottage was thickly muffled.

Another favourite saying of his was that to compose music was far worse for him than to bear children is for a woman, as it took longer than nine months and was much more painful. He would love to perplex interviewers with remarks such as that his eraser was more important than his pencil, or that he lived abroad to prevent people in England from finding out that he couldn't read or write!

He enjoyed staying in Amalfi, but not all the Sitwells' friends did because it was too remote, and very few visitors came in winter. William recalled with glee the upheaval caused by the arrival of an American tour of young ladies, one of whom took his fancy, a young musician called Miss Swift. 'Miss Swift was very swift,' he would say with a chuckle.

The Sitwells and their friends would often walk to the town of Ravello to lunch at the Hotel Caruso, which was owned by the same family as the Hotel Cappuccini. On their way they would pass the old paper-mills perched on the edge of the gorge above Amalfi. William could order his manuscript-paper there. Even today I buy my writing-paper from them, with the watermark of my choice. I have seen them hang up each sheet of paper to dry and have been deafened by the noise of the four-hundred-year-old wooden hammer that beats the paper flat. It is moved by a wheel turned by the rushing waters of the stream. On this walk William and his friends would cross small meadows enclosed by stone boulders where sweet grasses grow, which the local girls collect to feed to their rabbits. It is still a lovely walk today.

When William was sent down from Oxford he did not want to go back to Oldham to be, as he termed it, a cotton clerk. 'What the hell *am* I going to do?' he asked Sachie, and was told to come and stay with them in London, until he could find something more permanent. In fact, he stayed with them for almost fifteen years.

At the time William hoped a couple of months would be enough for him to find something to do. The Sitwells didn't want him to go to a music college; they didn't approve of that kind of training, because they thought it turned out composers of doubtful status. Everybody William knew seemed to be able to play the piano or the violin or could sing or do something. But he could not earn his living. To survive, William became a scrounger from Osbert, from Gerald Berners,* and from Siegfried Sassoon, and he would continue to do so for quite a time.

He stayed with the Sitwells, first in Swan Walk, where Mrs Powell, their charming housekeeper, looked after him like a mother and darned his socks. He lived in the attic, and used to eat bags and bags of black cherries and, according to Osbert, throw the stones out of the window on to unsuspecting passers-

---

* 14th Baron Berners (1883–1950).

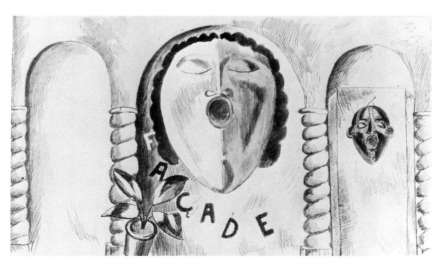

Original Front Curtain for *Façade* designed by Frank Dobson for the first performance
in the Sitwell's drawing room at 2 Carlyle Square, London, Sunday 24 January 1922

Frederick Ashton's ballet *Façade* with the original scenery and costumes by John
Armstrong. The first performance of this ballet was given by the Camargo Society at
the Cambridge Theatre, London, 26 April 1931. The original cast included Lydia
Lopokova, Prudence Hyman, Maud Lloyd, Antony Tudor, William Chappell, Walter
Gore, Alicia Markova, Pearl Argyle, Diana Gould, and the choreographer himself. It
went into the repertoire of the Ballet Rambert and later was added to the repertoire of
the Vic-Wells Ballet. The Sadler's Wells Company lost their scenery and costumes in
their flight from Holland in 1940, when they narrowly escaped the Germans

Frederick Ashton dancing the Dago in *Façade* with Margot Fonteyn as the Debutante, in front of the new backdrop by John Armstrong for the revised version

Osbert, Edith, and Sachie Sitwell, William, and a companion holding the sengerphone, possibly Neil Porter, the reciter, at the New Chenil Galleries, Chelsea, 27 April 1926

William photographed by Howard Coster, 1934

Hubert Foss with William at Symond's Yat, September 1932

Above, left, Baroness Imma von Doernberg, née Princess of Erbach-Schoenberg

Above, right, Alice Wimborne on a skiing holiday

Alice, wife of the 2nd Viscount Wimborne, née the Hon. Alice Katherine Sibell Grosvenor

by below. When the Sitwells moved to 2 Carlyle Square, which was not such a big house, there was still enough room for him in the attic, and he was given a piano. Osbert told me that in those days William got sick if separated from his piano; he would leave his room with great reluctance. The only money he managed to earn was by copying. Adrian Boult gave him some work. He wrote a couple of songs, 'The Winds' and 'Tritons', and even managed to do a piece for tenor and chamber orchestra, *The Passionate Shepherd*. He sent his publisher a little overture called 'Dr Syntax', which, as Eugene Goosens informed him, would never be performed because of its awful title.

I asked William whether Osbert had ever made advances to him while he was living in their house. He replied that yes, he had once done so, but it did not create an awkward situation. William had told Osbert that that sort of thing was not his cup of tea, and he had never asked again.

I thought that Osbert had Hanoverian features, as with his large nose and heavy chin he might well have been an early nineteenth-century royal duke. He dressed much more conventionally than his brother Sacheverell, whom I was to meet later, and was extremely well-mannered when he felt inclined to be courteous. But I had heard that Osbert could be very rude and crushing if he felt he'd been offended or treated with less respect than he thought he was entitled to. He was a bit of a tease, sometimes a rather cruel tease. I got the impression that he had, now and then, made life rather difficult for William.

Peter Quennell, the novelist and a friend of all the Sitwells and of William, says that William was often made by Osbert to feel that he occupied a rather secondary position in the Sitwell household. He remembers when a biscuit box had once been knocked over and William was told, 'Pick 'em up, pick 'em up.' William used to smoke thin dark toscano cigars that were very smelly, or at times have what the French call a *mégot* glued on to his lower lip. The Sitwells disapproved of this Bohemian behaviour. And they also certainly disapproved of all William's girl-friends. The story I best remember is when in 1927 William went to a party in nearby Chelsea, where he met a girl who was a very disreputable character, called Brenda Dean Paul. She is said to have been rather pretty, and to have looked like a Lely of Nell Gwynn. While she was dancing with William, she bit his lower lip which then swelled up. When Sachie's wife, Georgia, who was confined to bed awaiting the birth of their first child, Reresby, saw William, and heard him tell, roaring with laughter, that he'd just been bitten by this girl Brenda, she said she would miscarry if that sort of thing went on.

A story was put about by William's friend, the composer Constant Lambert, that William had committed suicide on account of the fagging at Carlyle Square. Constant had invented this after reading in the daily newspaper about a scandal of a boy committing suicide because of fagging at his public school.

Osbert could be very funny. He amused us with a series of extremely funny stories. I got the impression that he was very much liked by women, far more than he liked them. He liked women as friends, but I don't think he was ever in love with a woman, although William knew of various women who were certainly in love with him. But his brother Sachie, William told me, was always in love and had desperately wanted to get married, probably to get away from Carlyle Square. Osbert had not approved of his getting married at all. Partly because of this, William thought, the atmosphere at Carlyle Square was often strained.

William imagined them to be very rich; he soon discovered that they were dependent on their father, who was a rich baronet. Life with them was great fun. They knew everybody who was anybody in those days, in music, theatre, and high society, from Walter Sickert, Lady Cunard, Lord Berners, Sir Thomas Beecham, and Diaghilev, to the younger set like Gershwin, William's great pal Constant Lambert, and the novelists Peter Quennell and Ronald Firbank. Through the Sitwells William also met Siegfried Sassoon and John Masefield, the conductor Ernest Ansermet, and the composer Busoni. Indeed Carlyle Square was a centre of cultural excitement. William realized that the Sitwells were also intensely ambitious, and deeply concerned with the arts they practised. They felt it their duty to wage a battle against contemporary philistinism. Seemingly, it was tougher in those days, as there seemed to be many more philistines and they were more vocal than they appear to be today. This induced the Sitwells to adopt rather pugnacious methods to make their way and this pugnacity made them many enemies. They projected this quarrelsomeness on to the outer world and battled against the London critics and publishers whom they thought did not appreciate them sufficiently. They also had a great legacy of family quarrels. During the First World War their unfortunate mother, Lady Ida, guilelessly got involved with an unscrupulous money-lender, and their father did nothing to prevent her from going to jail.

They never ceased to fight their father, whom they used to call 'Ginger'. William found the quarrelling particularly trying, but certainly took notice of their cunning in dealing with their father. He told me the story of how, to avoid Sir George's never-ending stream of instructions and admonitions reproving Osbert for his expensive tastes and so on, he had invented a yacht, had a letterhead printed on stationery with the name of the fictitious yacht, and told Sir George that Sachie and he could write to him but that he could not write to them, because the vessel's ports of call were not known in advance.

When the Sitwell brothers bought the house in Carlyle Square, and William went with them, he met at dinner a friend of the Sitwells, Christabel McLaren (she became Lady Aberconway when her husband succeeded as the 2nd Baron). As she looked across the table, she got a sympathetic look back from William, and they became close friends. She would say to her friends in the city, 'I've got a young composer friend who's starving,' and they would give her £50. Though this happened quite often, it was not as often as William would have liked. He also found that quite a few musicians gathered there. Some William didn't like very much, like Heseltine (known as Peter Warlock), who led a tormented life, indulged in black magic practices, and eventually committed suicide. Others, like Constant Lambert, Patrick Hughes, and Angus Morrison, became great friends. William was four or five years older than Constant but there was not the slightest sense of jealousy between them. This was quite exceptional in their world. He often told me how beautiful a young man Constant was, and of how they liked to flatter each other and together would laugh a lot. Of course, musically speaking, they competed with each other. Physically, they were very different, William thin and fair, Constant becoming plump and walking with a stick because of the lameness he suffered as a result of an attack of Maltese fever caught in childhood that had also left his hearing impaired. They exchanged limericks and must have behaved like two brilliant but irrepressible school-boys. The main difference between them was that, although Constant loved the occasional grand party, he was much more at home in a grand pub-crawl. William, on the other hand, loved the *beau monde*.

Constant was completely at ease with all three arts—music, literature, and painting. His father had been a painter and he had been brought up in a painters' world, although he could not draw. He thought of music in terms of the other arts and was incredibly well informed. William would often pick his brains as he himself was very much concentrated on music. He was introduced to jazz by Constant, who greatly admired the black singer Florence Mills, who was then appearing in a Cochran revue in London. Another friend of those days was the pianist Angus Morrison, who described to me how a challenge would spur William into writing a new piece. The piano quartet which Osbert had heard William play in Oxford was composed principally because a rival, Herbert Howells, had made a success with his quartet. When he could not make up his mind about what sort of music would suit Edith's poems, he was told by the Sitwells that, if he didn't get down to work, they would ask Constant; hence *Façade*. Or again, when Diaghilev asked Constant in 1926 to write a ballet score, William felt that he should have been asked as well. Indeed Osbert and Sachie made elaborate arrangements to secure this commission, a luncheon party was organized, and William wrote to his mother saying he was going to see 'these Russians' and that the piece that he had written, that was in the form of a piano duet, was certain to be accepted. William was mortified when Diaghilev turned the piece down, saying he was certain William would go on to better things. This rejected ballet music he used the following year in his *Sinfonia Concertante*, maintaining thereafter that he had never been asked by Diaghilev to write a ballet score. When Constant, in 1928, had a success with his cantata 'Rio Grande' ('much better than anything I have ever written,' William used to say), this was the spur for him to write *Belshazzar's Feast*.

Both Constant and William had great success with women but William did not have many girl-friends as he probably could not afford them. He did tell me he was a late developer! The Sitwells adored Constant and he worshipped them. William remembered a weekend at Sachie's house in Weston, when they were utterly exhausted by Sachie's inexhaustible energy. He had sacked all the servants, rearranged the furniture, and jumped out of the car to stop two dogs fighting, chasing them as far as the horizon, and had then returned to the car and his discourse on Baroque architecture.

Constant was attracted to exotic females; he fell in love with a Chinese film star and married a half-Javanese beauty, known as Flo to his friends. William was godfather to their son Kit, who became the founder of the pop group 'The Who'. Both father and son had tragic lives.* William voiced great concern about Constant who even when young was already drinking much too much and would become an awful problem to his friends. When I met him in Lowndes Cottage he chuckled a great deal but the jokes were incoherent; yet William had once thought him the wittiest man he had ever come across as he always saw everything that cropped up in extremely amusing terms.

William loved going to *everything*. He went a lot to the old Lyceum Theatre, for instance; but, because he was always broke, he had to scrounge the five shillings for a night out on the town that he could never pay back. The trouble was that being a composer in those days made life very difficult. He would have starved really except for the luck of meeting the Sitwells, because he hardly made £50 a year.

Indeed to the end of his life, despite various ups and downs in his relationship with them, William never stopped being thankful to the Sitwells. It amused him to recall that the three siblings, Edith, Osbert, and Sacheverell, were supposed to be the result of exceptional family planning on the part of their parent, Sir

* See Andrew Motion, *The Lamberts* (1986).

George, who spent months preparing for each act of procreation. He would read books of especial beauty and artistic merit, recite poetry, and contemplate flowers, trees, and exotic colours for hours. Then, having eaten what he thought was the appropriate diet, he would announce to his wife, Lady Ida: 'I am now ready,' and the great act would be undertaken. Hence, Edith, Osbert, and Sacheverell.

As a house guest William seems to have been acceptable, and Dora Foss, the wife of Hubert Foss, William's publisher at OUP, remembers how gentle and sweet William was to Sachie's then very small child, Reresby, who loved him and always called him 'Willie Boy'. He also stayed at Renishaw, the Sitwells' country house which was supposed to be full of ghosts. Sir George had not allowed electricity to be installed; it was lit by gas. They all had to go to bed with a flickering candle. Most of the beds were four posters crowned with clumps of dusty feathers. The whole atmosphere was dark and foreboding. Sir George scoffed at the notion of ghosts but once, while climbing the stairs, he had expressed himself derisively about their existence and had been resoundingly slapped on the cheek by an invisible presence, to the astonishment of those present, among them William. After Sir George's death Edith had the house exorcised by a Roman Catholic priest.

As Peter Quennell has pointed out to me, to a lad from 'up North' the atmosphere at Carlyle Square must have seemed exotic and glamorous. What was clear to me was that, coming from the North, William had hung on to a certain shrewdness. As I came to know him more and more, I became convinced that he had never been taken in; I don't think his critical faculty had ever been asleep. It had been, I believe, an exchange of benefits on both sides and an education for William. Sachie had certainly liked having William around, and it must have helped William to be with people who had an appreciation of his talent and were seemingly at pains to cultivate it, to bring it out in any way they could.

6

Three Masterpieces

WILLIAM also, of course, met Edith, Osbert's older sister. She was ten years older than Sachie and an accomplished pianist. She had studied with a Mr Frederick Dawson, a piano teacher in the North Country. Edith had written a whole group of poems as a sort of technical exercise. The first one was 'Hornpipe'. She would recite them in front of a lot of their friends and either she or Sachie, perhaps it was both of them, suggested they would be much better with music. William agreed, but couldn't quite see what *kind* of music. In those days there was a lot of musical experimentation going on by composers like Stravinsky, Ravel, and Milhaud, works such as *Ragtime* and *L'Histoire du soldat*. It struck William that one of them, Stravinsky's *Berceuse du chat*, or even *Cocardes*, the songs by Poulenc with words by Cocteau, could be a model. So in November and December 1921 he worked on enough of the poems to make a little after-dinner entertainment, which Sachie called 'Façade'. Someone had said that Edith was clever, but only a façade, hence the title.

Angus Morrison stressed to me how William had at the time of *Façade* never heard Ravel or Schoenberg played, but he had certainly studied the works. Angus was a friend of both Constant and William and would meet them in Carlyle Square after concerts. He remembers seeing the score of *Pierrot Lunaire* in William's room; he also claims William pinched the odd tune from Ravel in some of his earliest works. William did buy as many scores as he could lay his hands on.

When William was writing *Façade* he impressed Sachie by his facility in writing music. He managed to churn out tunes day after day, even if some of them were borrowed. Sachie remembers having first heard the fanfare from *Long Steel Grass* played by an itinerant fortune-teller, in Syracuse. So, despite William's apparent lack of appreciation of words or poetry, the music he produced for the *Façade* poems turned out to be brilliant.

The L-shaped first-floor drawing-room in Carlyle Square was quite small so it could not hold more than a few invited guests for the first performance of *Façade*. It was Sunday, 24 January; William was nineteen at the time. He conducted and had only four players: a cellist, Ambrose Gauntlett; a clarinettist, a Mr Paul Draper who, after looking at his part, is said to have asked William if a clarinettist had ever done him an injury! Mr Herbert Barr played the trumpet and Mr Charles Bender most probably played the percussion instruments.

Osbert, who found recitation embarrassing, had the idea of putting the whole thing behind a curtain. He had Frank Dobson, a painter friend of his, design a curtain, behind which Edith and all the performers sat.

The next problem was that Edith's voice couldn't be heard above the music. So she had to speak through a hole in the curtain, with the aid of a megaphone. Actually, it was called a 'Sengerphone', after a man called Senger, who had used it to project his voice with greater force while singing the part of Fafner the dragon at Bayreuth. Sachie and William had asked Herr Senger for permission to use his dragon trumpet which was made out of papier mâché. At that first performance only seventeen or eighteen numbers were included; some of the more famous ones, like 'Popular Song', 'Polka', and 'Old Sir Faulk' came later. The invited audience of between twenty and thirty were flabbergasted. William, who had hardly ever heard his own music performed, used to say the audience had talked all the way through the recitation and had come to the conclusion that both Edith and he were off their heads.

Mrs Robert Mathias asked them, two weeks later, to do it again at her house in Montague Square. Then, the following year, the Sitwells thought they would do it, one afternoon, at the Aeolian Hall, in public. The Sengerphone could not be heard by anyone not directly in front of it; as a result, the performance was raucous and crude. William was very upset by the way the audience behaved, booing and hissing. He had not imagined people could react so violently and was shocked by this horrible reception. Noel Coward was in the audience and wrote a little parody on it entitled 'The Swiss Family Whittlebot', in which the poetess Hernia Whittlebot recited her poems with her brothers, Gob and Sago. Her manic script included lines such as, 'My brothers and I have been brought up in Rhythm as other children are brought up on Glaxo ...' This satire offended Edith, although she said she had never seen it. William had laughingly told her about it as he thought it rather funny, and would never forget how indignant Edith had become. *The Times* said, 'It is almost impossible to make words clearly audible through a megaphone unless they are spoken slowly and distinctly. Mr Walton's accompaniments ... are for the most part too spasmodic.' The little orchestra had grown to include a flute, clarinet, saxophone, trumpet, violoncello, and percussion.

William concluded that the three Sitwells were pleased with the uproar caused by the performance, especially Osbert, who liked a little notoriety and playing at being the bad boy of the family. But, looking back, he would say how it had embarrassed him and how, every time *Façade* was performed, there seemed to be a row, egged on by Osbert. The reviews were pretty awful—the journalists had interviewed a fireman on duty in the concert hall who was most indignant and said 'He'd never seen or heard anything like it in his life'; that was most certainly correct. The general feeling of indignation caused by the event made *Façade* famous overnight. It was not until 27 April 1926 that a performance seemed to work. It was performed in the Chenil Galleries in Chelsea, after a lot of revision; several poems had been rewritten, and others had been abandoned altogether. It became the talk of the town and Osbert got Diaghilev to come. Ernest Newman, reviewing the performance, said: '... as a musical joker he is a jewel of the first water ... the deft workmanship, especially in the orchestration, made the heart of the listening musician glad ...' At a repeat performance at the Chenil in June, Constant Lambert read the poems.

One performance in Italy caused a great stir. It was at the Sixth International Society for Contemporary Music Festival, in the Rozzi Theatre at Siena, on Friday, 14 September 1928. It was a morning performance which William conducted and Constant was the reciter. The audience liked 'Popular Song' so much (it was the first time it had been performed, having been written especially for Constant) that they had to do it again. Later in the performance the whole audience suddenly started an uproar. Things were thrown on to the stage, and people whistled, shouted, and protested in the name of Mussolini and the entire Italian nation. It was later explained to William that the Italian audience felt mortally insulted because in one of the numbers he had parodied Rossini! He had poked fun at a composer whom he personally loved, and would always do, above nearly all others. As a result, whenever he conducted the 'Swiss Yodelling Song' from *Façade* in public, he became a little apprehensive. William was amazed to discover that the Sienese had been offended by his turning Rossini *seria* into Rossini *buffa* at the end of the Yodelling song—a parodistic touch which would have surely enchanted the Maestro from Pesaro. Years later, over glasses of Strega in Rome's Piazza Navona, André Previn asked William whom he considered to be the finest composer. 'Rossini,' said William without hesitation. Next day André, puzzled and amazed, asked Jack Buckley, who had been with us, 'He was joking, wasn't he?' 'Of course not,' said Jack, who happens to be of the same opinion as William.

The curtain for the performance in Siena was designed by Gino Severini, and to get it painted in Florence was the *raison d'être* for a bit of *scena buffa alla Sitwell*. Osbert wrote about it in *Laughter in the Next Room*. It seems that William forgot the address of the scene painter to whom he had entrusted the Severini design, and knew only that his surname was Barone. As the day of the performance drew nearer and the curtain failed to arrive, Edith's mother, Lady Ida, told Edith to accompany her in the car to the hotel where they usually stayed in Florence. There she told the driver to obtain from the concierge a list with the address of every Barone in town. He returned with a list, and was told to drive to each address on it. But the list was of all those with the title of baron. When the imperious English lady accosted each of the surprised barons, of course none of them had 'my daughter's curtain'. In the end Christabel McLaren found the painter by sensibly sitting in the bar where William had met the young man until he turned up for a drink. She then forced a reluctant Sir George to allow the rolled-up curtain to be carried on the roof of the car back to the castle of Montegufoni, where they were all staying.

Even William's bizarre stories had not quite prepared me for my first meeting with Edith, in 1949. She had asked us to tea at the Sesame Club, and delighted me by saying that I had eyes like a Phoenician. Edith liked to describe her appearance as Plantagenet, William said. When William and she had worked together on *Façade*, William had started to flirt with Edith, but Osbert had quickly put an end to any romantic attachment by warning William not to court his sister; otherwise he would be shown the door.

She had had a hard life. She had disliked her mother intensely, and had escaped from her parents with her governess, Miss Rootham, who had encouraged and assisted her. They had run away together. Edith, immensely tall, looked to me exactly like one of those elongated statues around the main portal of Chartres Cathedral. But, in spite of her dramatic appearance, her conversation was very down to earth. She would interrupt a reading of her latest poem to talk about a quarrel with a neighbour who had a barking dog.

She did not appear ugly, as some people had described her to me, but extraordinarily elegant. Certainly she did not look like anyone else I had ever met. She had very fine hair, and always wore the most striking head-dresses to complement her long oval features, prominent nose, high forehead, and almost complete lack of eyebrows—they were so fair that she painted a line high above the eye. Her jewels seemed barbaric: Mexican breastplates in gold, with rings of large aquamarines encased in high settings. She also seemed to eat very little; a couple of lightly boiled eggs, served in a soup plate, was all she had for lunch. She chattered endlessly, and I came to think that she often invented situations to get her own back on whoever was not in her good books.

I was also struck by how strangely alike, physically, Edith and William looked at the time. Edith told the story of their likeness in this way. 'His profile and mine—(he will not thank me for saying this)—were so much alike in character and bone structure that many people who did not know us thought my two brothers, William, and I were three brothers and their sister. Indeed long before Pavel Tchelitchew spoke English (though he understood it), he said to me one day, "J'admire beaucoup la délicatesse de votre mère et vos frères envers Monsieur Wal-ton." I said, "Oh yes, they are delicate, all right. But why are you particularly struck by this?"

"Ecoutez, nous ne sommes pas des enfants!"

"No, alas."

"Alors, . . ., vous êtes un peu parents, n'est-ce pas?"

"No."

"Mais votre père" (hopefully) "est un boyard."

"Oh yes, he is one of the lads, all right."

"Mon père aussi était un boyard. Ma mère a montré beaucoup de délicatesse."

I was left pondering the situation. William was very displeased when this was repeated to him, saying he had been accused of being a buzzard!'

William's friend Constant Lambert invented and put about another story, of William being the illegitimate son of Sir George Sitwell and Dame Ethel Smyth, a lady composer whom Sir George knew well. She appears to have looked like a First World War tank and to have been of doubtful sexual orientation. In his wily way William was not averse to using this story to his advantage, as is evident from a letter to Hubert Foss, his publisher, written from Ascona in 1931.

My dear Hubert,
This is all very well. You know that my life is already an open book and I can't think of anything more which can with strict propriety be divulged to the public. However, as you ask, here goes.
Perhaps it is wiser (and more profitable) to cast a doubt about parentage, only born March 29th, 1902 . . .

Edith told me that William could be extremely firm with people who bored him. He would use his Lancashire accent for fun from time to time, as well as drop his 'aitches'. On one occasion an exceedingly affected lady named Eyre telephoned 2 Carlyle Square where William was living, disturbing him in his work.

'Oo's that?' enquired William.

'Mrs Aah', said the lady.

'Oo?'

'Mrs Aah.'

'Oo?'

'Aah.'

'Oo the 'ell?'

'Aah.'

'Osbert,' William called, 'there is a Chinese woman wants you.'

By contrast, I found William very patient with me. He put up with a lot of nonsense when I started nicknaming him 'Poppe-tino', and then changed to calling him 'Bobik', after seeing the National Theatre's production of Chekhov's *Three Sisters*, directed and acted by Larry Olivier with Joan Plowright in it too. Bobik is the name of the spoiled child in the play. To get me out of this bad habit, he gave me a piece to read called 'Travelogue of Flowery Catalogues'.

> Bobolink
> Bobolink
> Spink
> Spank
> Spink
> Bobbink
> Atkink
> Sprink
> Burpee.

So we returned to calling each other 'Poppet'.

In those early years William's struggles to compose were made worse by his inability to earn money. One person who helped him over the years, treated him like a son, and promoted his work to the best of his ability was Hubert Foss of the Oxford University Press. But this was before the time that publishers saw the wisdom of subsidizing their composers, giving them an allowance to enable them to live, and of spending money on promoting the works—as Boosey and Hawkes did with Ben Britten and Schott with Hans Henze.

William Walton

Hubert Foss headed the music department of Oxford University Press, which became William's publisher. Foss first heard about William and *Façade* from his future wife, Dora Stevens, a singer, and her mother, who had both attended the second performance at the Chenil Galleries in Chelsea. They were captivated by the work and by the pale, willowy, apparently shy composer. Soon after, on the advice of the Dean of Christ Church, William went to see Foss, and *Façade* was definitely assigned to OUP.

Foss was enchanted by William's airy nonchalance, and amused by the shafts of lightning and the acid touches which could suddenly illuminate his conversation. William was so hard up that on his first visit to stay with the Fosses, in October 1929, he borrowed Osbert's pyjamas, a most striking orange and black pair, but went with little else in his bag. Nevertheless, he always appeared to them to be immaculate and extremely elegant in what they later came to know were Moss Bros misfits. Both Dora and Hubert Foss became real friends, and William wrote frequently to them. They in turn wrote to him to encourage and advise on his work. As they would say, he needed to be petted and patted. From Amalfi William sent them a large net filled with little packets of raisins swaddled in vine leaves, which they thought a charming and delicious present. When he was in London, he often visited them in the country, and Dora remarked that, as he was most appreciative of good food, they took the greatest pains to give him the best they could afford, though he also loved simple things like home-made pickled shallots. When he got these, he could not stop eating them. William never lost his addiction to pickles. We always had bottles of pickled onions, walnuts, peaches, and different kinds of mustards in the kitchen. Our favourite one, to serve with *bollito misto* was *mostarda di frutta*, the northern Italian speciality from Cremona, made of many different pickled fruits in a sweet sauce.

Hubert and Dora Foss loved William's visits, and laughed at the gossip and comments on friends and foes with which he regaled them. But sometimes William went too far. On one occasion he wrote to them:

I hope you have enjoyed your holiday in spite of the adjacency of the Blisses. I love your descriptions of his glass-walled studio, and of course he is just like a moustachioed codfish, so he will be in the right environment. I hope it won't make his music even more watery.

Dora Foss was quite shocked, and complained to her husband that she couldn't understand what provoked such a letter, since she had merely informed William in a letter to him of their amusing visit to see Bliss's new music room.

Hubert Foss was a sort of nurse to William's musical off-spring, knew the works intimately, and loved them as if they were his own. William had never taken any exercise until the Fosses forced him to go on long walks and to play table tennis. They also introduced him to Sir Henry Wood, and asked Arnold Bax to dine so that William could get to know him better. Dora Foss recalls that Hubert would sit with William at the piano for hours. Sometimes William would play 'with his composer's technique', sometimes Hubert. In a letter to me, Mrs Foss, writing of those occasions, says, 'This is how we heard the great works growing.'

William wrote three songs for Dora to sing at a recital, and dedicated them to Hubert and Dora Foss. The first to be finished was 'Through Gilded Trellises'; a month later 'Old Sir Faulk' arrived, with a note from William saying, 'I am not sure you will approve of this one ... It ought to evoke a touch of lunacy in any programme.' The third song, 'Daphne', reached them with a postcard saying, 'It is not fit to be seen.' When Dora Foss sang the songs she was attacked by Edith because William had not told Edith he was using her poems, thus inadvertently placing Dora in a very awkward position.

Hubert went to all the International Society for Contemporary Music Festivals, and wrote home to Dora Foss how exciting these first performances of William's works were. William, on the other hand, felt that all the music played at international festivals of contemporary music in those days was outrageous; the advantage was suddenly to find himself in illustrious company. For example, among the other composers present or represented at Salzburg were Bartók, Janáček and Hindemith. Wicked William laughingly told me that Bartók was morbidly interested in the anatomy of ducks and forced his wife to dress as a 'ducky little girl'. She, however, bankrupted him by her passion for buying shoes!

William was shy of recalling those early years after *Façade*, when he had written two or three bits and pieces but nothing of any consequence to him. In London he managed to get a part-time job doing arrangements for Debroy Somer's Savoy Orpheans, but was much too slow for them. The only thing he remembered getting out of it was a free cup of tea, which for him in those days was quite a help. He also mapped out a monumental concerto for two pianos, jazz band, and orchestra, the 'Fantasia Concertante', which was never performed. He attempted some incidental music for a Chinese melodrama, *A Son of Heaven*, based on some writings by Lytton Strachey, which he subsequently abandoned because he thought it was too much like Gershwin.

In Amalfi William had also written a string quartet; some of it had been composed while he was at Oxford, but now he revised it and added a third movement, a scherzo. He would say that the Schoenberg–Bartók style he had adopted was horrible. It got lost in the post but reappeared two years later, whereupon he rewrote it. It was played first in London, at the Royal College of Music, and then a month later in Salzburg, at the 1923 Festival, on 4 August, by four gallant ladies, who tried their best, but couldn't do very much about it. It seems to have been a disaster! The poor lady cellist had a misadventure when she started to play, in that the end-pin of her cello gave way. The tension was relieved by the hilarious laughter that followed this incident. Anyhow, the quartet was considered by William to be an outrageous piece, and best forgotten. Indeed, he refused to have it published. An unnamed critic of the London *Times* wrote about it, saying,

It is a long work and it was very unfortunately placed at the end of a long programme. The impression it gave at a first hearing was that some passages might be rewritten with a view to making the work more grateful for the strings to play . . . the lengthy treatment in the scherzo of an apparently meaningless figure of two notes lost the attention of the hall and this was never regained . . . No one grudges

Mr Walton the performance of his quartet, but one may doubt the wisdom from the composer's point of view of forcing an immature work on the public notice.

This performance in Salzburg had a worthwhile sequence; it excited the interest of the great Alban Berg, to whom William had been introduced by Osbert as 'the leader of English atonal music'! Anyhow, Berg took William to see the even greater Arnold Schoenberg. They arrived at an inopportune moment. Schoenberg's piano displayed on the music stand several sheets of music-paper on which he was working. To be 'found out' composing at the piano clearly irritated him. He tetchily gathered up the material and put it away in a drawer. This made William feel even more nervous and shy.

The Sitwells were deeply involved in William's early music-making, starting with *Façade*, which amused and impressed them. Even if William had little appreciation of poetry, he certainly had managed to produce what Sachie termed 'a terrific noise'. Then in 1927 in Amalfi William completed *Sinfonia Concertante*, the first movement of which he dedicated to Osbert, the second to Edith, who thought it beautiful and like Ravel, and the last to Sachie. He wrote *Bucolic Comedies* to words by Edith, a theme well suited to his temperament.

They continued to take him on their travels and in 1925, while in Spain, he composed the overture *Portsmouth Point*. He was paid £20, the OUP undertook publication, and he dedicated the work to Siegfried Sassoon who had been generous to him for so long. It was first performed in London as a symphonic interlude in the middle of an evening of ballet given by Diaghilev's company and conducted by Eugene Goossens. It had been premièred six days earlier in Zurich, at that year's ISCM Festival. William recalled how difficult the London orchestras found it, because they said it changed time every other bar! Sir Henry Wood eventually asked him to conduct it himself, so he got Eugene Goossens to teach him, since he had never done any real conducting before. He had just half an hour's rehearsal and when he saw how many wrong notes there were in the parts he had to stay up all night rewriting all of them. He learned to conduct the work by heart, and would boast, in future, that he could conduct it in his sleep. Sir Thomas Beecham gave him a strong tot of brandy just before he went on to the podium, which may have helped.

Amalfi turned out to be especially important for William's work. There he composed not only the *Sinfonia Concertante* but also his early masterpiece, the Viola Concerto. Sir Thomas Beecham had suggested that he write a viola concerto for Lionel Tertis, which slightly perplexed William, who wondered why Sir Thomas thought he should be able to write such a work. Obviously he did, as otherwise I suppose he wouldn't have suggested it. William says that at the time he knew very little about the viola, except that it made a rather awful sound. The only piece of viola music he admired and knew was Berlioz's *Harold in Italy*, which he thought quite beautiful, although it was not very highly thought of in those days.

In the 1920s and 1930s very few people ever commissioned works. They just suggested a work should be written for so-and-so. In 1928 Sir Thomas had done just that by saying, 'It would be rather a good idea if you wrote something for Lionel Tertis.' William did so, and dedicated it to Christabel McLaren. When he had finished the piece, in Amalfi, he brought it back to England, and sent it to Tertis, who sent it back by the next post. William was very hurt, and disappointed, and didn't know what to do. Viola players weren't so plentiful as all that; seemingly he had done a lot of work for nothing. So he asked Edward Clark, who was in charge of music at the BBC, if he should turn it into a violin concerto as there was no point in having such a large work on his hands with no one to play it. Instead, Edward Clark sent the concerto to Hindemith to find out if he would like to play it. William had met Hindemith at the Salzburg ISCM Festival in 1923. When he gallantly accepted to play the viola concerto, William was delighted.

Paul Hindemith's publisher, Willy Strecker, the London manager of Schott, had made plans to launch Hindemith as a viola soloist—he was a wonderful player—at a Courtauld–Sargent concert. These concerts were funded by Mrs Elizabeth Courtauld, wife of Samuel Courtauld, chairman of the giant textile firm and William's future benefactor. In 1928 she decided that, after financing three seasons of international opera at

Covent Garden, she would turn her attention to symphony concerts. She appointed the young Malcolm Sargent as musical director. Believing that only the best was good enough, she then engaged the newly revived London Symphony Orchestra. The success of these concerts was to prove so great that each performance had to be given twice.

Strecker was furious to hear that Hindemith had instead agreed to play William's concerto at a Henry Wood promenade concert at the Queen's Hall. The first performance was to be in the 1928 season. Strecker wrote to Gertrude, Hindemith's wife:

Your husband should make himself harder to get. An appearance with Wood to play a concerto by a moderately gifted English composer—and that is what Walton is—is not a fitting debut. Wood's promenade concerts are, like their conductor himself, a worthy institution at which the playing is so-so and never a sensation of the sort I am hoping for.

Paul Hindemith played William's concerto for the best possible reason—because he liked it. He also respected Sir Henry Wood, recognizing in him a man of his own kind, one who set himself to make music competently and without fuss, in the most practical way, unconcerned by thoughts of personal fame, either present or posthumous. Playing William's concerto endeared Hindemith to the British public more than any number of Courtauld–Sargent concerts would have done. William was obviously immensely relieved, and would later admit that he had been much influenced by Hindemith's own Viola Concerto, even 'borrowing' several bars.

In fact, so pleased was he that he offered to conduct himself, although he soon realized that this was a mistake. The orchestral parts were all wrong—bars were missing, notes were wrong—and, as with *Portsmouth Point*, there was practically no rehearsal time allowed for the promenade concerts in those days. The first rehearsal was a shambles. Again he had to stay up all night and redo the parts, so he was not feeling his best next day (3 October 1929). Anyhow, it delighted him to see how well the work went down.

William used to say that Paul's technique was marvellous, but that his playing was brusque; he was a rough, no-nonsense player. He just stood up and played. Tertis was at this performance in the Queen's Hall. William had a letter from him later, saying he was sorry to have turned it down, and that he would play it eventually. This he did, first in Liège at yet another Contemporary Music Festival and then at Worcester, where William met Elgar in the lavatory. He didn't much care for William's work, and was heard to mutter that William had murdered the poor unfortunate instrument! The great man was only interested in hearing from William what the horse racing results were.

Hindemith remained a good friend. He and William met again in Berlin in 1936, where William was to attend a performance of his own First Symphony. William had decided to be present at the concert, despite the advent of Hitler. He knew that Hindemith was by then being persecuted; apparently his wife was partly Jewish. When William rang him up he was told, 'For God's sake, don't talk, just come to see me; meet me somewhere for lunch.' William realized that his life was becoming quite impossible. He could not even come to hear the symphony because, if he had done so, there would probably have been a demonstration in his favour, and heaven knows what would have happened. He didn't dare go out into any sort of public place, even to the Hochschule where he had worked, which was by then practically deserted, with very few pupils. Hindemith had none. He played William the concerto he had written for something called a trautonium (it is still unpublished), which sounded like a George Robey joke. It appears to have been an odd electronic instrument which could play like a piccolo on one note and a tuba on the next; it was comical, and full of possibilities. Hindemith had a great sense of humour.

In the early 1930s William was still living with the Sitwells in Carlyle Square and was wondering what on earth to do after the Viola Concerto. He was thankful that the Sitwells put up with him. He told me how nice they were about it, never once reproaching him for his inability to make a living. However, although he was not super-sensitive about it, he had started to worry a little. Now Sir Thomas Beecham came to the rescue again. He prompted Edward Clark to get in touch with William.

The BBC wanted a work which would have broadcasting appeal, so the subject had to be something that everybody knew about. Osbert was consulted about this, and feelers were put out. He came up with the idea of the 'Writing on the Wall', which he said everybody knew about. William was the one who didn't. He got mixed up with Nebuchadnezzar, and thought the Israelites had gone out to eat grass. Imagine! Belshazzar eating grass! Osbert set about finding a libretto for this. I know Christabel claimed she did all the work of research and selection of suitable extracts from the Bible, but William was definite that it was Osbert's work.

What Sir Thomas needed was a work for a large chorus for the Leeds Festival, of which he was in charge. So the two commissions fused into one. William had believed Sir Thomas would conduct himself, but instead he got the young conductor Malcolm Sargent to give the first performance. When Sir Thomas saw the score he said, 'You do seem to have got everything in. The work might not be heard again, so why not throw in a brass band; there are such excellent ones around.' William thought it rather a good idea, so he included two brass bands for good measure.

William wrote most of *Belshazzar's Feast* in the stables of Sachie's house at Weston, in Northamptonshire. In the stables he was more or less out of earshot—he made the most awful din on the piano. The 'writing on the wall' caused William terrible trouble. Sachie was greatly amused to see William's discomfort when, on opening the *Daily Express* one day, he saw the writing on the wall facetiously reported as not 'Mene Mene Tekel Ufarsin', but 'Amy, Amy Sempel MacPherson'. William was singularly unamused by the joke. Amy MacPherson was a hot gospeller of the time who called on the faithful in her evangelical temple to donate paper money because neither she nor the Lord God liked to hear the jingle-jangle of small change. To make sure her congregation could be 'weighed and not found wanting' she ordered them to peg their donations to a clothes line strung across the hall. Sachie thought that, though William did not appreciate the joke, nevertheless the incident had inspired him to finish his work and not be himself 'found wanting'.

William knew from experience how difficult it was to sing in tune, and to sing unaccompanied, in tune, and rhythmically was, he thought, almost impossible. Luckily Malcolm Sargent knew how to control a choir. William may or may not have liked his conducting, but admitted he could deal with choral forces. They ate out of his hand. Contraltos and sopranos all adored him. Sir Thomas was also well known to be good with choruses, at whose expense he coined one of his famous utterances, 'Now, ladies and contraltos, if you will look to your parts, you'll see where the gentlemen and tenors come in.' These sayings amused William. What did not amuse him was the first performance of *Belshazzar's Feast*. The pace was too slow. In a way he was pleased that it was not performed immediately again as the ladies of the choir were in open revolt about the impropriety of singing words like 'concubines'!

However, the BBC liked it. When King George V died, they asked William to write a coronation march for George VI. This commission worried William as he wondered if, after Elgar, one could write such a thing. He did not think it possible until someone said, 'You know the speech in *Henry V*? There's a whole line of titles for Coronation Marches.' The actual bit with the titles is in Act IV, Scene i:

> I am a King that find thee, and I know
> 'Tis not the balm, the sceptre, and the ball,
> The sword, the mace, the crown imperial,
> The intertissued robe of gold and pearl,
> The farcèd title running 'fore the king,
> The throne he sits on, nor the tide of pomp
> That beats upon the high shore of this world—
> No, not all these, thrice-gorgeous ceremony,
> Not all these, laid in bed majestical,
> Can sleep so soundly as the wretched slave ...

William wrote *Crown Imperial* for the coronation of George VI and *Orb and Sceptre* for the coronation of Elizabeth II. With a wry smile he would say that *Bed Majestical* would be for Prince Charles.

7

First Symphony

IT was Hubert Foss who thought it a good idea, after the success of *Belshazzar's Feast*, for William to attempt a large-scale orchestral piece, and this induced William to think about a symphony. After all, *Belshazzar* is symphonic in construction. This was the birth of the First Symphony, although it took him a very long time to get the first bars down, making him think that only a bloody fool would try to write such a work.

William spent a weekend in February 1931 with a society hostess called Edith Olivier (a distant relative of Larry Olivier's) at her country house, The Daye House, Quidhampton, in Wilton Park, near Salisbury. He annoyed the assembled guests that evening by complaining that he was so poor as to be quite unmarriageable. Among the other guests were Rex Whistler, and an American girl who admired him, who had brought Baroness Imma von Doernberg* to stay the night. Imma was strikingly beautiful and full of fun; she had been married in 1923 to Baron Hans-Karl von Doernberg, twenty-six years her senior, but only ten months after the marriage her husband had died. She and William almost immediately fell in love. Imma's royal English cousin Princess Alice described her as 'the most alive and buoyant person imaginable'. Siegfried Sassoon found her 'pretty, sweet, lively and courageous ... with a tall, graceful figure'.

It was not long before William and Imma went off on holiday together, to Ascona in northern Italy, and from there William wrote to his friend Siegfried Sassoon:

---

* Born 1901, daughter of Prince Alexander of Erbach-Schoenberg and his wife, née Princess Elizabeth of Waldeck and Pyrmount. Through her mother, Imma was a first cousin of HRH Princess Alice, Countess of Athlone, and of Queen Juliana of the Netherlands.

You will have received my postcard stating our safe arrival. Imma only just got out of Germany in time. You will have read the new decree about people leaving the country. She has £15 which has to last her for two months; after that she is uncertain of what she gets. Consequently, she can't afford to stay here after I leave on September 6th. I'm afraid that this will be the last time for long ahead that Imma and I are together. It is too sad for me to dwell on.

Two months later, however, Imma was still there and William was writing to Sassoon:

Imma is very busy learning stenography, and I have been correcting hundreds of pages of parts. The worst of that is over, and I have been able for the last ten days to do as I like. I have been lent a canoe, and so spend most of the day paddling about on the lake and swimming.

Consequently, I am looking and feeling the picture of health. Imma is not going to Zurich until November and may not then, as she is not allowed as an alien to get a job, but she has work with Frau Pulver at graphology. But that won't bring in much. She heard yesterday from her brother-in-law that the Doernberg estate can't pay anything for some time to come, and her father also will have to discontinue the small allowance he has been giving her. All of which is very depressing for her, and her nerves are consequently in a rather bad state. But she is much better than she was a month ago. . . .

Worry about Imma's increasingly precarious financial state was made worse by her unpredictable health. In May 1932, for instance, she was seriously ill with a tooth infection, which caused her great pain, as the infection had spread to her bones and all over her head. She and William had to make a hasty dash to see doctors in London.

When they got back to Ascona, he wrote again to Sassoon, of his own poverty this time, as well as of the first creative result of his love for Imma:

Life has been very worrying, and such things as symphonies have fallen far into the background. However, as it is already decided that a performance of it is to be given next March 27th, I suppose I shall be able to get away with it soon. You must be sick of guaranteeing overdrafts, but I want you, if you will be so kind, to guarantee mine for £300. The reasons being these: quite simpl[y], I won't involve you in any expense; I will pay the interest. Life is just possible here at the present rate of exchange. If the pound goes down it becomes impossible. Therefore, as I hope and expect to be here for most of this year, I should feel very much safer about it if I had between £200 and £300 here always in the Swiss bank. If I have to be in England more than I expect, it can easily be moved back; but, all the same, I should like some here, as Imma's financial position is becoming more and more precarious and she will perhaps at times have to rely on me for support entirely. And I am only too willing that she should, as you must realize how much she means to me.

Apart from mentioning for the first time a date for the possible performance of the First Symphony, this letter shows Siegfried Sassoon's willingness to help with guarantees of overdrafts.

In the next note, of 2 June, William writes: 'We came back here two days ago and her Highness is beginning to be her usual sweet self.' Later in the letter he says:

Imma is going to stay with Neil McEacharn at Pallanza for a few days on Saturday, so she can lead a life of luxury. I am not going. For one thing she is in a very nervous condition and it will be better if she is alone, as she more or less will be, as it is an enormous villa and she will have her own suite and need hardly appear—even for meals— unless she wants to. And I must get down to this Symphony.

It is understandable the joy William felt when Christabel's inspired intervention provided him with his first financial stroke of luck. He wrote to Siegfried:

Dear angel Lill Courtauld has left me in her will the magnificent sum of £500 per annum for life, and with the disposal of the money eventually. It seems quite unbelievable. It is too marvellous for words. I can hardly realize what it means for my life, and really to everybody else to whom I have been a willing burden.

Although in this letter William clearly states that the money was a legacy from Mrs Courtauld, he told me that it was given by Sam Courtauld at Christabel Aberconway's behest. The confusion seems to spring from the fact that the funds originally came from Mrs Courtauld's estate.

In early October 1932 William had to leave England in a rush, recalled to Ascona by Imma, who was again ill. This made it impossible for him to be present at the recital on 10 October of the three songs that he had dedicated to Dora and Hubert Foss, and which were to be sung at the Wigmore Hall by Dora. In writing to his publisher, he says: 'Imma is getting better slowly and will be able to stay in Pallanza, further down the lake in Italy, with some rich friends, to recuperate.' He added that he had decided to christen the symphony 'The Unspeakable' or 'The Unwritten'—only time would tell which.

No wonder the prospective conductor, Hamilton Harty, wrote to Hubert Foss in February 1933: 'Why don't you go over to Switzerland and wrest poor William's baroness away from him, so that he can stop making overtures to *her* and do a Symphony for *me* instead! Very funny!'

In June Hubert met William in Amsterdam, where both were attending the annual gathering of the International Society for Contemporary Music. Constant Lambert conducted *Belshazzar's Feast*, which, according to Foss, was a huge success. William had taken with him the first two movements of the symphony, which he showed to Foss. Foss wrote to Dora: 'Willie's looking thin. He talked today about whether it was bad for him to be so much away from England and I told him we thought it was.' Later, he added: 'Willie's Symphony is most exciting. Really on the big scale, and in the clearest symphonic manner. Just like Beethoven and Sibelius, and yet more personal. Rather tragic, and the second movement really sinister.' And in another note to his wife: 'Imma couldn't get away, so he's leaving Monday.'

In September 1933, back in Ascona, William wrote directly to Harty:

I'm sorry I've been so slow in producing my symphony, but actually I don't think it is any the worse for it; in fact, I hope and think that it promises to be better than any work I've written hitherto, but that may be only an optimistic reaction to the months of despair I've been through when I thought I should never be able to write another note. However, the 1st movement is finished and the second ought to be in another ten days or so. But having disappointed you once, I feel chary about fixing any date for its ultimate completion, but it ought to be ready sometime for next season (1934).

I must say I think it is almost hopeless for anyone to produce anything in any of the arts these days. It is practically impossible to get away from the general feeling of hopelessness and chaos which exists everywhere, however one may try—so you mustn't think I'm an exception, and one capable of compassing all difficulties and producing a masterpiece. But I'm trying my best.

William was impressed by Imma's apparently extraordinary power to heal. Once, when he broke his nose in an accident, she made the bruise and swelling disappear overnight by laying on her hands. The symphony dragged on by fits and starts for three years and William decided that Imma's healing powers could also help him to work.

I think that it was because of the time it took him to write the symphony that William always remained so defensive about it. He did explain to me that he wrote the slow (third) movement first, or, at least, most of it. The theme had originally been a quick one, composed only a couple of weeks after the first performance of *Belshazzar*. It was to have been the first movement but as it didn't work out it became the slow third. As was usual in his composing, he had an idea of the end and when he was writing the slow movement he had already thought of the finale.

The great symphonic composer of the time was Sibelius. William couldn't help but know all his symphonies well because one or another of them was played at every concert he went to. It was, I know, particularly Sibelius's Fourth and Seventh symphonies which influenced him. The Seventh has only one movement and he sometimes regretted that he had not followed Sibelius's example. Had he done so he would have saved himself a lot of trouble and anxiety but he did want to write a very classical symphony and he was delighted when someone pointed out that his opening very strongly resembles that of Beethoven's Ninth.

Everyone became very impatient with him, so he returned to England. There he used to go round to Angus Morrison's house in Chelsea and play what he had just finished. Angus told me how William never brought a sketch, always a finished piece. The slow movement of the First Symphony had a scherzo in the middle. Angus told William that it held up the progress of the movement and was unnecessary. William tore out the offending pages on the spot and gave them to Angus.

When the first movement (which was quite a good symphony in itself) was finished, William thought it was too long by about fourteen minutes. He would joke that, had he been a little more economical, he could have written four symphonies.

Yet again William found refuge to work at Sachie's house at Weston. Foss brought Hamilton Harty there, and Harty asked if he might do the first performance. In fact, the first performance was announced long before the work was finished. Instead of being firm and insisting that they couldn't have it until it was really completed, William allowed himself to be talked into permitting a performance of three movements. This was a mistake as people would later say that the last movement was an appendage; that is, of course, nonsense.

The fact remains that, when William finished the third movement, he got stuck and seemed incapable of completing the work. He had already drafted much of the fourth and last movement, but was unable to finish it to his satisfaction. Hamilton Harty must have been a kind and patient soul to have put up with all the delays before the first performance. Originally scheduled for 19 March 1934 the première at the Queen's Hall had to be postponed repeatedly. Harty wrote to Hubert Foss in September 1934:

Dear Hubert

Ecco! Il Duomo! as the little Fiesole tailor said to me after the 12th fitting of the suit he was trying to make for me. (I had, at last, in despair, professed myself satisfied, and he was as sardonic as he dared.) Poor little man—it was a frightful suit.

I shall not be sardonic, but very thankful, when I say these words to Willie Walton—but he, poor boy, is right to wait until he is quite satisfied. I do so hope (and think) it is going to be all right this time.

But what a difficult accouchement! No matter—pass the chloroform, Nurse—these are the authentic pains!

Yours ever
Hay

By now Imma, William's first true love, had left him and moved in with a Hungarian doctor, Tibor Csato. The doctor later claimed that she had abandoned William because at that time she found him impotent. If this was true, I can only assume that it was caused by their financial worries and Imma's anxieties, ill health, and intransigence. Certainly William marked the second movement 'with malice'; was that, too, a reaction to Imma's departure? Later, when War broke out, Imma was living at Kensington Palace, and her royal relations persuaded her to marry Captain Neil McEacharn, with whom she had often stayed at his beautiful estate, the Villa Taranto at Pallanza. Not only was he a very wealthy man, but, by giving her British nationality, he allowed her to remain in Britain and saved her from internment during the War.

William described the problems which delayed his finishing the symphony thus:

I changed horses, so to speak. A great mistake to change horses crossing streams. Imma left me, and I found beautiful, intelligent Alice. She was very kind, full of all the virtues. Moreover I even got on very well with her husband, Lord Wimborne, a Privy Councillor, who had been Viceroy of Ireland. One of England's richest industrialists, he was a steel magnate. The family seemed to like me, I don't know why.

Alice, who was very musical, played the piano quite well, certainly better than William. Together with other of her friends, like Garrett Moore, who became Lord Drogheda, she organized concerts in Wimborne House. The only member of Alice's entourage who disliked William was her pekinese. At mealtimes William would force this miniature dog to sit in an empty tureen at the centre of the table. The enraged little creature often bit him.

William lamented how the world of Ashby, the Wimborne's country estate, completely disappeared after the War. It was a luxurious life, replete with footmen and champagne, and he loved it. Emerald Cunard* was once staying in Ashby as a guest of the Wimbornes, and had just come down from her room around 11.45 in the morning when she saw the footman

---

* Lady Cunard, widow of Sir Bache Cunard, 3rd Baronet, and herself a noted society hostess.

apparently waiting for her with a half-bottle of champagne on a silver salver with a glass and a dish of sandwiches. She went up to him and said, 'How very nice, this is just what I fancied,' only to be told, 'No, milady, this is for Mr Walton,' as the footman disappeared up the stairs.

As to the difference in age between William and Alice, I was told by Alice's daughter-in-law, the present dowager Viscountess Wimborne, that even at the time of her death her mother-in-law had looked twenty years younger than her age; she added that her parents-in-law led independent lives, getting together only for entertaining, whether in London or at Ashby. The family accepted that Alice liked men younger than herself, and Lord Wimborne knew that in William she had a special friend. Maybe he thought their relationship was platonic, but in any case it was not until Lord Wimborne died, three months before the start of the Second World War, that Alice acquired a small London residence—Lowndes Cottage—and there became thoroughly involved in William's life and that of his friends.

According to William, Alice also became very jealous of his other women friends, and, when widowed, offered to marry him. William told me he could not allow her to do so. After a lifetime of being the exquisite Lady Wimborne, he could not allow her to become Mrs Walton. When Alice died in 1948, she left William £10,000, as well as Lowndes Cottage, which became our first home.

The inspiration to complete the symphony and finish the last movement undoubtedly came from Alice Wimborne, although—not for the first time—the necessary environment was provided by the Sitwells. The fact that Sacheverell Sitwell's house in Weston was quite close to the Wimborne estate at Ashby St Ledgers, near Rugby, was more than convenient. They left him working away at Weston quite alone, or so they thought; even the cook was on holiday. But when Sachie returned in August from a trip abroad, the taxi-driver who picked him up from the railway station told him that he had driven Mr Walton to Ashby every day.

At the end of August William telephoned Foss to say he had finished the symphony, but was unsure of the last movement. Therefore, the London Symphony Orchestra, with Harty conducting, performed the incomplete work in December 1934. The first-night party, after the performance, was held at Wimborne House, beside the Ritz Hotel in London. Dora Foss describes the occasion thus:

After the first performance of Walton's Symphony on December 3rd, 1934, Lady Wimborne gave him a sumptuous supper party at Wimborne House. It was a never-to-be-forgotten experience. We passed through a series of ante-rooms till we came to a large salon where we were received by Lady Wimborne. Huge pyramids and columns of white lilacs and lilies rose from the floor; champagne cocktails; and I got entangled with mine and my handbag, trying to shake hands with Lord Wimborne in the middle of this spacious room, with no flat space near on which to park my drink.

We then moved into the supper room where we sat at a number of round tables. I counted thirty-five guests and seventeen footmen. The tables were massed with yellow roses in silver tankards; we drank soup out of silver plates and ate the most exquisite food. After supper, we moved into the vast music room, with its fantastically lovely crystal chandeliers lit by hundreds of candles. It was a scene of great splendour and beauty—yet as a *party*, it was ineffably dull. Siegfried Sassoon joined Hubert and me and we sat together on a brocaded seat and contemplated the magnificent room and the distinguished company. 'This is Rome before the Fall,' Siegfried Sassoon said.

From Weston, William wrote to Dora Foss in July 1935:

Dear Dora

Thank you so much for your letter and the delicious cream. In spite of having progressed a little with this last movement, I feel at the end of my tether and am longing to get off to Denmark for a few days. . . . As a matter of fact, I'm not at all sure that I shan't have to begin this movement all over again, and only a chance remark of the gardener's wife as she brought in the famous ham, saved me from destroying it already. 'How pretty your music is getting—it sounds just like a great big band.' Considering that it is more than likely she knows what she likes more than I know what I like, and perhaps it may be a piece for the mob at any rate, I thought I'd keep it to see what Hubert thinks on Monday. But on the whole I feel pretty gloomy.

It soon became clear to the Sitwells that their protégé had flown. Osbert met Lord Wimborne in London, and, upon enquiring after Alice, was told, 'Oh, Alice has gone to Denmark with Willie.' William had still been living part of the time at Carlyle Square, but, when Osbert heard about this new relationship, he asked William to leave the house. Alice was a particularly close friend of theirs, and, after all, they were all very aristocratic. They managed to set a lot of people against William at that time. He was very happy, but they were very, very disagreeable. Whatever the reason, Osbert took good care to discredit William and Alice with their London friends. He even wrote to a friend, 'I saw Willie and Alice walking down King's Road looking slummy.' As William said, it would have been almost a physical impossibility for Alice ever to look slummy. Many people have told me that she was always impeccably turned out and looked years younger than her age, so I am sure Osbert was just being spiteful.

After these attacks William hardly ever spoke to the Sitwells until after we got married, almost fifteen years later. William maintained that they resented his new-found independence, but, according to Angus Morrison, the split between William and the Sitwells had another cause. The arrival of David Horner in Carlyle Square had made the difference, since, for the first time, Osbert publicly acknowledged that he was a homosexual, and Horner wanted William out of the house.

In 1935 the completed symphony—the first fruits of William's and Alice's relationship—was a notable success. After the first performance, on 6 November, Alice gave an even grander party, with royalty present. Dora Foss wrote:

It was regally done and was meant, I suppose, to be a triumphant sequel to the concert, yet it didn't seem to have anything to do with the music. It was just a terrific social occasion. Willie had had a whole page about himself in the *Evening Standard* that day, and I remember Mrs Constant Lambert unhappily bemoaning the fact that Constant had no rich patroness to procure him such attendance from the Press. We were able to tell her that it was through Hubert's agency that the article had appeared and not through aristocratic influence—which somewhat consoled her.

William had a more pertinent view: 'I felt I had arrived at last,' he told me.

Edwin Evans, Leslie Howard, William, Dora Foss, and Hubert Foss at Rickmansworth in the 1930's

William conducting a rehearsal of the Viola Concerto with the Henry Wood Symphony Orchestra at the Queen's Hall, London, with Paul Hindemith as the viola soloist

Robert Helpmann as St George (the Red Cross Knight, personifying Holiness), and Margot Fonteyn as Una (personifying Truth) in the original performance of *The Quest* choreographed by Frederick Ashton with costume and decor by John Piper, first performed at the New Theatre, London by the Sadler's Wells Ballet, 6 April 1943

Drawing of William by Michael Ayrton, Capri, 1948

Portrait by Foujita of my mother, Alejandrina Passo de Gil, with my brothers Harry and Gonzalo, myself, and a cat, *c*. 1931. Tsuguharu (Léonard) Foujita (1886–1968) was a Japanese artist, one of whose works fetched £627,000 at Sotheby's in June 1987

My mother, brothers, and myself in Buenos Aires, 1932

Our church wedding, Buenos Aires, January 1949

On 7 November, the day after the performance, he wrote to Sir Hamilton Harty from his house at 56 South Eaton Place:

Dear Sir Hamilton

I should just like to let you know how very grateful I am to you for the infinite trouble, care and energy you put into the performance last night. There is no way of describing it except by that well-worn word 'inspired'. But it is certainly true in this case. . . .

The public and critical reaction to the completed *First Symphony* seems, in retrospect, to have been extraordinary, and it quite gives the lie to William's repeated insistence that the critics were always cruel to him. One headline said simply: 'Historic night for British music.' Arthur Hutchings, in the *Musical Times*, wrote later of the thirty-three-year-old composer: 'Today English music holds a place of dignity and distinction, with promise of a rising school of composers under an exemplary leader. . . . One can say for certain that we shall from now on wait for every work of Walton, as we once did of Sibelius, in the certainty of getting something of permanent value.' The redoubtable Sir Henry Wood wrote to William's publisher, Hubert Foss: 'What a work, truly *marvellous*, it was like the world coming to an end, its dramatic power was superb; what orchestration, what vitality and rhythmic invention—no orchestral work has ever carried me away so much.' The composer John Ireland was even more succinct. In a letter to William after the first recording was released, he said: 'It has established you as the most vital and original genius in Europe. No one but a bloody fool could possibly fail to see this.' And to set the seal of musical approval on the symphony, Furtwängler and Mengelberg, acknowledged to be the greatest conductors of their day, both sent for the score, as did George Szell, who was already in America.

The *Radio Times*, in a preview of the work, gave William what was probably his best review ever. Headed 'Unique World Première for a New Symphony', and under the byline of Edwin Evans, it said:

That William Walton should have taken so long over the composition of his first symphony need occasion no surprise. It is not even a record.

Balakirev began his first symphony in 1866 and completed it in 1898. In comparison with that precedent, Walton has been a lightning worker. The circumstances that directed general attention to the time occupied upon it was that he allowed the work to be announced for two years running in the prospectus of the London Symphony Orchestra before it was completed.

Expectancy having thus been aroused, it was necessary, or at least expedient, to allay it by performing the three completed movements on December 3, 1934, after which they were included in a Courtauld–Sargent programme last April. The musical public, being thus reassured as to the existence and the character of the long-promised symphony, was quite content to await its completion at the composer's leisure. If the premature announcement had done any harm, which was doubtful, it was now remedied.

The fact is that the symphony has become a formidable undertaking. Gone are the pleasant days of such charming but non-committal symphonies as were frequently produced in the eighteenth century, when composers wrote half a dozen of them at a time. Beethoven put an end to all that. After his 'immortal nine', composers were bound to take a more serious view of their responsibilities to the form, with the result that some, like Brahms, waited until they were middle-aged before attempting one, and yet others, like Tchaikovsky, nearly broke their hearts over their first attempt.

Nowadays a composer, unless he is reckless, does not sit down to write a symphony unless he feels *that* within him which will produce something worthy of the form, and is confident of his power to realize his conception. The remarkable thing is not that Walton took time over this symphony, but that at the age of thirty, he should have felt the time ripe to attempt one. Now, at thirty-three, this confidence has proved justified. November 6 should prove a memorable date.

The number of movements in a symphony was once fixed. Lately it has become variable, but Walton, whose mind turns more and more to pure classicism (without the 'neo'), favours the older usage. His symphony has therefore four movements. In their character and in their relation to each other they follow the classical precedents, but internally they are developed in the light of modern experience. The first movement, for instance, is not divisible into exposition, development, and recapitulation. It grows organically as do the later symphonies of Sibelius. Its particular virtue—apart from the high quality of its musical content—is shapeliness achieved without the aid of the props and stays supplied by conventional 'musical form'. This shapeliness is not arbitrary, but the expression of a masterly constructive mind.

The Scherzo bears the inscription *presto con malizia*. Malice in English implies spite, but I fancy the composer had in mind connotations such as those of *malicieux* in French, as applied to the wit that touches a weak spot—in short, irony. This movement links the Symphony to the Walton we knew before it was written. It harks back to Rowlandson and 'Portsmouth Point', not to mention works written since. I cannot understand why it has been called macabre. Pungent would be my word for it.

The *adagio con melancolia* is contemplatively lyrical. Like the first movement, it grows organically, but the strands of the growth, being lyrical, are more extended. The melancholy expressed in it is profound, yet not depressing, because of the inherent beauty. There are sounds in nature that have that quality. They are sad, but one is more affected by their beauty than by their sadness. Apparently, however, it was otherwise with the composer. He is inclined to blame the mood which produced this movement for his tardiness in proceeding with his Finale. And now the Finale is ready for performance. In fact, it has already been performed, and I was present at its world première on Sunday, October 13, when Walton played the entire work from the orchestral score to an audience of five. Walton is not a great pianist. . . .

In the Finale the composer reverts—as other composers have frequently done—to a tighter, formal conception. The divisions, imperceptible in the first movement, are here clearly defined. There is a *maestoso* which forms prologue and epilogue, a group of short motifs and figures which collectively represent the first subject, and a pair of themes which combine to form the second. Of these the first is introduced fugally, after which the second enters quietly in contrast. But on its reappearance it assumed the premier role, and the other theme is reserved for the *stretto* (or drawing together of the themes) which works up to the return of the *maestoso*. The end is declamatory, an eloquent summing-up, a statement of conclusions, as befits the end of such a work.

In the strictly musical sense I feel confident that this will be hailed as a splendid Finale to a great work. Such doubts as remain to be settled by an orchestral performance, are mainly psychological. The three movements hitherto performed ended with a huge, and rather soul-searching mark of interrogation. Has Walton, in producing a masterly movement which fills all the musical requirements of a symphonic finale, still left that question unanswered? The language of subjective music begins where the power of words leaves off. The perception of its meaning rests with the individual listener. If he apprehends it, he still cannot communicate it, still less explain it to others. Only the music itself can do that. We shall know more next Wednesday ...

William always reckoned that this article said all there was to say about his symphony, with the addition perhaps of one footnote which speaks volumes about William's dislike of pomposity. A second performance of the new symphony was given at Oxford, and William was asked to address an undergraduate musical society after the concert. One of the students asked him rather solemnly what had prompted him to incorporate a fugue in the last movement. His reply, as remembered by a friend who was there, was as follows:

Well, ... when I got to the middle of the movement I was stuck, so I rang up a friend at the other end of London to ask if he had any ideas. He suggested a fugue. I said I didn't really know how to write one, to which he replied that there were a couple of rather good pages in Grove's Musical Dictionary on the subject. So I had a good look at Grove ... and wrote the fugue.

The 'friend at the other end of London' must have been Constant Lambert.

'Symphonies are a lot of work to write,' William told me. 'Too much. One has to have something really appalling happen to one, that lets loose the fount of inspiration.'

8

Music for Films

WHEN William began to write music for films, he was able to save money. He then bought a small house in South Eaton Place. Indeed the temptation of (and the need for) ready cash sometimes diverted him from what he considered his more serious compositions. The film *Escape Me Never*, produced by Herbert Wilcox and starring Elizabeth Bergner, for which William wrote the music in 1935, helped to pay the mortgage during the composition of the First Symphony, but, as he would say, it nearly drove him to a lunatic asylum.

In December 1937 William was operated on for a double hernia at the London Clinic. He was therefore delighted when, in the new year, Alice took the Villa Cimbrone, above Ravello, for a holiday, and William just tagged along. Alice was very good at making him work, and would get very cross when he mucked about. This 'holiday' proved significant in William's life, for it was at the beautiful Villa Cimbrone that he wrote his Violin Concerto, which had been commissioned by Jascha Heifetz.

William was thinking of writing a piece for clarinet and violin that Benny Goodman and Joseph Szigeti had asked him to do, when Spike Hughes, an old friend, introduced him to Heifetz at the Berkeley Hotel in London, and, when Heifetz asked him to write a concerto, William was delighted and accepted. It had been William Primrose, the viola player whom William had met at one of Alice's musical parties, who had suggested to Heifetz to contact William. The viola concerto was by now thought successful, and Heifetz was keen on having a work written especially for him.

Villa Cimbrone had been built by Lord Grimthorpe in the early 1900s; its famous long walk ends in the Belvedere where the cliff falls precipitously away revealing a thousand-foot drop. It commands the most exciting view of the sea. Lord Grimthorpe had spared no expense. Directed by his ex-valet, he employed local craftsmen, who copied works of art from Villa Rufolo and other old palaces in the town. He peppered the garden with statuary: a standing figure of Ceres, a bronze Mercury, a marble statue of Venus in a grotto, a group of nymphs, a young Bacchus, columns from Paestum, two bronze gazelles, and a Donatello David enhanced various corners of the garden. He transformed a vineyard into a magic garden, where the air is rich with the fragrance of myrtle, sage, and thyme.

No wonder William found it irresistible. He worked in a little room above the crypt, another lovely feature of this idyllic property, made to look like an enchanted forest of *Tufo* columns through which a magnificent view of the coast and the sea can be glimpsed.

The year before Alice and William came to stay, Lord Grimthorpe had let the house to Leopold Stokowski and Greta Garbo, and William told me that journalists were still on the look-out for that famous couple.

From Ravello, while working on his Violin Concerto, William wrote to Hubert Foss, of the crossroads facing him:

This is a letter I am writing for the sake of easing my mind. In the last fortnight I have had weighty decisions to make. I do hope you will think I have acted rightly. What has happened is as follows. About a fortnight ago, Bliss, authorized by the British Council, wrote me, for the moment in strictest confidence, asking me to write a Violin Concerto for the concert in New York's World Fair (in June 1939), adding that three others were being asked. Himself for a Pianoforte Concerto, Vaughan Williams for a choral work, and Bax for an orchestral work. Terms being £250 for a first performance only. No other rights being asked for, except maybe the dedication. Also a £100 extra for a trip to New York. I replied in the affirmative, stipulating that Heifetz should play the first performance. The British Council's terms not clashing with Heifetz's, I could try and kill two birds with one stone, for he can do whatever he likes about the work after the first performance. (I have not heard that the British Council will accept Heifetz or demand a British violinist.) . . .

Everything in the garden seemed lovely. I settled down to it, determined to undertake nothing else until it was finished. And knowing what I am like, it is not any too much time. Next occurs a telegram: 'Please undertake music "Pygmalion" film. Terms 550 guineas.' I answered no. This started last Thursday and has been going on ever since, Pascal the producer not taking 'no' for an answer.

It takes too long to describe the temptations brought in front of me, the telephone calls (I might as well be Garbo), but I persisted in saying no. The most difficult one to refuse is the offer of the next two pictures at the same if not a higher price, which means refusing £1,650 within the next twelve months. But to accept would mean refusing the American offer, for I should have to return now. There is about thirty minutes music in this film, which is going to take a month to get through, and at least one other film could be ready by Christmas and that would mean another month—quite apart from the distraction and settling down again to the Violin Concerto.

But, as I say, I've turned it down. Though if it is a wise decision, I am in some doubt.

Consider the British Council's American proposition again; financially, with what I shall get from Heifetz, I am not out of pocket if it concerns this one film. But there are other doubts as well. Heifetz may not like the work; he may have other dates and be unable to play it. This I have not had time to find out, and at any rate Heifetz is hardly likely to commit himself until he has seen at least part of the work. At the moment there doesn't seem much to show him. Of course, I suppose in the case of Heifetz refusing, I can always find someone else, but it would be bad I think for the work.

What, however, seems to be the greatest drawback is the nature of the work itself. It seems to be developing in an extremely intimate way, not much show, bravura, and I begin to have doubts (fatal for the work, of course) of this still small voice getting over at all in a vast hall holding ten thousand people. (Perhaps) my original plan to have the first performance with Courtaulds in the 1939/40 season at Queen's Hall is not the best after all. At least there would be some in the audience who would know what I was talking about. ... Under the American conditions, however good the work may turn out to be, I can't see it being a justifiable success at that particular performance, and that means the end of it, and most of my works in America for some time to come.

Anyhow, I think I can leave the idea of refusing the American performance for a little while, at any rate till the end of July. But as it is, it all boils down to this; whether I am to become a film composer or a real composer. I need hardly say that no-one likes refusing the prospect of £1,650. . . . Nevertheless, I should like your approval and views, especially on the American question. Even if I come to refuse, I believe I am right about the film decision. Sorry to bother you with such a long letter.

Love to you both, William.

The lucrative offer to write the music for the *Pygmalion* film, which William rejected, was eventually taken up by Arthur Honegger. No one hearing the lovely Violin Concerto could ever doubt for one moment that William made the right decision, but, as usual, writing it gave him a lot of trouble. Once again, he couldn't finish the last movement. He said he didn't know how to make the violin part elaborate enough, and therefore worthy of Heifetz. In a panic, he thought he had better give it instead to Fritz Kreisler to play. Eventually he was satisfied that he had exhausted the possibilities of what one could do on a violin. Yet he always thought of it as a rather intimate piece, a bit like the Elgar concerto; as a matter of fact, it is in the same key.

In May William wrote to Hubert Foss that at last he had 'dropped' the first movement. He had been bitten by a tarantula, a rare, dangerous, and unpleasant experience, so to celebrate the occasion he had made the second movement into a kind of tarantella and indicated that it should be played 'Presto capricciosamente alla napolitana'. He writes in the letter, 'quite gaga, I may say, and of doubtful propriety after the 1st movement!'

Nine months later, on 4 February 1939, Dora Foss wrote to her husband (who was in New York) saying that William had telephoned her in despair about the Violin Concerto. To change the subject, she had asked him what he was going to work on next. William had said that he was going to learn composition, starting with chamber music: a duet, a trio, a quartet, and onwards. Dora had told William not to be so silly, adding that no one else would be likely to do a better job. 'Oh, I've no doubt about that,' William was reported as having said. Then, a month later, having sent Heifetz the still incomplete score for his approval, William received a cable saying: 'Accept enthusiastically.'

In the event William withdrew the Violin Concerto from the concert sponsored by the British Council at the World's Fair in

New York. He explains why to a friend, the conductor Leslie Howard, in a letter sent 28 March 1939:

Dear Leslie

I'm sorry not to have answered your letter before but what with having to give an unexpected performance of my symphony and all this bother with the British Council I've had rather a chaotic and distracted ten days.

As you may have seen I've withdrawn my Concerto from the World's Fair not as is stated because it's unfinished but because Heifetz can't play on the date fixed (the B.C. only let him know about ten days ago!) Heifetz wants the concerto for two years and I would rather stick to him. But actually I'm afraid there is little to be said for either the British Council or myself, so keep this 'under your hat'.

So I'm out of the World's Fair altogether. I understand that all the music programmes barring those of the B.C. have been cancelled and that nothing is happening at all.

Unfortunately I know very little about American conditions, but I am going over sometime soon to work with Heifetz on the concerto probably the same time as you, and I most certainly will scout around and unreservedly reccommend [sic] you, which for once I can do with a clear conscience. . . .

William and Alice sailed for New York on the SS *Normandie* which William described as 'a miracle of a ship'. The object of the journey was to see Heifetz. He took the manuscript of the Violin Concerto with him but he found that Heifetz seemed more interested in planting the garden. 'He didn't even play the piece through,' William told me, 'although he did later jazz up the last movement a bit.' William tried to play it to him, but he couldn't get his fingers in the right places.

William wasn't at the first performance, which took place in Cleveland, Ohio. War had been declared by then and the house in South Eaton Place was bombed flat. There had earlier been a bomb scare, in the middle of which the score of the Violin Concerto had actually got lost. 'A pity it was ever found, really,' was William's wry comment. Heifetz's own copy of the score, complete with his bowing marks, was later lost in the Atlantic, sunk during a convoy crossing.

An amusing incident took place when William and Alice

were in New York and went to visit the Fair. For a small fee, students would wheel visitors around the vast exhibition grounds. The day was hot, so William took off his jacket and hung it on the back of the wheelchair. Very soon, it seemed to him, he and Alice were attracting rather too much attention. William suddenly remembered that the suit he had bought cheap, as a tailor's reject, had on the inside pocket of the jacket the name of the original client. It just happened to have been His Royal Highness The Prince of Wales, briefly Edward VIII.

Had the War not intervened Alice would have built a house on the cliff below Villa Cimbrone on a point known as 'I Quattro Venti'. William spent hours planning it and building a replica out of matchboxes glued together. He nostalgically kept the drawings of the house of his dreams.

William's work to help the War effort was hardly successful. He tried driving an ambulance, but found such a heavy vehicle beyond his powers, as to change gears one had to double declutch. Having distinguished himself by driving the ambulance into a ditch several times, he just waited to be called up like everybody else. But, as he had written music for films before—including *As You Like It*, with Laurence Olivier, in 1936—he was asked to write scores for propaganda films. He wrote the music for *Went the Day Well*, and for *The First of the Few*, the story of the man who designed the Spitfire. In the end he did half a dozen films; this was the only way he knew of really making himself useful.

William vividly remembered the end of the War, with the crowds rejoicing in the streets. He broke his determination not to drink when he met a friend, the film director David Lean, in St James's Park. They celebrated and congratulated each other on having survived!

9

Laurence Olivier

WILLIAM first met Laurence Olivier in 1936, when he starred with Elizabeth Bergner in *As You Like It*. The film's editor had been David Lean. Larry says he remembers William very well; he found him slender and good-looking, with a dashing air produced by William wearing a trilby hat, turned down in front. Larry got the impression that William rather looked down on him for being merely an actor. He was struck at the time by how pale William looked. He describes William in these words:

pale green hair, pale green face, palest ice-blue eyes; I would hear him going 'tim plim bim bim bim' on the piano, then stop for a bit, then write about eighteen lines of music; that tiny little twiddle he had done with his hand on the piano produced the most gutsy, bash and crash and bang you have ever heard in your life. All this did not transpire from his face or personality when you met him. You only saw the exterior that was remote, rather chill; I think he found refuge in this simulation of eccentricity. I could imagine him even walking on to a concert platform in this studied manner.

Larry was Orlando to Elizabeth Bergner's Rosalind. William remembered that it had not been love at first sight between these famous actors. Larry objected to her German origins and her Eton crop caused him to remark that she was still in the age of puberty, deciding whether to be a boy or a girl. He admitted, none the less, that she looked stunning on the set, appearing out of her caravan in a glorious evening dress with flowers in her hair. Larry thought she had taken a fancy to William as he had also written the music for an earlier film of hers, *Escape Me Never*.

Seven years later, in 1943, Dallas Bower, a distinguished producer with whom William had become friends when working for the BBC, approached Larry with the offer of reproducing on film his famous interpretation of *Henry V*. The remarkable collaboration between Larry and William really started then. It was still the middle of the Second World War, and *Henry V* was thought to be a suitably patriotic theme to inspire Britain towards the final victory. Dallas Bower had said to Larry, 'I want you to do *Henry V* and produce it with me as a director.' This offer did not go down well; nor did the next suggestion: Dallas remaining the producer, with Larry given the chance to direct as well as act the main part. Poor Dallas ended up as an associate producer, with even his shooting script radically altered. As Larry put it, 'The first job of a producer is to select a director, and I selected myself. I was ambitious, and I wanted the lot.' Dallas Bower had worked with William in 1942 on a radio play about Christopher Columbus for the BBC and so recommended him to Larry for the music.

Larry tells me that at the time he was still in the navy and he didn't really know William at all, except that he had written the music for *As You Like It*. Dallas Bower came to see him, and said, 'You must use this chap called Walton for the music.' Larry queried, 'Walton?' 'Yes,' said Dallas, 'he's a bit modern, but writes a good tune.' Larry replied, 'Modern, . . . yes, oh very good. That will be splendid. A real modern musician. Thank you very much.'

William would say that Larry had definite ideas about the music, and thought he knew what he wanted. A famous instance was Larry saying, 'Now this is a beautiful tune I've thought of—dum de dum de dum.' 'Yes,' William retorted, 'it is a lovely tune; it's out of *Meistersinger*.' Now Larry says that he never attempted to tell William what music to write, but William always swore that he did.

As for Larry's thoughts on William's music, they are best expressed in his own words: 'William knocked out the most fantastic score for *Henry V*; why it didn't win every award throughout the film industry, I'll never know, because it's the most wonderful score I've ever heard for a film. In fact, for me the music actually made the film; otherwise it would have been a nightmare. For instance, the charge at Agincourt. It was 1943, so to get a horse that anyone could sit on, you had to go to

Ireland. And even then, the only way you could get enough horses was to allow the farmers to ride their own horses. So the farmers were the knights in the charge scene. But the charge scene is really made by William's music.'

Both Larry and Dallas had wanted the music for the battle scene written before the filming began, so that Larry could arrange the acting to the music. The guide track for the Battle of Agincourt was recorded by Roy Douglas on the piano in July 1943, but it was never used. Roy Douglas worked with William often, writing out piano reductions of his scores, and correcting and supervising the orchestration. In the end William was required to fit the music to the finished film. Six months later, he wrote to Roy Douglas: '*Henry V* is being more of a bloody nuisance than it is possible to believe. Our masterpiece [the piano recording] went for nothing—no attempt whatsoever has been made to use it.'

Notwithstanding what Larry says now, the music for the charge at the Battle of Agincourt was a real problem for William. 'Ten minutes of charging horses,' William wrote ruefully to Roy Douglas. 'How *does* one distinguish between a crossbow and a long bow, musically speaking? The whole work was pretty grim, although I managed it quite well.'

It took eight weeks to film the battle sequence because of bad weather. Larry had to get up at five o'clock every morning to be fully made up because later in the day he was the director as well as the principal actor. He has often told me that the idea of shooting that scene made him terribly unhappy; he was really very worried about it. To start with, nobody believed in *Henry V*—that is, they couldn't imagine how it could ever be a success. People thought it was cranky to put Shakespeare on the screen and they couldn't understand why Rank should have backed it. However, the actors liked the idea, though the cameraman did not. Poor Larry felt that Bill Wall, the chief electrician, was the only one who truly understood what he was getting at, apart, that is, from William, who trusted Larry completely. Larry recalls that, when he first heard the Passacaglia for the Death of Falstaff, months and months before he really started shooting, he suddenly realized he had a great film on his hands because he found the music so moving and so exactly right.

There were endless delays and crises when funds were lacking. In January William told Roy Douglas of his irritation: 'I need hardly say they are not yet off the floor and won't be till mid-Jan. . . . Everything is at sixes and sevens and I seem to get no chance of settling down to the music; and of course (at the end) there is going to be the usual hell of a rush.' A week later William wrote, 'I'm now in the thick of *Henry V*; about fifty-five minutes of music, and very difficult. I wish I'd never taken it on . . . in spite of filthy lucre.'

In 1948, just before William and I met, William and Larry worked together on *Hamlet*. Larry had filmed it in black and white. He now says he did so because he did not want the film to look 'too pretty'—he saw it as an engraving rather than an oil-painting—but in fact he was in the middle of a strenuous dispute with Technicolour, who were the only manufacturers of colour film at that time, and could not obtain the colour film stock he required; hence the 'decision' to shoot in black and white.

William was known to everyone on the film set as 'the Doctor', so Helga Keller, one of the assistant film editors, told me later. She remembered William as being ultra-charming, with an amused smile permanently around the corners of his mouth, while he sucked his inevitable pipe. When Helga had to telephone William with changes in the music requirements, which had to be adjusted with every cut, William always thanked her profusely, and went on to ask if she had a boyfriend and if she was in love with him. She was frightfully flustered by this, and never knew quite how to take William's jokey remarks. His phone calls apparently became legendary in the cutting room. 'Helga, the Doctor's on the phone!' became a constant source of amusement. William had a brilliant way of scoring beneath dialogue, Helga told me. He managed to hit the tone of Larry's voice exactly, as if it were just another musical instrument only needing the accompaniment of his particular orchestration. Helga remembers William bringing to the cutting room a set of records of *Henry V* as a Christmas present. He had queued for an hour at the record shop to buy it, which was typical of his sweet shyness, because he could have requested the record company to send him a set.

Helga remembers the feeling of delicious excitement on hearing the music performed for the first time, especially the beautiful theme for Ophelia. William was to use this again years later in *Troilus and Cressida*. Helga and Larry, who were seated in the same row at the performance of that opera, turned to each other when they heard Ophelia's theme, raising their eyebrows in recognition. *Hamlet* had been a difficult film for both of them. Larry was made up as a blond and saw himself as a Dane, according to William, a Great Dane. William felt compelled to do his best for a person like Larry; *Hamlet* won the Oscar for the Best Picture in 1948. After the usual troubles over finding people to put up the money, the success was such that the British Council circulated both films all over the world. When I joined the Buenos Aires office of the Council, one of the first special occasions was the showing of *Henry V* to invited guests.

There was a strange sequel to William's film relationship with Larry, which also, incidentally, spelled the willing end of William's career as a film composer after fourteen films in all. William had agreed to compose music for a feature film about the Battle of Britain, feeling this to be a fine patriotic subject. The producer, Harry Salzman, better known as the producer of the original James Bond films and the same Harry Salzman who had once rented our house in Lowndes Place, showed William a rough-cut of the film. William was determined to write something rousing and British, something people would remember. It also amused him to discover that the German armies had marched into battle to the accompaniment of music by Wagner; William felt he could make good use of this. Malcolm Arnold was now a close friend and offered to help.

Malcolm was to conduct the recording sessions, as well as help orchestrate some of the music. Guy Hamilton, the film's director, told us after the recording sessions that he was delighted with William's score, and we returned to Italy feeling that a good job had been completed. Imagine our astonishment, therefore, when, some weeks later, one of the London evening papers telephoned to ask why Ron Goodwin had been asked to redo the music for the film.

William was hurt to the quick. The film company had decided that William's score was not long enough to issue as a gramophone record. William had written to the exact length he had been instructed, and it fitted the film perfectly. But 'it would not have been impossible to write some more,' William told me; 'as it was, someone else took over.' For weeks afterwards he couldn't sleep at night; the anguish over his discarded score was devastating.

Laurence Olivier, who appeared in the film as Air Marshal Dowding, was furious, especially since William had written the grandest of patriotic tunes, which 'out-gloried any he had written before, whether for Kings or Coronations' (as Edward Greenfield, who had been present at the recording sessions, wrote in the *Guardian*); this tune was to underline Larry's last appearance in the film as victory in the skies was assured. Larry told United Artists that he would have his name removed from the credits unless they retained some part of William's music. Eventually the producers compromised by agreeing to use five minutes of the air-battle music. William's only consolation was when he read in *The Times*, after the première in September 1969:

handsomely shot, soberly put together, but weighed down by a platitudinous score from Ron Goodwin. The only sequence of the rejected Walton score, the Battle in the Air, turned down allegedly because it was not long enough to fill an LP, is not perhaps vintage Walton, but at least lifts the film with moments of sharp excitement.

The Oliviers were the most exciting people I met when I came to London. We spent wonderful weekends at their country house, Notley Abbey. William told me how Vivien had spent weeks in bed at Notley to cure her tuberculosis, and how she had started by disapproving of this rather grand place, thinking it too pompous. Larry had been knighted in 1947. He particularly enjoyed being in the country and landscaping the grounds. William and Larry had quite a few things in common. They had both been choristers; they both bought Bentleys as well as a William Etty oil-painting ('the poor man's Titian,' as they liked to describe their Ettys); they shared a lady masseuse called Miss Chandler; they had the same doctor, Amando Child; and they both did eye exercises with a Miss Scarlet. William admired Larry, and I believe he emulated him whenever he could.

Vivien was especially fascinating, the most beautiful woman I had ever seen: feminine, exquisite, with good taste, and a knowledge of how to run a house and amuse a house party. Above all, she was a star, fascinating audiences. She spoke five languages and loved music, flowers, and cooking.

We would arrive with other guests on Saturdays, after their matinée and evening performances, for a seated, sumptuous meal. The table would be decorated with bowls of floating passion-flowers, and we would be served exquisite food and wine. Larry used to droop by three in the morning, but Vivien never tired. The house was always full of flowers from the conservatory. I vividly remember our room, with curtains chosen to match the sheets, as well as the breakfast set, and the colour scheme continued down to the loo paper. It was sybaritic.

Despite parts of the house being very old, Vivien did not think twice about tearing out an ancient staircase and replacing it with a handsome one, bought at a house sale, that she liked better. She also loved the garden, and I enjoyed gardening with her when I was there. What a difference from Argentina, where actors would not have been thought suitable people to meet! In England I marvelled at how lucky I was to be friends with these two most talented and beautiful actors.

10

Ischia

By October of our first year in London William was beginning to pine and wish to escape from the English winter. In February, two days before landing at Tilbury, he had already surprised me by announcing that we were not going to live in London. He had fallen in love with the area around the Bay of Naples on his first trip abroad with the Sitwells over twenty-five years earlier, and there he intended to settle down for six months of every year to do some hard work. After the War, William complained, he had found he was doing nothing except sit on committees, which effectively stopped him from doing any work, so he decided that we must try and go to Italy, to Amalfi, or somewhere around that part of the world, where he had worked before. We went to Thomas Cook's to find out where we might go, and they told us it was quite hopeless; there was nothing to rent, because the place had been bombed flat. But then somebody behind the counter remembered a lady who had a house in Forio, on the island of Ischia. So William said, 'Well, let's try that.' So we did.

Little did we realize what we were letting ourselves in for. The house recommended by Cook's had belonged before the War to a Countess Stead, an Englishwoman and a Papal countess, but had now passed to her daughter, Mrs Marret, whom we met in London. She had not visited the island since before the War, but assured us that the 'Convento San Francesco', as it was known, was eminently suitable. It had a most beautiful piano, she added, and a caretaker-cum-housekeeper who would do all the shopping and cooking. We could pay her the £5 a week rent in London, and it would cost us only 30,000 lire per month for the caretaker's salary, and the same again for food. As we were only allowed £5 each for foreign travel in those days, we stuffed a hot-water bottle full of £1 notes sufficient to survive for six months, and another hot-water bottle full of tobacco for William's pipe, and set off in the Bentley.

The Bentley, together with Lowndes Cottage and the housekeeper, had been the asset William had been most keen to boast about when courting me in Buenos Aires. But when we reached London, it was nowhere to be seen. We were reduced to using his old Sunbeam Talbot, which had to be towed home most evenings as it was on its last legs. The Bentley had been delivered on the eve of William's departure for Capri and, knowing that he would then travel to Buenos Aires for the Performing Right Society conference, he had lent the car to a friend, the film composer John Woolridge, whom he admired for his heroism during the Battle of Britain. John was an RAF 'ace' pilot. The MGM studio bosses were very impressed by John turning up to work in a Bentley, so he was naturally loath to part with it. He played on the unfortunate incidents when William had ditched two ambulances during the War to try and convince William that he couldn't possibly drive such a car, as he claimed it needed an expert driver. He returned it to us, reluctantly, when I rang him up to say that, if he thought William wasn't able to handle the car, I felt sure I could, since I had been driving since the age of nine. William had the same weakness for fast cars as Puccini. He delighted in racing the Bentley down to Naples on the then fairly traffic-free motorways of Italy, to test how fast the car would go.

This journey began badly: I was very sick crossing the Channel. However I enjoyed Monte Carlo where we stayed *en route* and where I played roulette at the Casino and won enough cash to pay for our hotels and meals. The car had a very small boot so our luggage was piled up on the back flap, held together by leather straps. Thieves tried to steal the suitcases by cutting the straps when we were caught in a traffic jam near the port of Genoa. We stayed with Osbert Sitwell in the castle of Montegufoni, the property south of Florence bought for him by his father. Sir George had even built a village, close to the house, for the many families that had once occupied the different rooms of the castle, in order to get them out of the main building. Osbert was eventually to live more or less permanently in Montegufoni.

The castle was situated on the top of a hill, so the view of the countryside with its vineyards and olive groves was enchanting, especially from the windows of the tall, frescoed sitting-room. In the centre of the room a large round table covered with an old shawl was piled high with books, and there was a bowl full of letters and cuttings from newspapers. Upon arrival we were offered a lethal home-made vermouth that Luigi (manager of the estate and cook-cum-general handyman) concocted by mixing miniature bottles of essence of vermouth with grape alcohol distilled from the local grapes. I am ashamed to admit that in Ischia we used to offer our horrified guests a similar mixture. It was poisonous stuff, but then so was the Montegufoni brand.

Osbert was always interested in improving the property. Upon Luigi's advice, he had bought up all the best land in the neighbourhood for the excellence of its wine, and had begun to sell it under the 'Sir Barone Osbert Sitwell' label. He installed a modern oil-press in the castle's extensive cellars, which, until then, had been empty. The new oil-press meant that all the neighbours brought their olives to him to have their oil made for them, and a flourishing business developed.

Lunch was usually taken on a side terrace, provided the weather was fine, with an old fountain dripping water into an oval basin built against the house. The terrace was flanked by huge terracotta pots with lemon trees, some of which I was told were a hundred years old. Pale blue plumbago was trained to grow up the faded terracotta-tinted walls.

On that first visit I was surprised to discover that Osbert spoke little Italian. An old lady retainer was being tiresome, and he could not convey to her what he wanted to say or understand her high-pitched answers. To William he was always affectionate, although he did tell me on a later visit how offended he had been when William had chosen Christopher Hassall as the librettist for *Troilus and Cressida*. Osbert despised Christopher for his association with Ivor Novello.

Eventually we arrived in Naples, our port of embarkation for the island of Ischia, some ten kilometres off the coast. But when we told the Cook's official in Naples that we wished to ship William's Bentley over to the island, he just looked at us in amazement. 'Impossible,' he declared. A sailor suggested that we motor north to the port of Pozzuoli. We hoped for better luck there. It was, after all, the port at which the Emperor Caligula had determined to ride his horse, which he had already promoted to consular status, across the bay to Baia. Perhaps good fortune would smile on us.

We drove our lovely Bentley to Pozzuoli over the worst-pitted road I have ever seen, through the grimy steel-smelting industrial development of Bagnoli, which was started by the English before the War and was later developed into a large complex by the Italians. Pozzuoli may be the birthplace of Sophia Loren, but my illusions about the glorious bay of Naples were well and truly shattered. The port was, and is, the biggest fish market of the area; and, as Italians like to buy their fish alive, the dockside was nothing more than a collection of wooden tubs containing every kind of shellfish and eels, some of which leapt out of the tubs and frisked about on the great stone blocks of the quayside. We realized that the whole area was alive with desperate people who would doubtless be ready to knife us. Eventually we were shown a very small boat that took meat to Ischia. It actually had on board two live cows of uncertain age.

The captain said he had not been asked by anyone to transport a car over to Ischia since before the War, when Ischia boasted two motor vehicles, one belonging to Senator Parodi Delfino, the other to Countess Stead. A crowd soon collected around us to witness the unusual embarkation. My Italian was almost non-existent, but, with a few Spanish words, much sign language, and some money, we persuaded the captain to put two long planks across the stern of his ship. Inch by inch, I drove the Bentley on to the planks. 'Avanti! Avanti!' shouted the captain.

On the quayside, the betting was that I would plunge into the sea. I could see only the vast expanse of the bay above the bonnet of the car, and was quite terrified. William didn't help by suggesting that I plug the exhaust of the car with a cork, because he feared it would dip into the sea when the small steamer left the quayside, since the car hung on the planks well out over the sea. The cows were shifted to one side of the boat, and we were just about to cast off when the port police appeared and declared that we could not take the car to Ischia. Our European green card (an insurance document) said plainly that we could drive all over Italy, so I informed the police in Spanish that, since Ischia was part of Italy, we were taking the car over. I turned to the captain and ordered him to steam away, leaving the uniformed port policeman irate, helpless, and waving our documents in the air.

It turned out that the house we had rented was on the opposite side of Ischia from the port. The car thus proved to be essential since there was hardly any form of public transport. The Convento, enclosed in a fretwork of stone arches draped with creepers and flowers, looked idyllic. It was built by the side of the church of San Francesco. We were offered a glass of home-made vermouth by Pasquale Castaldi, the caretaker, whom William at once dubbed 'Don Pasquale'. The caretaker did not realize that this was the name of an *opera buffa* character and thought we were showing him an exaggerated respect, as the title 'Don' implied that we regarded him as an aristocrat at least! I ran through the house in great excitement, noticing in the bathroom a great marble bath with a carved mask above it, in the garden oleanders in bloom, and in the music room a 120-year-old Érard piano—which William insisted had not been tuned since the day it was made. The large sitting-room with many high windows looked out to sea and to the village of Forio, and from a window balcony looking into the adjoining church I could hear Mass.

We had a good laugh when I discovered that not only the mask but also the bath was decorative: there were no taps. The bath had been used only once in the last years, when the bishop had been a guest there. The water to fill the bath had been heated in copper cauldrons over a wood fire in the garden, and had then been brought in wine vats on the head of Don Pasquale. Such an enormous effort was appropriate only for bishops, he informed us; no one else could expect such treatment. The electricity supply, moreover, was perilous in the extreme. The electric bulb above our bed was connected by two bent wires which were supposed to hitch on to two similarly bent wires that hung from the ceiling. If one managed to get the right wires touching each other, all was well; otherwise, the main fuse blew.

The water we washed in had wriggling mosquito larvae in it. Worse, the kitchen, which was in the middle of the house, had no water. Pail upon pail had to be carried up from the water cistern in the entrance drive, which collected rain from the flat roof. The chimney flues had been neglected, and many of the bricks had become dislodged, thus providing an easy way down for the many rats which infested the hill behind the house, *en route* to the wooden ice chest where our food was supposed to be kept fresh. Every time I tried to cook, a large rat would jump out from a side range, or out of the fridge in the side of which the rats had eaten a hole. Such was our honeymoon!

But we survived. Don Pasquale explained to us that the Convento was in such a sorry state because Countess Stead was British, and therefore the house had been considered enemy property during the War years, and had been taken over by the Italian government and administered by the Banco di Napoli. Most of the window-panes in the rusty iron windows were broken, and in place of the missing curtains Mrs Marret had thoughtfully sent Pasquale some silver-coloured rubber which he had cut and hung up. This had come from the barrage balloons which had floated over London to stop the approach of low-flying enemy aircraft. But the smell of hot rubber, when the sun was full on the windows, was quite unbearable. So was our bed. It looked splendid enough, but its mattress was capricious. The springs had a life of their own, and would often get loose from their binding and hit us deftly in the ribs in the middle of the night, waking us up.

The roof tiles of the entrance hall were badly damaged. We curtained off this small area with army blankets, as it seemed easier to heat with charcoal braziers than the long main room. Don Pasquale improvised a settee by extracting the back seat from the old Lancia car that Countess Stead had left in the entrance drive; this he propped on bricks, so I had a seat where I could embroider. It maddened me to find that the rain came through the tiles, and forced me to move my seat and embroidery frame every time it rained.

The day after landing on Ischia we realized that the island lacked petrol pumps; as our Bentley had to be fed fifty litres at a time, we had to persuade Don Pasquale to get his brother—a fisherman—to sell us the drums of petrol which the authorities had allocated to him for fishing. I'm sure Pasquale thought we were mad, as all foreigners are supposed to be. The islanders loved inventing stories about the eccentric visitors who now and then settled on their coast. One of these tales particularly appealed to William. Don Pasquale told us that the son of one of these foreigners, instructed by the local boys, was found by his mother dallying with a nanny goat. The horrified lady locked the youngster up in a derelict wine-cellar. That afternoon she sailed her boat to visit an American friend who lived on the opposite side of the island in a Moorish-style villa, said to have been so built to harbour an errant Indian princess. On hearing the story, the friend determined to free the prisoner. She saddled her white mare and galloped all the way to the wine-cellar, returning to her Arabian Nights house with the lad. She later took the young man to Africa, where she owned extensive plantations. William thought the story fitting for an island colonized by the Greeks in 800 BC. Even now, he informed me, the old Greek saying of, 'Women for duty, boys for pleasure, and goats for ecstasy!' held true. The Convento had a fine library of old books. One of these books recorded the fact that one of the Steads had gone down in the *Titanic*, but had subsequently narrated the experience to a medium, who had written a book telling what Stead had experienced on his voyage to the next world.

The great advantage of the house was peace and quiet. For six months in winter there were no foreigners on the island at all, and William found that he could work without interruption. Our only distraction was visiting Naples to take a bath, go to the Opera, and buy fresh food. The people of Ischia kept mainly to their Mediterranean diet of fish, pasta, dried beans, goat cheese, tomatoes, and figs. If we wanted different vegetables, meat, or butter, we had to send a courier to Naples. We soon discovered that the island was primitive in other ways. Once we were taken by a friendly priest to a high plateau beneath the twin peaks of Mount Epomeo, an extinct volcano. Don Pietro, who is an archaeologist and lover of nature, told us that a few years previously an aeroplane had crashed there. When the police had reached the site of the wreck on the morning after the accident, they had found that everything of any value had already been taken away; ears had been cut off for their ear-rings, and fingers were missing where presumably a ring had been. A thorough search was mounted in the cottages and villages nearby, but nothing had ever been found. In later years we braved these same hills to collect ferns and plants that only grew at those heights, to furnish rare specimens for the garden at the new house we were to build, La Mortella.

The Convento was just too uncomfortable for a repeat visit, so we started to look for an alternative house. Don Pasquale offered us his wine-cellar, 'Casa Cirillo', higher up on the hill. Having been abandoned for years, it had no roof or electricity, but it looked out to sea and had thick, comfortable-looking walls and a well-head in the entrance hall. He told us that this was the very place where the horrified foreign lady had imprisoned her bestially inclined son.

William and I agreed that anything would be better than the leaky Convento. We had not realized, however, that Don Pasquale, having survived without a salary during the War years, was now anxious to secure a job for himself. By offering us the ruined wine-cellar, he hoped to work for us *for ever*. At the time this arrangement suited all three of us; in exchange for a nine-year tenancy agreement with Don Pasquale, we undertook to rebuild the place and to employ him. It was our first experience of building a house and our master builder was just eighteen. There was no proper road to the wine-cellar, but we managed to drive the Bentley up the widely spaced stone steps without damaging it. We had to spend a second winter in the Convento while the building was in progress. We reroofed part of Casa Cirillo's roof terrace to make a music room for William, and installed plumbing, electricity, and a garage. When the Ascot cylinder-gas hot-water boilers, brought from London in the back of the car were fixed in the two bathrooms we built, they were ceremoniously inaugurated by some of our neighbours, who were agog with the novelty of hot water coming out of taps.

The local carpenter made a sturdy bed, a cupboard, a large work-table for William, and one for the dining-room. We had a lot of trouble getting the windows and doors to the terrace to shut. The ironmonger believed it was essential for fresh air to come in through the gaps he had left; otherwise, he declared, we would choke in the house. Pasquale brought a lot of straw, out of which I made the mattress. William was delighted to help with the painting of the furniture, and we enjoyed visits to Naples to hunt for second-hand chests of drawers and discarded gilded wooden candlestick-holders, which I repaired and converted into lamps.

So as to have running water, we installed an electric pump in the water cistern where rain-water collected. We planted a walk in the garden, arched over with orange and lemon trees and bordered with blue hydrangeas. I even began to grow vegetables, including spinach, which sprouted with such profusion that we tried to give it away. This proved impossible, since Pasquale and his family thought that everything, including the rabbits, would die if given these green leaves to eat. At last I had no rats to contend with or water to carry. The view from the terrace was lovely, and on it I could dance—more like leaping around, it was—to my heart's content.

For several years we commuted between London and Ischia—six or more months on the island, a few back in London. All worked out well until we thought of helping Don Pasquale to make some extra money. He had added a pair of twin girls to his family, and, as we were generally in London in the summer, we suggested that he find a summer tenant for the furnished house, provided he personally took care of the property. That way he could not only work, but also keep the rent.

Unfortunately, he let the house to a well-known film star, Alida Valli. Don Pasquale had never seen 'showbiz' life before; cascades of champagne, motor boats and cars, constant visitors, and a very, very good time being enjoyed by all. He started to wish that more film stars would take the house, and that the boring British couple with whom he had made the initial arrangement would depart. Thus, on our return from London, we found a sour, confused man determined to get us to leave by being extremely disagreeable. Our contract was a word-of-mouth agreement sealed only by a handshake. A three-month siege began; Pasquale had clearly not counted on the formidable Argentine wife of the gentle English composer. I persuaded the mayor of Forio, who was a lawyer, to speak to Pasquale and ask him to sign a proper contract. Pasquale boasted of being honesty itself, but it took three months of melodrama before he signed. He went on hunger-strikes, and cried on his knees. He stacked the sideboard with unwashed dishes. He threatened to leave our employment. Eventually he signed the lease, but soon after resumed his campaign of making life untenable, so we had to ask him to leave. This caused a tremendous crisis. He wrote us a menacing letter saying that, before sacking him from employment in his *own house*, we ought to have known that he would take revenge. He went on to admit that he knew he shouldn't be doing such a thing, but that, unless we paid him the sum of 700,000 lire (more than two years' salary), he would denounce us for not having paid his social security stamps. We had allowed him to keep the social security booklet in good faith, and had paid for the stamps regularly, a thing very few people did at the time. Of course, we ignored the threat. The labour inspector duly arrived at the door of Casa Cirillo, and, since he looked like a thug and was armed, I shut the door in his face. The mayor came to our rescue again. One was not allowed to be insured if one worked for oneself at home, so Pasquale had no right to his social insurance. His letter was used to prove that he had been employed in his own house. It was touch and go. I believe my hair started to go white during this trying contest of wills. However, this appeared to please William, as, in future, hotel receptionists stopped asking him to which room his daughter's suitcases should be sent.

There was a happy sequel to our years of soured relations with Pasquale when we returned the keys of Casa Cirillo to him a year before the end of the lease, together with the one million lire we had charged Malcolm Sargent for that last summer's rent. We had, by then, moved to San Felice, one of the newly rebuilt cottages on our new property. Pasquale was so overcome by our gesture that he expressed the wish to give William a present, and asked me what William would like. Never thinking for a moment that he would accede, I told him how much William loved the fifteenth-century wooden carving of a madonna that had hung above our bed in Casa Cirillo. Pasquale had bought this carving from an old lady in the village, and was very attached to it. To our surprise and delight, he came next day to see us, with the madonna tucked under his arm. She now hangs over the bed at La Mortella.

But life on the island was enjoyable. I liked shopping. I learned Italian quickly, and I liked talking to the local people. I enjoyed cooking, and there was always my embroidery to keep me entertained. The walks up rough tracks looking for wild asparagus and earth orchids were our afternoon *divertissement*. In spring amusing people appeared to rent or occupy their houses for holidays. We met and made friends with some of them. Camillo and Lidia Casati came each year to Forio to shoot quail, and celebrated William's birthday with us on 29 March. The Marquis Camillo Casati Stampa di Soncino was the half-brother of Cristina, Lady Huntingdon, daughter of his father's first wife, the legendary Marchesa Luisa Casati, an intimate friend of D'Annunzio. Her portrait was painted by Augustus John and by Boldini, among others. William remembered having seen her in Venice wearing white make-up to show off her large limpid eyes, heavily made up in black. She could not pass unnoticed, as she generally held a boa constrictor, was draped in leopard skins, and led her hounds on a golden leash. In her impoverished old age she lived in London, and was helped by old friends of her brilliant youth, such as Harold Acton and Lord Berners.

The Casatis came to a sad, tragic end. Camillo and Lidia separated, and, by those mysterious ways available to the very wealthy, they obtained a Vatican annulment of their marriage. Their only child, Anna Maria, lived with Lidia, who died of cancer a few years later. Camillo married Lidia's best friend, Anna, for whom he also managed to contrive a Vatican annulment. Several years later, in Rome, Camillo murdered Anna and her latest lover, and shot himself.

While for William life on Ischia was ideal, because he could work undisturbed, for me it was sometimes a battle for survival. What I perceived as the local mentality was the biggest problem. I was only twenty-two and good-looking, so the villagers thought I must have married William for his money. In their view, this was the only reason why a young woman would marry an older man. I was also the only woman on the island who drove a car, something thought quite immoral by the islanders, I later discovered. It never occurred to us that my driving the car could be frowned upon. William, in any case, was too busy working to come shopping with me. Moreover, negotiating the narrow island roads was a different feat from racing the car down the Italian highways, which was what greatly amused him.

My parents came to visit, as did my older brother, Harry. William got on well with him. Harry's generation was the first in Argentina to realize the importance of running their country estates scientifically. His speciality was animal science, and, in particular, the eating habits of cows. This amused William no end, and he became very fond of a photograph of Harry's cow, into whose side a window had been inserted, so as to take samples of the cow's fodder at different stages of decomposition. Harry used to tell us that this cow liked him. Whenever he opened the window in its stomach to take samples, he would scratch the inside, and the cow would show its appreciation by mooing away. William was particularly keen to know how Harry managed artificial insemination with his cows. But Harry was too shy to allow us to see these photographs. He later became dean of a college of agriculture in Argentina, and today still devotes himself to research.

William was not the first artist to come to the island. Among other notables, Ibsen worked in Casamicciola in the last century, and Toscanini used to come for the radioactive mud baths. When Augustus John, well known as a portrait painter and for his legendary way of life, visited the Stead family, he found the grey lava of the island hills did not inspire him to paint. All visitors to the island, including the mainland Italians who come from what the local people term *il continente*, are known as *stranieri* (foreigners). One who had a house for years and we enjoyed seeing was Mollie, the American widow of the last Earl of Berkeley. Her nephew Lennox Berkeley and the writer L. P. Hartley were among her frequent visitors. She also had a castle in Assisi, a tower in San Geminiano, a *palazzo* in Venice, and a flat in the Palazzo Borghese in Rome; but she loved her little

Ischian cottage. Germans too have long favoured Ischia. The painter Bargheer had a house in Forio when we came, and a school of young local painters formed around him. One of them, Gino Coppa, later painted William's portrait.

In London we met another painter who made his second home in Forio, Prince Henry of Hesse (Enrico d'Assia), a son of the late Prince Philip of Hesse and Princess Mafalda, daughter of King Victor Emanuel III of Italy. Princess Mafalda died tragically in Buchenwald. It was Enrico's relation Princess Ludwig of Hesse and the Rhine,* 'Aunt Peg' to many of her friends in the musical world, who introduced us to him.

Enrico told us over lunch how he and the group of foreign artists who would meet at Maria's Bar in the piazza of Forio were fascinated by the aura of mystery which surrounded the 'invisible composer' and his wife, who led such a secluded life that no one had ever met them. They had glimpses of me, the exotic young woman—Spanish, they thought—emerging from the stately Bentley when Pasquale took me to the bank in Forio on our first winter's stay.

We liked Enrico immediately, and asked him to come and see us when he next visited Forio. When he arrived at Casa Cirillo, he found me pulling up weeds in the front patch of ground, looking like a peasant with a handkerchief tied under my chin. We had met in elegant town clothes, and he did not recognize me. He asked if Lady Walton was at home. I replied, 'Yes, she is.' He then said, 'Can I speak to her?' When I answered, 'But you are speaking to her,' he blushed purple, and we couldn't stop laughing. He built his own house on a hill near Casa Cirillo, and became our favourite neighbour.

Wystan Auden had come to Ischia the year before us; he had been on the look-out for a place in the sun, just as William had, one that was far enough away from visiting friends for him to be able to work quietly. He lectured in America for six months a year, and spent the spring and summer in Forio. We usually did the reverse, spending winter on the island; but we met when our visits overlapped. Wystan and Chester Kallman took a house on the outskirts of the village of Forio. It had a garden where

* Née the Hon. Margaret Campbell Geddes.

Chester grew vegetables. He and Giocondo, the young Forian who helped in the house, cooked the meals.

Wystan was oblivious to personal comfort, so much so that he ignored the fact that the central room of the house he and Chester had taken had lost its roof and was open to the sky. The old beams were still in place, curtained in creepers. Lucina, the cat Wystan loved and immortalized in verse, lived in a Neapolitan-style cupboard which had lost its doors, and she produced kittens among his sweaters. Books and papers littered the kitchen table, which was cleared only for meals. Wystan dressed in very simple clothes: a shirt over baggy trousers and a pair of worn-out espadrilles. Generally, he preferred to go barefoot. This habit of not wearing shoes appeared hilarious when we saw him years later in Salzburg, all dressed up in a dinner-jacket and black tie, shuffling around in slippers. Even so, he had a quiet dignity, an elegant presence, and his humorous face was ridged with deep lines. Half closing his eyes to avoid the smoke of the cigarette usually held in his hand, he would bend towards one to converse, often shaking with silent mirth. We used to meet in the piazza in the front of the town hall for outdoor opera performances. I well remember one wild evening when a whirlwind took off with the backdrop of Nagasaki, and Mme Butterfly fled in terror.

A table at the left-hand corner of the vine-clad terrace of Maria's Bar was always reserved for Auden. Actually called the Bar Internazionale, this bar belonged to Maria Senese, a one-time 'lady of the town' from Naples. Maria, who blacked her greying hair with boot polish, was particularly kind to foreign artists, and would be very patient over them settling their bills. Here Wystan's friends congregated at midday, when he would walk down to the piazza to collect his post after a full morning's work, and again after supper. It was not unusual to spot Stephen Spender and Christoper Isherwood there too, and it was amusing to notice how Truman Capote was made to hang around, not daring to approach until Wystan appeared to want to meet him.

Auden immortalized Maria in verse:

> How serene and jolly it is to sit here
> Round a table under the stars of summer
> Laugh and gossip over wine or stregas

William Walton

Yankee, Limey, Kraut, Foriano, Roman
Ladies, Gentlemen, and the third sex, join me,
Raise your glasses, drink to our Hostess crying
VIVA MARIA

Wystan was extremely kind to William when the last act of
Troilus was being anxiously fashioned, and the librettist Christopher Hassall needed help writing the sextet. Wystan wrote it
out for him. He was also kind in other ways. Although he was
not a Roman Catholic, the priest of the small church opposite
his house knew that he could call on him to help unfortunate
families. Moreover the expensive harmonium, and the new
shrine and missal in the church are further evidence of his
generosity.

Wystan's companion, Chester Kallman, was a source of
scandal. Don Pasquale regaled us one morning with rumours of
an orgy that had taken place at Wystan's house, while he was
away in New York. We had been asked by Chester to dine with
some of his American friends, among them a talented painter,
Carlyle Brown, and his lovely wife, Marjorie. After we left to go
home, Chester invited a young Forian to entertain the guests.
Pasquale informed us that the young man was given a shower
and then covered in eau-de-Cologne. After a lot of wine was
imbibed by all, the youth had sexual intercourse with everybody
present. What surprised us was to be told by Pasquale that the
young man had been paid double by the girls. The poor youth
had then had to jump into the sea to get the scent of the cologne
off his skin. Otherwise, said Pasquale, he could never have gone
home to his one-room family house, lest his family suspect that
he had been up to no good. As it was, he caught a terrible cold,
and the village people enjoyed spreading this gossip. One of
Chester's ephebes was a brawny fisherman known as 'Rocky';
another, slighter in stature, earned the nickname 'Scendiletto'
(bedside mat).

I did not find Chester attractive. Tall and blond, with light
green eyes and thick lips, he looked a bit like a Rugby player. He
was an excellent cook, and there is no doubt that his collaboration in Forio with Auden on the libretto for Stravinsky's opera
The Rake's Progress led to one of the masterpieces of contem-

William photographed with me
before leaving Lowndes Cottage
for a party at the U.S. Embassy,
London 1949

At the Royal Opera House,
Covent Garden, at the first
performance of *Troilus and
Cressida*, 3 December 1954

William and Laurence Olivier on the set at Denham Studios, during the filming of *Hamlet*, 1948

William watching me work at my embroidery in Casa Cirillo, Forio

Christopher Hassall, William, and Malcolm Sargent with the score of *Troilus and Cressida*

Toscanini's daughter, Contessa Castelbarco, Nicola Benois, myself, William, Pietro Zuffi, and Maestro De Sabata at the first performance in Italy of *Troilus and Cressida* at La Scala, Milan, 12 January 1956

With David Webster at the opening of the Stockholm season at Covent Garden, 30 August 1960

Weighed down by plants purchased at the Chelsea Flower Show for our garden in Ischia, London 1962

Maria Callas, William, and I on the terrace of Casa Cirillo, our Forian home, in 1957

William, still using a crutch, Vivien Leigh, and myself with a stick, Covent Garden, 1957, after our motorcar accident

porary opera literature. I remember him telling us that, as Stravinsky had never listened to any music by Puccini, he had sent him some records to inspire him, along with some words for Igor to set as an aria. Stravinsky came to Ischia to visit Auden at his little house in Forio. Wystan was in a panic, and consulted Maria, the *padrona* of the Bar Internazionale. She was of the opinion that the important item of the meal should be the cake. So Wystan ordered a superb cake, to be made by the local pastry shop and delivered on the day. When it arrived, not knowing where to put it—his table was, as usual, littered with papers— he sat it on the outside loo, which had a curtain drawn across its doorway.

Stravinsky arrived, and said he was much looking forward to the meal. Wystan was really interested only in the quality of the wine, but to reassure his guest, whom he knew was more of a gourmet than he was, he drew back the curtain to show off the *pièce de résistance* of the meal. Stravinsky, taken aback, was amazed that the cake should be in such a place. Wystan told us that he simply could not understand why Stravinsky was shocked at where the cake had been enthroned.

In 1957, when he won the Feltrinelli literary prize, Auden moved to Kirchstätten, near Vienna. He had become disenchanted with life in Forio as it had become a noisy tourist centre, and the inhabitants had given up their traditional ways and became grasping. The local authorities also started to pester him with requests for payment of taxes, which they levied on all of us foreigners with devastating effect. As for William and me, the tourist boom did not affect us, as we had never indulged in the café life. Our friend the accountant Nino Mattera dealt with the tax officials in a simple, Byzantine fashion. Perhaps because of this, we stayed, while most of the other early foreign residents abandoned the island.

The last time Wystan came to dine before leaving Forio, he surprised us by arriving in a jacket and tie, with shoes over which he wore a pair of grey spats! We couldn't believe our eyes, and immediately made it clear that we had not invited a party to see him off; it was only us. He replied serenely, 'Why! I am not elegant. I have only dressed to come to see you.' I never found out if he was pulling our leg.

William Walton

He brought me a little book entitled *The Naming of Wild Flowers*, by Gareth H. Browning, with the following dedication:

Let your floral vistas Broaden
Happy Birthday dearest Susan
is wished by Wystan Auden
Chester Kallman too.

Wystan and our friends the Casatis would never miss the three days of festivity in May when the village of Lacco Ameno celebrates the feast of Santa Restituta, patron saint of the island. We liked to think of her as the Christian version of Venus (her name means 'to be returned', restituted from the sea). She is believed locally to have been an African princess martyred in Carthage in AD 304, whose body was swept up on the beach in a half-burned-out boat by a powerful sirocco wind, the wind which often covered our terrace with red sand from Africa. The band in the bandstand built on the piazza, the sea illuminated by a thousand floating candles in coloured cartons, the hills flickering with tiny oil-lamps, and the midnight firework display attracted the eager population of the whole island. William, taking advantage of the crowds following the procession of the saint while she blessed the fields and the sea, would naughtily pinch the bottoms of passing pretty girls. He used to remark that, far from objecting, they actually expected such attentions!

The streets would be lined with kiosks selling delicacies, such as pig's snout with a large lemon stuck in the open jaw or *torrone* (hard toffee with almonds). We all admired the antique statue of the saint, her dark mien contrasting with her pale golden habit.

Another visitor to Ischia in those early days was Herbert von Karajan. He used to come for the radioactive cure which had made the island famous. Most conductors, he told us, suffered from bad backs. With his girl-friend, Eliette, they would scamper back and forth on their Vespa scooter, she seated side-saddle, her long blonde hair blowing in the wind. It was a strange courtship. The music world did not believe that he would ever divorce his wife, Anita, to marry this girl. When she used to ask me what it was like to be married to a musician, I would think, 'Poor thing, she will never find out.' But Eliette was immensely patient with Herbert, whose idea of a good holiday was to get up at five o'clock in the morning, go for a walk up to the summit of the extinct volcano Mount Epomeo, then sail round the island and have several hot mud cures, which would have exhausted most normal human beings, and all this before breakfast. We noticed that Eliette was always seasick when out on the boat, but she never complained. When they finally married, it amused William that the first thing to go was the boat, exchanged for a very expensive-looking ring. William asked Herbert one day what he would have liked to do if he had not become a conductor. He replied, looking William straight in the eye, that he would have loved to have taken William's appendix out! William used to quip that Herbert had stopped conducting English music when the English tanks moved out of Germany after the War.

The Italian writer Alberto Moravia rented a peasant's house in Forio with his companion Dascia Maraini, while his estranged wife, Elsa Morante, also a successful writer, rented a fisherman's house near the beach, where she welcomed local youths. Among the other annual visitors were Roberto Ducci, who was to become Italian ambassador to Great Britain, and his pert Polish wife Wanda, the painter Aldo Pagliacci, Dylan Thomas's widow Caithlín, Mussolini's daughter Anna Maria, and the Australian painter Mitti Risi. One unforgettable regular visitor to Forio was Mrs Constance Mappin, widow of one of the owners of Mappin and Webb. She was usually accompanied by her dog 'Mosquito' and an enslaved young man called John Pollock, who wrote a *roman-à-clef* about Ischia called *The Last Boat*, and followed her everywhere.

Mrs Mappin spent most of her waking hours in the little restaurant on the town beach in Forio run by an expatriate former GI, who had married the sister of Auden's and Kallman's Giocondo. She occupied her time between dry martinis by writing a new will every few days. Each will began, 'I, Constance Violet Marguerite Mappin, being of sound mind, ha, ha, ha . . .', and had a certificate attesting to her sanity, issued by a local *Dottore* who was, in fact, a vet. The wills were replete with insults to her heirs and outrageous stipulations; in one, she left a large bequest to a Conservative MP on condition that he join the Labour Party.

We met Frau von Stohrer, the formidable widow of the wartime German ambassador to Spain, who was credited with trying to tempt the Duke of Windsor with an offer of the Crown of England if Germany invaded Britain. She had built her large house on a beautiful site which she had acquired through the good offices of Mussolini's ill-fated son-in-law Ciano. In her house we met Ciano's widow Edda, who was Mussolini's favourite daughter.

At a party at Wystan's house in 1953 we were introduced to a brilliant young German composer, Hans Werner Henze. Hans was then only twenty-seven, about the same age as me. He had come to live on Ischia after he had won an Italian Radio prize for his setting of a Kafka story, 'The Country Doctor'. The money from this prize had allowed him to leave Germany and travel south. His publisher had provided him with a small allowance to work abroad, so he rented a room in a peasant cottage, not far from Casa Cirillo.

Hans was very excited about meeting William. It seems that he had heard William's First Symphony at the age of seventeen, and the music had made an unforgettable impression. Although enlisted in the Nazi army at only sixteen, he had somehow retained his good humour; he was then exceptionally good-looking, with light blue eyes and blond hair, very precise in his gestures, and tidy. He had a knack of getting people to serve him. Lucia, the peasant lady in whose house he had rented a room, was already a willing slave. She soon became very possessive in exchange for her dedicated care of him, and later made a tremendous scene when Hans decided to move to Naples. She cursed him with terrible oaths, which worried and frightened him. He became convinced that she could harm him, even at a distance.

William discovered that Hans had even less money than we did. On one occasion I met him in our local bank, and found him in great distress. He was supposed to go to Rome to produce his latest opera *Boulevard Solitude*, but lacked money for the journey. The work had already been produced at the San Carlo Opera House in Naples, with great success, so William suggested that I take the few traveller's cheques which we kept in case of an emergency and leave them in Hans's cottage, with a note to say that we hoped the Rome Opera House would eventually pay him; until then, we wished him the best of luck. Hans got to Rome where he was very amused to learn that, at the première there, Igor Stravinsky, who was in Rome and wished to hear his new work, was turned away by the ushers because he was not wearing a black tie.

At that time Hans lived very simply. His cottage didn't even have running water; he had to go to Forio, where a small *pensione* allowed him to take a free mineral hot-water bath, as in winter there were no tourists. He was also diffident about food, unlike William who, although he had a very discriminating palate, was quite happy eating his mother's favourite dishes, Lancashire hot-pot and tripe and onions. We introduced Hans to lobster; he was too polite not to eat it, but he didn't really enjoy it.

William tried to educate Hans, gastronomically speaking; he once insisted that Hans and he should leave the train to Venice in the town of Bologna for the sole purpose of offering Hans a meal at the famous Pappagallo restaurant. They were on their way to hear several modern works performed at La Fenice opera house, including Prokofiev's *The Angel of Fire* with Dorothy Dow in the leading role, the same soprano who would disappoint William when she sang the role of Cressida in the Milan production of his *Troilus and Cressida*.

Life on the island gradually became easier. Petrol pumps arrived. Water could be bought by the truck. An energetic grocer started up a mini-Fortnum's in the next door village of Lacco Ameno; Arcangelo was his name, to us a real archangel. Only the Post Office did not improve. They didn't even know how many stamps should be put on letters to England. The post sometimes arrived, and sometimes did not. It was a complete gamble.

Ischia has changed since those heady days. Flocks of goats used to pass the front of Casa Cirillo. Groups of young women, returning from the hills, would carry enormous bundles of forage on their heads, walking barefoot and resting their mounds of tightly packed grasses on the dry stone walls while they regained their breath. Long wooden carts, pulled by what looked like miniature horses, would labour up the rough track beneath the house, hauling wine barrels. I remember one occasion when William and I both lost our coats on the mountainside while we were out on a picnic. When we searched the path we had come along, not a trace of them could be found. Our guide told us not to worry; he would ask the parish priest of the area to mention in the Sunday sermon that his friends had lost their coats, and that, if anyone had found them, please to bring them to the church. We never thought this would work, as poverty was then extreme in that area and our warm coats would have been a useful addition to the people's simple garments. But, to our great surprise, the coats were returned anonymously. I wonder whether, with the great influx of tourism on the island and the new prosperity, that would happen now. I'm sure that, had William and I come to Ischia today for the first time, we would have been less eager to make the island our permanent home.

Some time after we left the Convento, it was leased by an old Englishman, a brother of the Earl of Clanwilliam; he had served as a cavalry officer in the Boer War. He and his plump little American third wife wintered in the Bahamas, and spent their summers at the Convento San Francesco. William and I often watched him drive rather dangerously in their long, old-fashioned, American station-wagon, always very erect at the wheel, his aristocratic features crowned incongruously by a round, white, American sailor's cap. The local people referred to him as 'l'Ammiraglio' (the admiral). One day, in the main street of the village, he backed his unwieldy vehicle into an empty baby carriage, smashing it. With extraordinary presence of mind, a woman standing by grabbed the nearest baby she could find and dumped it, howling, into the wrecked pram. By the time the octogenarian driver had got out to see what damage he had done, a gesticulating crowd had gathered, and he was appalled and scared. He quickly handed over a considerable sum of cash. This money was later amicably divided three ways between the owner of the wrecked pram, the mother of the baby, and the astute woman who had created the dramatic scene by throwing in the baby. The whole village had a good laugh over this. The 'admiral' was clearly not used to navigating in Mediterranean waters.

When the painters and writers and most of the early group of eccentric expatriates left, wealthier visitors came, and the price of property rose. Prince Said ibn Hussein, a brother of the Hashemite kings of Iraq and Jordan, bought a house in Forio. His capacious Turkish wife, who wore flashy, valuable bracelets and rings outside long colourful gloves, travelled about the island in a *moto-carozella*—a little two-seat open carriage attached to a Vespa motorcycle. Millionaire German industrialists came; American remittance ladies came; millionaire Italian industrialists came with their yachts; British peers and peeresses came; a galaxy of international film stars and starlets came; and Rizzoli built a luxurious hotel. Visconti bought and refurbished a castle. Royalty came from Greece and Sweden, and ex-royals from Romania, Austria, Yugoslavia, Bulgaria, and every conceivable former German state. The niece of British Prime Minister Anthony Eden came, and married an Ischian boatman. As for William and I, we continued our tranquil life, unaffected by the glamorous comings and goings. We worked and planned, and dreamed of future work and what plants to grow.

11

Other Composers

IN the early years of our marriage William's compositions
emerged at a steady rate. The very first was the Sonata for Violin
and Piano, written for Yehudi Menuhin and Yehudi's brother-
in-law, Louis Kentner. William finished it during our first year in
Ischia, at the Convento San Francesco. Yehudi and his wife
Diana, her sister Griselda, and her husband Louis Kentner were
old friends of William and of Alice Wimborne. In late 1947,
when William and Alice were in Lucerne, Alice was taken very
ill, and William wanted to have her examined by the best
doctors possible. Foreign currency was then still very restricted
for Britishers abroad, and, as Alice couldn't get money out of
England, William had to beg Yehudi to lend him some Swiss
francs, which he would repay in London. Diana told me that a
wicked gleam came into Yehudi's usually innocent eyes. 'I'll
give you anything you like, William,' he said, 'in return for your
writing me a sonata for piano and violin. Lou [Kentner] and I
can give the first performance.'

William promised, but Yehudi was so impatient to see
William start work that he led him firmly by the hand to the
nearest music store, pulled him into the shop, and bought a
quire of manuscript-paper and half a dozen of William's favourite pencils. By chance, Ben Britten's new opera *Peter Grimes* was
being premièred at the Lucerne Opera House, and the window
of the music shop was full of scores by Britten, whom William
considered a rival. A large photograph of Britten was propped on
a chair. Without looking to right or to left, William, clutching
his quire of paper and his pencils, reached into the window of
the shop, picked up the photograph, and put it neatly on the
chair seat, face down. Then he dusted off his hands with

satisfaction and left. Yehudi has never forgotten this incident as they were so amused by it.

Recalling that time in Lucerne when Yehudi had commissioned the Violin and Piano Sonata, William told me how grateful he was for Yehudi's generosity in advancing the money for the work, so that he could pay for Alice's medical examination. It caused him great pain to remember how the doctor they had consulted had said she had got cancer, completely contradicting the opinion of Alice's London doctor, an eminent old German called Plesch, who had said there was nothing wrong with her at all. It is possible that in those days it was difficult to ascertain if a patient had cancer. In any case, it was too late for treatment to benefit her by that time. Her death was preceded by weeks of agony that haunted William for the rest of his life.

Yehudi kept his promise about playing the first performance of the Sonata. He and Kentner gave it at a Sunday night concert in the Drury Lane Theatre of all places, in February 1950. William dedicated the work to their wives, the sisters Griselda and Diana.

Diana told me how William shocked her the day after her marriage. Yehudi was giving a recital in Leicester with the pianist Gerald Moore. As an encore, he had launched into the Bach D minor solo partita. William, who was there with Diana, said in a loud whisper, 'O God, not that Chaconne again! Come on, let's beat a retreat.' Diana, the embarrassed new bride, had had to say, 'No, William, you go if you want, but my place is here!'

Throughout William's life relations with other composers were far from simple. When he spoke of Ben Britten he sometimes described him as his 'junior partner'; William deplored and could not understand Ben surrounding himself with what he saw as a court of admirers and hangers-on. Such a life would have stifled William, and he imagined that Ben's followers were often the cause of ill feeling between them. He admired the artist in both Ben and Peter Pears. Indeed, in 1950, when *Façade* was performed by Edith Sitwell and Peter Pears at the newly founded Aldeburgh Festival, resulting in a recording made four years later, it remained among William's favourites. At a special concert at the Maltings in Snape to celebrate

William's seventieth birthday, Peter recited several of the poems to Fred Ashton's ballet version of *Façade*, after which William wrote to Ben:

It was really most noble of you to provide such a handsome birthday present. . . . As for Peter, he was superb. He must record it again for there isn't, in spite of the numbers made, a vaguely good one among the lot. In fact, one has to go back to the one he did with Edith years ago.

While it is true that William considered Ben his great rival, they respected each other. In our early days in London Ben and Peter were among the first to invite us for a weekend. William was much amused by the way they enthused over my embroidery, and this prompted him to ask them if they knew the story of two of their friends, well-known musicologists who lived together in an old mill and had trouble with the fire. One asked the other to add more wood to the fire, since it was dying down. The request was ignored. After repeated requests, the other got up petulantly and threw a great log on the fire, which immediately put it out. The first was outraged, and in a high-pitched squeal said, 'How like a man!' As with others of William's stories, the only one to laugh was me. Ben and Peter were not amused. As for me, I was quite perplexed to see that Ben and Peter shared a double bed, a situation which I would now take in my stride, but which shocked me at the time.

One day Ben took us for a ride in his vintage Rolls Royce, and we just happened to pass a boys' school. Ben asked William if he was interested in little boys. This was a perfectly innocent remark, but William replied, no, he was only interested in little girls. Again, Ben was not amused. These anecdotes might make it sound as though William was narrow-minded and judgemental. He was neither; he was just an incorrigible tease.

Christopher Hassall once told William that he had found a wonderful actor to play the lead in a play he was writing for the Edinburgh Festival. William enquired who it was. When Christopher answered 'Britten', William groaned. 'Oh no,' he said, 'don't tell me he can act as well.'

William's admiration for Ben pre-dated the Second World War. As early as 1937 he had written to him after hearing a performance of the *Variations on a Theme by Frank Bridge*: 'I should like you to know how very excellent I thought them. . . . It is really a fine work.' And this was long before the twenty-five-year-old Britten had had any serious recognition. William even arranged a private performance of the *Variations* at Wimborne House. 'I do hope that the rehearsals will be enough,' William wrote to Ben, 'as the piece sounds rather difficult, and a doubtful performance would do a lot of damage to a work where every note tells. Let me know what you think. With many congratulations.'

Later, in March 1941, when Ben returned from the United States, it was William who offered to speak on his behalf at the judicial hearing for conscientious objectors. At first Ben had said he was ready to help in a non-fighting unit during the War, but in court changed his plea to not wanting to do any War work at all. William, who was disconcerted by this change, was left with only one line of defence—namely, to stress what a crime it would be to stop this young composer from working on his music. The judge turned on William, and enquired what authority he had to assess the so-called national importance of Britten's music. William replied, with bare-faced bravado: 'Well, your Honour, if you don't know who *I* am, there is no point in continuing this hearing!' The judge let Ben off; probably he thought he ought to have known who William was.

After the War William renewed his acquaintance with Ben, although by this time each was touchy about the achievements of the other. William had sent him a fan letter after *Peter Grimes*, saying it was just what English opera needed, and that it was an extraordinary achievement; even so, he got into trouble over a recording of the opera. At that time the British Council had a recording panel, for which William was a consultant. When asked whether *Peter Grimes* should be recorded, William replied that, as the funds available were so scarce, something less commercially successful than *Peter Grimes* should be selected. Britten was much offended. The opera was not recorded for another ten years.

None the less, William was acutely aware of Ben's success in the field of opera, and was full of admiration for what was being attempted at the Aldeburgh Festival, the revival of local music-making of the highest standard. In 1950 William wrote to Ben: 'I should like to have a shot at a chamber opera or a piece of some kind for you. It seems to me that there is a real future for that medium from all points of view.' At the time he had already started work on *Troilus and Cressida*, which had grown into something more than a chamber opera.

When in 1969 William asked if he might write a series of variations on the Impromptu theme of Ben's Piano Concerto, Ben agreed. Subsequently they were both irritated when Ben's publisher, Boosey and Hawkes, tried to cash in on William's royalties.

William's high spirits, especially in dealing with other composers, sometimes knew no bounds. Once, returning from Prague, he spotted the Hungarian composer Zoltán Kodály and his ancient wife at the airport. William told me how he had hidden behind a pillar, and how, when the plane stopped to refuel in Frankfurt, he had kept out of sight to avoid Kodály. 'He's got the evil eye,' he had explained to Alice Wimborne, who was with him. All the way to London, William sat with his fingers crossed.

In London it was easier to avoid Kodály, and William thought he had got away with it. Imagine his vexation, therefore, when, at a Composers' Copyright Banquet at the Mansion House, he found himself seated next to Kodály. William promptly turned his back on Kodály, and focused all his charm on the lady to his right. The worst moment came when a loving-cup was passed around, and over the rim of the cup he saw Kodály's eyes scrutinizing him. William muttered a few words in an invented tongue, pushing the cup at Kodály, and turned again to his neighbour. He left as soon as he could, and telephoned Griselda Kentner to say, 'I've managed to avoid that awful old Kodály without his knowing it.'

The next day, Kodály—normally a taciturn and silent man— rang up Louis Kentner, spluttering with rage. 'I know that Englishmen can live in the desert for years and never speak to each other,' he said, 'but what I am going to tell you now, you will not believe. I saw Walton and a lady in the airport in Prague, and again when we got out at Frankfurt. I imagined he was frightened or nervous of flying, and accepted his avoiding me. When I then attended the banquet at the Mansion House, I was surprised by my neighbour turning his back on me during the whole meal. Just imagine my indignation when, soon after this man left, the lady who had been on his right said to me, "I had such an interesting talk with Dr Walton." "Dr Walton?" I queried, "Where is he?" "He was sitting next to you, Professor," she replied. 'I am mortified,' complained Kodály.

Kentner tried to apologize, saying, 'You know, Professor, William is a very shy man.' Kodály snorted. 'I will of course tell him,' added Kentner, 'but you must believe it was unintentional.' When Kentner reported this to William, William, realizing he had gone too far, tried to make amends by sending Kodály a copy of *Belshazzar's Feast*, dedicated 'with homage to Zoltán Kodály'; but there was silence from Budapest.

When William subsequently married me, the twenty-two-year-old Argentine girl whom he had met only a few weeks earlier, Kodály sent Louis Kentner a postcard with the newspaper cutting glued on, and wrote, 'We are much interested in the doings of your friend Walton. To have married a young girl on such short acquaintance does not seem to me to be the act of a shy man. I should rather say of a bold one.' The delicious aspect of this story is that Kodály was himself renowned for such farouche behaviour, and to be outdone at his own game was too much for him.

William's sense of humour often incited disapproval. When he was staying in Amsterdam during 1933 for a meeting of the International Society for Contempory Music, Hubert Foss had written home to his wife, saying that he and William had been to an exhibition of old instruments. 'William behaved abominably, of course,' wrote Foss, 'beating all the drums in an ecstasy and turning a plaque of Richard Strauss to the wall.' On another occasion, when attending an exhibition of modern painting in 1936 which Osbert Sitwell had arranged in London, William painted a smoked herring red and stuck it on to a surrealist picture with a pin. Then he waited by the picture, listening to the favourable comments on this work of art. The owners of the gallery did not realize what had happened until some days later, when the fish started to rot and smell. In Graham Sutherland's biography by Roger Berthoud, published in 1982, a reference is made to a painting of a kipper with a real kipper attached, a memorable item of the Surrealist Exhibition of 1936! William relished the fact that his addition to the original should be recalled forty-six years later.

At least this wasn't as bad as a time when William and Rex Whistler took Margaret Whigham* to a ball. When he danced with her, Whistler put a banana in his pocket. William decided he must follow suit. But to outdo Whistler, William put a banana in *each* trouser pocket, and danced with Margaret Whigham. William told me that on another occasion he did this when dancing with Oliver Messel's pretty married sister, Anne Armstrong-Jones, later the Countess of Rosse and mother of Lord Snowdon.

On occasions even I felt flustered by William's behaviour. We once accepted an invitation to stay for a weekend with the art critic Bernard Berenson at his villa, I Tatti, on the hills above Florence. In spite of thick fog, and the difficult drive over the mountain passes from Bologna—the auto route had not then been built—we managed to arrive just before lunch. The venerable Mr Berenson was seated in a large carved armchair, with a group of admirers at his feet who were so gushing and obsequious that William instantly took against the whole situation. When Berenson started talking about music, William decided to escape. The moment lunch was over, and all had retired to rest, William said we were leaving. I tried to dissuade him, but he told me that, if he was forced to stay, he would make sure he was 'bloody rude' to everyone. I packed in a hurry, and we crept down the dark wooden staircase and had our hands on the front door handle when a lovely secretary popped out of a side door and said, 'But where are you going, Sir William?' I desperately hushed her and said, 'Please don't disturb anyone. It has been such a lovely luncheon, but now we must rush. Osbert Sitwell is expecting us. We're late as it is.' She looked amazed and said, 'But you were to stay the night!' 'Oh dear,' I replied, 'we hadn't realized!' She just wouldn't let us go, and woke up Berenson, who looked us up and down in astonishment, and insisted on showing us every cypress and shrub in his garden. Previously Berenson had often come to

* Later Mrs Sweeny, and subsequently the third wife of the 11th Duke of Argyll.

Ischia for the mud cure; but after this he never called on us again, and wrote to friends in London to say that he was convinced we were deranged. But William was as happy as a child who'd just got away with a prank. He couldn't stop laughing. Osbert, on our arrival a day earlier than expected, was equally amused.

12

Invitations and Honours

In October 1952 the Arts Council commissioned William to write a march to celebrate the coronation of the new Queen, Elizabeth II. Remembering the line from *Henry V* that inspired *Crown Imperial*, he called the second coronation march *Orb and Sceptre*. He was paid £50 for it by the Arts Council.

In November of the same year, Dr Mackie, later Sir William Mackie, organist of Westminster Abbey, persuaded William to compose a *Te Deum* for the service. William could not resist the opportunity to use the Queen's Trumpeters, so he agreed. He insisted that the Archbishop of Canterbury give him permission to set the whole text, instead of a short version, as first suggested, which he thought would be undignified. By 17 January 1953 both works were finished, and in mid-March William flew to London to go through the scores with Dr Mackie. On this same visit he conducted some recording sessions, which included the new coronation march, well before its first hearing at the Abbey.

We were commanded by the Duke of Norfolk, the Earl Marshal of England, on behalf of the Queen, to attend the coronation service. I was in the seventh heaven! It also amazed me to discover that the Duke of Norfolk, who was in charge of this most important ceremony, was a Roman Catholic.

William had to travel to London some weeks earlier, as the University of Manchester was presenting him with an honorary doctorate of music. This meant that I had to drive the Bentley from Ischia back to London alone. I met my father in Paris to collect Mama's diamond necklace, lent to me so that I could have it mounted as a tiara.

Needless to say, the actual coronation was extraordinary. William and I left the house early, as we had been instructed to be at the Abbey by half-past nine. William wore his Oxford gown of a Doctor of Music. He filled the round velvet hat with its large black brim and soft top with miniature bottles of whisky to sustain himself through the long ceremony. The cream-coloured silk gown trimmed in shocking fuchsia pink was tremendously chic, I thought. I felt that he was outdressed only by the maharajahs from India, with their magnificent jewelled plumes sticking up from their turbans.

The north and south transepts of Westminster Abbey had an extra floor set up in them so as to seat double the number of guests. From the upper level we had a very clear view of the ceremony. Beneath us we could see the peers on one side and the peeresses on the other, the foreign rulers and ambassadors in court uniform, forming a colourful tapestry.

Seeing the Queen before her actual crowning gave my heart quite a turn. She looked so young and appealing in her simple white gown, divested of all ornament, as she turned first to the right and then to the left, asking to be accepted by the assembly as their sovereign. After this touching moment she was robed and appeared in great splendour. The crown of state looked far too heavy for such a slender person, and I began to wonder if she could ever carry it on her head. 'She is the most touching thing I've ever seen,' William said. 'The *Orb and Sceptre* I wrote for her is goodish—not as good as *Crown Imperial*, but I did my best.' The Queen's Trumpeters, standing on the clerestory with long silver trumpets and banners, made a dramatic impact when William's *Te Deum* was sung.

Friends have since asked me how the congregation survived all those hours without the facilities of a lavatory. But the Abbey was well supplied with prefabricated cubicles, and the way to them was discreetly signposted.

A few days later we were at Covent Garden for the first performance of *Gloriana*, Britten's opera written in honour of the coronation. The house, full of distinguished guests and foreign representatives who had come to pay homage to the new Queen, seemed awash with flowers—garlands running from chandelier to chandelier, coming together in a central tent of white silk and green laurel leaves. William had been asked by David Webster, the general administrator of Covent Garden, to rescore the national anthem for this gala performance. But John Pritchard, the conductor, was so overcome by the excitement of the event that he became very flustered. As soon as he saw the Queen enter the royal box, he gave the first beat for the orchestra to start up the national anthem. Alas, only half the orchestra started; the other half, knowing that the whole of the royal party had to be in their places before the music could begin, just sat and waited. Pritchard, who had his back to the orchestra, could not control the shambles that ensued. The general public and the Press thought that William had deliberately distorted the national anthem to upset the evening for *Gloriana*—professional rivalry with Britten, in other words. As a few of the courtiers thought the same, William was beset by irate gentlemen at the ball in Buckingham Palace a few evenings later. We had to ask David Webster to write to the Queen's private secretary to explain that this discordant version of the national anthem was not William's fault. But William was inconsolable, and the ball at Buckingham Palace, which should have been the greatest treat, was a misery for us.

London visits were delightful. I loved being pampered by Frieda, our housekeeper in Lowndes Cottage, and William could see his friends. Frederick Ashton, or Fred, as William liked to call him, had worked together with William in the early days. In 1931 they adapted seven numbers of *Façade* for the Camargo Society, with Lydia Lopokova, Alicia Markova, and Fred himself dancing and Constant Lambert conducting. The ballet included ten numbers when Fred choreographed it for the Sadler's Wells Ballet in 1940. It drew rave notices in the 1949 tour of the company to America when Moira Shearer and Fred danced the tango; the ballet was then reduced to nine numbers. In 1935 Fred choreographed *The First Shoot*, a short ballet that William wrote as part of a revue for C. B. Cochran with a scenario written by Osbert Sitwell and with designs by Cecil Beaton. As William ironically observed, 'there is more money in this sort of music than in writing a symphony'; a ballet version of *Siesta* followed the next year, with Robert Helpmann. In 1940 Fred asked William to orchestrate some Bach selections suggested by Constant Lambert; the ballet was called *The Wise Virgins* and was first performed by the Sadler's Wells Ballet with Margot Fonteyn, whom Constant tenderly loved, and Michael Somes. Rex Whistler designed the scenery and costumes and, though the critics had not approved, it was a success with the public. It had been a long and fruitful collaboration as each trusted the other's artistic judgement. William was not basically attracted to the art of classical ballet despite his affection for Fred and his admiration for his choreography.

When I first met him in London, Fred was slight and dark. He delighted me by speaking in Spanish. He was born in Peru and has never forgotten the language. When he moved, whether to show the dancers when or how to do the steps, or merely to walk across the room, it was almost as if he became airborne. He has an extraordinary instinct for timing, and, if he had not been a dancer and a choreographer, William was sure he would have been a clown—he is such a wonderful mixture of sadness and childish delight. Fred also loved gardens, and spent many hours patiently pruning into animal shapes the topiary at his house in the village of Eye in Suffolk.

Fred disapproved of our living in isolation on Ischia. He was terrified that Ischia was about to suffer an appalling earthquake; and when he came to stay, he could not leave soon enough to set foot on more solid ground.

After the War Constant Lambert had been put in charge of the revived Sadler's Wells Ballet, which was to be housed at the newly opened Covent Garden, on which, in 1945, the publishing firm of Boosey and Hawkes had acquired a five-year lease, with the specific intention of encouraging English opera and ballet. Not unnaturally, Constant suggested to Boosey and Hawkes that his old friend William Walton might be just the man to advise a committee on this. 'Opera was very much in the air in London at that time,' William told me. 'Ben had written *Peter Grimes* for the Sadler's Wells Theatre in Islington, and I thought it was not a good thing for British opera to have only one opera by one composer. I thought it my duty to try and write an opera.'

William contributed to a remarkable document which proposed a radical reorganization of musical life in London, and in particular at Covent Garden. He and the rest of his committee wanted Covent Garden to become the permanent State theatre for opera, ballet, concerts, drama, and films, with Sadler's Wells Theatre and the Old Vic as its satellites. It also stated that, until the Henry Wood Hall was built—the Queen's Hall, home of The Proms, had been bombed during the War—The Proms were to have their temporary home at Covent Garden, in preference to the Albert Hall. Some fifty leading industrial concerns were to be invited to contribute £500 per annum each for five years, with the Treasury contributing a pound for each pound. The Government's share, for some extraordinary reason, was to come from the National Health Services Bill! The establishment of such a national theatre, the report went on,

would mean the virtual creation of a new industry at a time it is most needed. . . . It would create employment, directly and indirectly, for some thousands of people. . . . With the eventual advent of a forty, or even a thirty-hour week [this was written in 1945, when the average working week was in excess of fifty hours!], people will have more leisure and better education, and be inclined to expect higher standards in entertainment than the commercial theatre might normally supply. The phenomenon of a new and vast audience for music . . . cannot be doubted, opera being virtually unknown to the younger generation.

In this and many other paragraphs, the proposal was way ahead of its time and remarkably prescient.

Chapter 4 of the memorandum began:

All opera [at Covent Garden] is to be sung in English, with the exception of the international season. The repertoire should be as catholic as possible, and contemporary opera should not be allowed to suffer the neglect it has in the past. Particular regard should be reserved for opera by our own composers, with the few already existing obtaining a permanent place in the repertoire as soon as possible. . . . The rarity of English opera is partly due to the conditions existing in the past—to find their works fobbed off with, at most, half a dozen performances was not exactly encouraging to composers.

The question of how to obtain both a livelihood and the necessary leisure in which to compose was also dealt with. An 'advance on royalties' scheme was devised, 'to enable the composer to fulfil his destiny'. Such words must have come straight from William's heart.

None the less, when I met William, more than three years after the report had been written, he had still not written his opera, and this delay worried him. He could not decide on a subject and, having quarrelled with the Sitwells, he couldn't ask Sachie or Osbert for help. Stanford Robinson at the BBC suggested Christopher Hassall as a librettist. William knew of him as a writer for Ivor Novello. Christopher thought of one subject after another for William to consider; Alice Wimborne prodded both of them to make up their minds and was delighted when Troilus and Cressida came up, not in the Shakespeare version but based on a poem by Chaucer taken from Boccaccio's *Il filostrato*. She thought the subject would suit William's music well.

The libretto remained a continuous problem. Time and again William just could not come to terms with the words that Christopher sent him. Ernest Newman, a music critic and writer William much admired, found the libretto too full of long words. William was disconcerted, but secretly he agreed. Hassall lived in Hampstead, in north London, and we were in Ischia, which gave sufficient time for William's temper to cool between exchanges. Their correspondence would fill a book; William used to say that Christopher was maddening, because he could not distinguish between a trite line of verse and an inspired one. He came to believe that Ivor Novello had taken possession of Christopher's soul. Even though William believed that Christopher never got the libretto right, some of it sounds quite spontaneous and beautiful despite the weeks, or rather the months, of rewriting. If Christopher sent some lines which William thought were wrong, and some even made him feel sick, we had to wait for the post, which in those days could take weeks, to know if Christopher had interpreted William's suggestions and written what he longed for. Unfortunately there were no private telephones on the island at the time.

But when Christopher came to visit, all would be immediately forgiven. He would take my mother out to the village café for steaming cups of chocolate. He would quiz me about spaghetti—he believed that I actually grew spaghetti, like asparagus, and from then on William never stopped ragging him about my going out into the garden to dig up some spaghetti for lunch. Christopher was very good-tempered. At one time he had been an actor. He had been extremely good-looking in his younger days but, by the time I met him, he had allowed himself to get quite chubby. However, he still had the most beautiful speaking voice.

Writing the music took even longer than getting the libretto in order. William started on the second act, which he wrote in about three months. The libretto of the first act was a shambles, and how to get all the characters to come on at the right time was complicated and took a long time.

When William was struggling to finish *Troilus* in London, Larry lent him the gardener's cottage while we stayed at Notley, so that he could work in peace. Vivien was then recovering from her first serious breakdown, and we could keep her company.

In February 1953 Vivien was in Hollywood, filming *The Elephant Walk*. Larry was staying with us at Casa Cirillo when he received a telegram to say that she was sick, and would he go to her at once. The studio had started to worry when she had not turned up for work. He immediately flew to New York and on to Los Angeles, where he found Vivien balancing on a balustrade at the top of the staircase in the house she had rented. She was quite naked, and thought herself to be a bird ready for flight. Larry told me that he could not make out if she was play-acting or really mad, so he carefully went up the steps, talking sweetly to her, and managed to grab her. She became so violent that, in order to sedate her, the doctor and nurses had to wind a wet sheet around her. Back in London she was put to sleep for three weeks, after being subjected to the first of the many shock treatments she was to endure for the rest of her life.

Larry returned to Ischia with William, via Rome, on the Comet. Soon after, this plane broke up and crashed into the sea near Elba. Larry looked quite worn out by Vivien's desperate condition, so we tried to distract him by taking him round the island in a fisherman's boat to visit the coves and beaches where hot water bubbles up into the sea. We also went for long walks up rough paths enclosed by the dry stone walls where mosses and ferns, cyclamen and wild violets grow in the crevices. We took him to the top of Mount Epomeo, the extinct volcanic peak that, rising out of the sea over millennia, formed the island of Ischia. If we chanced to pass a wine-cellar, the islanders would be certain to offer us a glass of wine and dried figs, which we enjoyed enormously. Ischia was at its most enchanting.

Before long, however, news of Vivien's illness became international knowledge, and Larry's presence on Ischia was discovered. We decided that the only defence from the Press was to disappear, so I suggested that we explore the south of Italy by car. As journalists were already at the gate of the house, we made our escape with Larry out of sight on the floor of the Bentley, covered with a rug, with me sitting legs crossed, Indian-style, on top of him. It was hilarious. Then, instead of taking the steamer to Naples, we drove to Lacco Ameno, where our Don Pasquale had a brother who was a fisherman. After much persuasion, he took us in his open boat, seated on upturned boxes, to the nearest point of the mainland, Torregaveta. The journey was hazardous, as we had to cross several miles of open sea in far-from-settled March weather.

We had tried once before to cross the bay in the fisherman's boat, when William had wanted to hear Berg's opera *Wozzeck* at the San Carlo Opera House, and we had missed the daily steamer. But hardly had we left the beach when the boat was hit by a huge wave and almost sunk. We had returned to the beach crestfallen and wet.

Larry was looking forward to the trip, mentally following the Roman armies down to Brindisi, where the tall Roman column that marks the end of the Via Appia rises, and whence the Roman armies embarked for Egypt and the East. Our itinerary was planned so as to reach a post office each night, where we hoped that news of Vivien would await us. But the idea of travelling incognito with Larry was, alas, absurd. The moment he opened his mouth, someone was certain to come up and ask, 'Non siete Laurenzio Olivier?' Even disguised in dark glasses with a Basque beret, it was useless; in those days, films were not dubbed, and people turned in the street simply because they recognized his voice. The only place where Larry was not recognized was crossing the piazza in front of the basilica in

Ravello. It was invaded by a troupe who were filming, with John Huston as director.

William, convinced that we would all die of food poisoning, refused to eat shellfish, which is a speciality of the coastal regions we were visiting. Taranto, for instance, is washed by the sea on one side and by a salt-water lagoon on the other—perfect for oyster-beds and mussel nurseries, so Larry and I gorged ourselves on these delicacies while William frowned.

Part of the enchantment of this trip was to see, early in the morning in the high mountain villages, women coming down to market, holding piglets under their arms. They walked like empresses, with baskets on their heads, wearing petticoats of red, the overskirts held together in a bustle at the back. One Sunday, Larry and William insisted on going to a high pontifical Mass. Both had been choirboys and regarded the ceremony as excellent theatre: altar boys swinging incense, the bishop and his acolytes gliding up and down the altar steps, arms moving in slow motion, the stiff hierarchical figures clad in white linen surplices edged in lace over red cassocks, and all to the high-pitched sound of chanting.

To return to Ischia, we again embarked on the fishing boat from the port of Pozzuoli. As we had been to hear a performance of *Götterdämmerung* at the San Carlo Opera House it was the early hours of the morning and the port police would not, at first, allow us to embark. I solved the problem by inventing a sob story of how 'la mamma' was so ill that we were forced to cross to the island at this unsuitable hour. Larry was most amused, and we were allowed to depart. Happily Vivien recovered, and Larry returned to London where we were soon to join them at Notley.

On these visits to Ischia Larry would tell us of his experiences in Hollywood. How he hated Billy Wilder for bullying the actors. Wilder found Larry pompous, stagey, and English upper class; he had lost his temper with Larry when shooting *Wuthering Heights*. Larry had upset Merle Oberon during an impassioned speech, when a bit of spit landed on her cheek. The star had quit the set in a great huff. Wilder had tried to make the peace and brought Merle back to the set but was doubly irritated when

Larry, always the stern professional, said only, 'Over with your tantrum, dear?' This, Wilder considered, was hardly an apology. His manner changed considerably when he directed Larry in *Sister Carry* after Larry had made such a success with the Shakespeare films. On this occasion he went out of his way to be polite, but Larry never forgave him.

In August 1953 William was invited to conduct at the Hollywood Bowl. We crossed the Atlantic on the *Île de France*. Its name amused William because before the war it had been a German ship. It was small but comfortable. We took the cheapest first class cabin and were very relieved when the purser, who was a music lover, offered to move us into one of the luxury cabins which happened to be empty. On board we met Ed Gilmour, the journalist who for years had represented the Associated Press in Russia, and his Russian wife Tamara, who after a long wait had finally been allowed to join her husband in America with their two daughters. A ballerina, she had fallen in love with this American journalist and been imprisoned in consequence. He got permission to marry her through his many political connections, thereby freeing her from prison. After Eddy went to the United States to ask President Roosevelt to intercede with Stalin to allow his wife and children to leave Russia; he was not allowed a re-entry visa to Russia. Poor Tamara had lived through months of terror, discriminated against even by the American Embassy staff, who thought she might be a spy. Every morning she had seen footsteps in the snow outside her balconies, tell-tale signs that she was being watched by the KGB. Her family had one prized possession, a beautifully cut, pear-shaped aquamarine, fashioned by Fabergé; when she was allowed to leave, they gave her this stone as a parting gift. William fell under the spell of this lovely woman, dressed in a slinky, long black dress, which showed off her figure to perfection, adorned with only this pendant stone on a gold chain. We became the greatest of friends, and met in New York and again in London where they settled. So, what with the comfortable cabin and the congenial company, we had a very enjoyable crossing.

After a few days in New York we took the 'Super Chief', a deluxe train; the journey took three days. On our first night we were having supper in the restaurant car when the waiter asked us if we were going to continue drinking as we had done up till then. We had drunk the train dry, he said, and he would have to telegraph the next station and have some more bottles put on board. The absurdity was that we had each drunk only three mini-bottles of Californian white wine, little more than three glasses.

When we reached Los Angeles and the Beverly Hills Hotel, William was convinced that someone had made a mistake. He had been told we were going to be put up at a hotel, but he never expected such a grand establishment, with shopping arcades, antique shops, picture galleries, swimming-pools, and a large garden with self-contained bungalows. We approached the desk and asked if we were expected. A young man, all smiles, came round to welcome us, and took us to a magnificent corner suite with a sitting-room adorned with red ginger flowers brought from Hawaii. He was a Walton admirer, he said, having sung *Belshazzar's Feast* in his college chorus, and promptly produced his score for William to autograph.

Jascha Heifetz, for whom William had written his Violin Concerto, gave us a lavish dinner and invited Joseph Mankiewicz, the famous film director, thinking he might get William a contract to write some film music. William had never heard of the film director, and, imagining him to be a musician, put his foot in it by enquiring what instrument he played. At the end of a delicious dinner we were introduced to the Heifetz's old cook-cum-housekeeper, whom we congratulated on the splendid meal. On leaving, we saw to our surprise that a van had come to collect the dishes. The whole meal had been brought in from outside. The nice old cook had merely ordered the menu. This was proof of how different life in America was from ours in London. I had cooked for three days with Frieda, our house-keeper, to entertain Jascha and our friends in Lowndes Cottage after the concert when, for the first time, he had performed the Violin Concerto in England.

Arthur Rubinstein invited us to a luncheon but, as we did not know Los Angeles and the distances were enormous, we were very late. Somehow William felt that we were responsible for Mrs Rubinstein's miscarriage not long after. He thought the irritation of waiting for us must have caused her a great deal of anxiety. Worse was to come. That afternoon we were to have tea with Stravinsky. Aldous Huxley drove us there. We were late again, and found a furious Robert Craft on the doorstep. Stravinsky was only interested in finding out from William how much he got paid for a film score. When he heard how little William had earned from the score of Olivier's film of *Henry V*, Stravinsky declared then and there that he would not write music for films. A few years later William was highly amused to watch the televised version of Stravinsky's *The Flood*, for which he knew the composer had been paid $25,000 for an hour-long work, though he had managed to produce only eighteen minutes of music. The rest of the hour consisted of advertisements for tinned spaghetti and shampoo. 'The old hyprocrite,' William said.

William insisted on visiting Forest Lawn, a grotesque ceme-tery made famous by Evelyn Waugh's book *The Loved One*. Scent exuded from recently watered lawns, and muzak ema-nated from the trees. A large sign said: 'Unseemly laughter will be prosecuted.' A museum in the grounds housed an oil-painting described as 'the longest in the world'. It was unveiled electronically while Wagner's overture to *Die Meistersinger* was relayed through loudspeakers. We were informed that, if we signed a contract guaranteeing that we would be both married and buried at Forest Lawn, we would get a 50 per cent reduction.

The immense outdoor stadium known as the Hollywood Bowl, where the concert which was the main purpose of our visit to Los Angeles was performed, had a large fountain between the orchestra and the public. William found it disquieting to be at such a distance from the audience. But he did enjoy conducting the Roger Wagner Chorale, a small group of about thirty-two singers specially selected for their good looks and professional-ism. They generally sang in television shows. William had to stop the orchestra after the first few bars of *Belshazzar's Feast* because some of the players had not come in. He felt that they had done it on purpose, as the orchestra had been tiresome during rehearsals. This was his first American appearance as a conductor of his own work. The concert included the *Sinfonia Concertante* and *Belshazzar's Feast*, a special *Façade* suite which William had arranged for the occasion, and *Orb and Sceptre*, first heard in June at the coronation of Queen Elizabeth II at Westminster Abbey.

One of the festive occasions during the Los Angeles stay was a supper given by the Screen Composers Guild. William's younger brother Alec, and his wife Nancy, came from Vancouver to be with us, and drove us to the party. On arrival our hosts asked me what William would like. It did not occur to me that the question referred to food and drink, so I replied that he was certain to enjoy being seated by a very pretty girl. This caused some consternation as the seating at our table had to be rearranged. After dinner the Hollywood String Quartet, renowned in its day, performed William's quartet. This embarrassed William, as he felt it was imposing on the guests. On the contrary, André Previn, then just twenty-four, remembers the occasion vividly.

For Christmas of 1954 we were again guests at Notley Abbey, together with Rex Harrison, his wife Lilli Palmer, and Peter Finch. Larry and Vivien had met Peter Finch on their six-month tour of Australia, and had asked him to join them to give this young actor the chance to develop his career. Peter succumbed to the fascination of Vivien and I had the distinct feeling that Larry, while setting off the Christmas fireworks, was pointing a rocket directly at Peter, but reluctantly changed his aim at the last minute and shot the rocket up into the evening air.

Vivien still had her ups and downs; sometimes she was sorry for being so tiresome. She knew full well that she often made a fuss about things she ought not to. It was sad to see how, increasingly, she came to disregard Larry's feelings.

A calf was born on the farm, and Larry insisted on calling it Waltonia. I remember Larry saying to me at the time, 'In all the music William wrote for me, indeed in all his music, there is an inner vibrance. Not afraid of the brass, is he?' he added with a chuckle. 'An energy twin to sexual energy. I'm sorry if this sounds a little over dramatic, but I believe it to be true. I think a lot of our energies match our sexual energy. I'm not talking about results, in either case. But I think it is very much the same thing; that exuberance, that spirit, that heart-quickening feeling, belongs in the same area of human nature. Certain types of actor have that quality; it has something to do with sex, but it has a lot more to do with love. It's a very vibrant sort of love; it's not a soft kind of love at all. And William's music is the strong kind of love.' Paradoxically, that was the quality I remember most clearly between him and Vivien when I first met them, but now, following Vivien's illness, that strong kind of love was no more.

William and Larry were now discussing what sort of music Larry wanted for *Richard III*. He had finished shooting on 8 January. I remember him asking William to write a celebratory march for Richard III's coronation. He said that something like *Orb and Sceptre* would do very nicely. William replied that maybe he could think of another such tune, but he complained to me: 'I have never been asked to write a march with only thirty-one bars!' The music recording sessions were to end on William's birthday, 29 March, but, after he had worked for three months like a fiend, never once putting his nose out of the house, I was quite hurt when Larry asked William to redo a sequence on the very night we were planning to celebrate his birthday. Larry was a severe taskmaster, and rebuffed my plea to let William off for the night, saying, 'A job is a job, and birthdays are a waste of time.'

Larry was thrilled with the music for *Richard*, but William felt he was repeating himself. He would say, 'Of course, Shakespeare repeats himself the whole time, battle after battle after battle. And that was rather the way I was feeling about *Richard III*. I can't do any more battle music, I told Larry, or charges, or anything of that kind. One charge is very much like another.'

Nevertheless William was pleased when *Richard III* won yet more Oscars. 'Actually, we won three Oscars in all, plus three other nominations,' Larry boasts. 'And I desperately wanted to do *Macbeth*. Alexander Korda wanted me to, and William had already sketched the music, based on some tunes he had done for a Gielgud stage production of the play back in 1942. But once again, I just couldn't get the financial backing. The reason, the money men said, was that the bank rate had gone up to $7\frac{1}{2}$ per cent! After that I began to feel a bit too old to undergo the painful effort that producing, directing, and playing the leading part involved. When I couldn't get the money, I thought that, well, perhaps I'd had it. And I had.'

13

Troilus and Cressida

IN September 1954 the manuscript of *Troilus and Cressida* was finished, dated, and dedicated 'To my wife'. It had been a long struggle. William's natural affinity and love for singing were uppermost in his treatment of the story. In William's own words *Troilus* was 'more a work of duty than pure inspiration. Part of the trouble was that I didn't know enough about the mechanics of opera writing to be able to say what I really wanted to. Nor did I know enough about the theatre, or what might work theatrically. So I began to rely on Christopher Hassall, because he had a lot of experience of performing these things for Ivor Novello; whatever one might think about them, they had given him practical experience, or at least, so I thought. I was trying to write a romantic opera, Pucciniesque. I felt that opera should have tunes to sing. Unfortunately, I don't seem to have ever found the voices to sing in *Troilus* that I dreamt I would.'

With the score of *Troilus* completed, our troubles really began. William had wanted Elisabeth Schwarzkopf to sing the part of Cressida, and had written it with her voice in mind. She was a beautiful woman as well as a marvellous singer. Both of us admired her and Walter Legge for creating the Philharmonia Orchestra and Choir. William delighted in conducting them when recording his own music for EMI.

Elisabeth seemed to us to travel incessantly, singing here, there, and everywhere. The music world tended to think that she was Walter's slave, her professional life relentlessly organized in an exhausting schedule. But Legge always maintained that it was Elisabeth who decided on her career, and that she was only happy when singing. Blonde and blue-eyed, she always looked superb on stage. She moved with grace and, though never thin, was tall enough to look elegant. She made no pretension to taste and fashion, except in her passion for shoes.

In 1949 the feeling against Nazi Germany was still so strong that Walter had had a few anxious moments introducing her to the English public. The establishment of the Philharmonia by Elisabeth and Walter Legge not only greatly enhanced their reputation, but also made it possible for their close friend Herbert von Karajan to travel to the United States, where he had a great success conducting the orchestra; otherwise he might have had difficulties because of his political affiliations during the War.

In 1950, to William's dismay, Walter came to visit us on Ischia, and verbally tore *Troilus*'s libretto to pieces. This happened when William was working on the difficult first act. He was devastated, and took weeks to recover and to be able to work again. William, however, stayed on good terms with Walter, both because he respected his professional ability, and because of Walter's absolute control over EMI recordings of classical music. Though friendly, the relationship was never easy.

I confess I wasn't much help. I remember exploding with rage when Walter belittled the efforts of Rafael Kubelik, who had been appointed musical director and principal conductor of Covent Garden. The policy of the Opera House's Board was to form an English opera company. Kubelik accepted to work towards this goal and wanted to encourage a group of English singers and to urge the creation of new works sung in English. Walter did not believe in opera in English, and was undermining Kubelik's resolve. I tried to make Walter see that his job was to encourage artists, not to demolish their self-assurance, as he had tried to do with William on that first visit to Ischia. I apologized afterwards for my outburst, but continued to resent his crushing dictatorial manner.

William handled Walter with calm assurance, refusing to take offence. I well remember our dining with Walter the evening before William was to conduct *Belshazzar's Feast* in the Kingsway Hall for an EMI recording. Walter announced over dinner that he had engaged a young, well trained, German conductor to do the sessions. Seemingly William could not conduct his own work to Walter's satisfaction! He added that William's name would still appear on the records as if he had conducted. After a pause, William replied, 'Well, in that case, there will be no recording.' William conducted himself. Walter took his revenge by not paying him a fee.

Elisabeth was not allowed to sing Cressida. This hurt William deeply; after all, as he told Walter, he had taken five years to compose the work especially for her. The excuse was that her English was not good enough and her voice not suitable for the wide range that William required. In retrospect Walter may have been right, because when William recorded *Troilus* later—and in this recording she was allowed to sing the part of Cressida— the recording sessions had constantly to be interrupted to allow her voice to rest, as well as to check her English diction. As for William's ability as a conductor, even Walter remarked how impressed he was that William could bring in the orchestra again and again to redo the same passage without varying the tempi, thereby avoiding making the end result sound like patchwork. Eight years after *Troilus*, Elisabeth at long last premièred a work by William, the *Song for the Lord Mayor's Table*, commissioned by the Worshipful Company of Goldsmiths. Christopher Hassall again chose the text. Elisabeth's English was no better then than it had always been.

Relieved though William was that Elisabeth Schwarzkopf was allowed to sing Cressida for the first recording, he felt her loss deeply at the first performance at Covent Garden. The rehearsals for that first performance were a nightmare. William discovered more than 238 errors in the orchestral parts. Not for the first time in his career, he became exasperated at the waste of time involved in correcting wrong notes. He decided he must leave Oxford University Press, and have his work published by Boosey and Hawkes, the rival publishers who had been wanting to sign him up since before we met. I was told by Roy Douglas, who had worked closely with William for three and a half years, reducing almost the entire score of *Troilus* for piano so that OUP could publish a vocal score, that William had telephoned late one night, after a frustrating rehearsal, to say he had decided to leave OUP. Douglas used a great deal of tact to smooth things over. But to me William said that he would never change

William rehearsing with
Hermione Gingold for
their riotously received
performance of *Façade*
at a Promenade concert,
19 October 1965

William conducting

Peter Pears, Cleo Laine, and William at a recording of a BBC 2 'Workshop' programme, 25 May 1968

William conducting Yehudi Menuhin with the London Symphony Orchestra at a rehearsal for the 70th birthday celebration concert, Royal Festival Hall, 28 March 1972

William with André Previn in Rome in 1974, photographed by our friend George Mott on the day of the RAI Walton concert to celebrate the 70th birthday. The programme included the Violin Concerto played by Kyung-Wha Chung, and *Belshazzar's Feast* with John Shirley Quirk and ninety members of the London Symphony Chorus

William at work, La Mortella, 1978

Impromptu photograph by Cecil Beaton who greatly admired my hat

publishers because of his indebtedness to OUP for publishing *Façade* when he was still young and unknown.

William knew that the conductor appointed for the première, Malcolm Sargent, had not learned the score. He was rehearsing the first act without having the faintest notion of what the last two acts contained. He had instructed the publishers not to send the rest of the manuscript, as he was not yet ready for it. So William went to all the singers' rehearsals and conducted them himself. Moreover, Malcolm complained to William that his musical script was illegible; he was too vain to wear spectacles, and as a result could not see the score properly. After rehearsals I often drove Malcolm back to his flat near the Albert Hall. On the way I had to fend off the advances of this incorrigible womanizer, who insisted on fumbling under my skirt, by steering with one hand and determinedly but politely removing his hand when it went beyond my knee. I did not wish to appear rude, in case he behaved in an even more cavalier fashion towards William's opera.

The rehearsals at Covent Garden went so badly that William finally complained to David Webster, the general manager. Malcolm's choice of the Hungarian soprano Magda Laszlò to sing Cressida was acceptable, voice-wise, but ridiculous on account of the language problem. Having lost Elisabeth Schwarzkopf because her English was not perfect, we were now reduced to me coaching Magda Laszlò in English! She looked and sounded lovely, but no one could understand a single word she sang. The libretto was not given a chance of being heard.

William went through agonies throughout the weeks of rehearsals, and, when Malcolm eventually tried to alter the score, William said that enough was enough. David Webster, however, could not bring himself to ease Malcolm out and allow William to conduct himself. By chance Jascha Heifetz happened to be visiting London while the rehearsals were dragging on, and offered to help William by attending a rehearsal and later agreed to come to supper with Malcolm. After dinner the ladies left the dining-room. Soon after Malcolm came out in tears, saying, 'What have I done? What have I done to you?'

William told me later that Jascha, in his dry and direct way, had remarked, 'I hear, Sir Malcolm, that you are planning a tour of America in the near future.' Malcolm replied that he was looking forward to making new fans in the United States. 'Well,' Heifetz continued, fixing him with a steely glare, 'unless you make the effort to learn the score of *Troilus and Cressida*, for it was plain to me today that you were sight-reading, I will make it my business to make your tour a perfect misery. I shall tell everybody who counts of your shameful and unprofessional behaviour towards this opera.' Alas, this shock treatment was to no avail. Malcolm seemed to prefer producing 'rabbits out of hats', and would not learn the score. The singers were frantic; each time Sargent conducted, they said, he changed the tempo, so they never knew what to expect.

Covent Garden again employed Malcolm Sargent to conduct the revival of *Troilus* in the early 1960s. Again William implored David Webster not to do so. But David ignored William's advice, so as not to offend Malcolm, a friend from his early days in Liverpool.

Yet Malcolm was one of William's oldest musical champions. He had conducted the first performance of *Belshazzar's Feast* in the Town Hall in Leeds, and, later, the première of William's cantata *In Honour of the City of London*. Despite the *Troilus* experience, he continued to conduct first performances. In September 1956, for instance, he conducted the *Johannesburg Festival Overture* in South Africa. Malcolm was dark and handsome, and there was always a flurry of activity from the bevy of beautiful girls who ran his professional and private life. Malcolm had been distraught at the death of his daughter from polio at a very early age. This had somehow blighted his married life. William thought that this was part of the reason why Malcolm encouraged the rumour that he was irresistible to ladies. He was also great fun to meet, as he always had a fund of amusing stories, and loved being the centre of attention at any gathering. He was obsessed with royalty, and generally had either a cousin or a niece of the Queen, or at least a foreign monarch, at his dinner parties. The gossip was that he kept his hair dark by dyeing it, and he appeared to wear a corset to keep his waist trim and slim. The carnation in his lapel was *de rigueur*.

Malcolm was so jealous professionally that this led to misunderstandings. William once conducted *Belshazzar's Feast* as the second half of a Commonwealth festival concert at the Albert Hall, after Malcolm had conducted the first half. We were to dine together afterwards, and we were delayed by fans wanting William to sign their programmes. On reaching Malcolm's flat for dinner, he asked me how many young people had been waiting outside the artist's entrance, adding, 'Of course, you know they were expecting *me*.' He was probably right, but why say it? William would also be irritated by Malcolm boasting loudly after a first performance of a work by William that he, Malcolm, had just 'delivered another baby' for us, which embarrassed William, who would have liked to throttle him for not having learned the score properly. But, as Malcolm was the main conductor of William's works, he felt he could never really say what he thought.

As it turned out, the reviews of that first performance of *Troilus and Cressida* were good, except for the one in *The Financial Times*; the audience was delighted and William got an ovation. He gave Magda Laszlò a pair of eighteenth-century pendant ear-rings to thank her for all the trouble she had taken. Many of our best friends were present at the first night, as were Maggie Teyte, the famous lyric soprano, and the pianist Harriet Cohen. According to William, the latter had been very keen on him when young and had been convinced, because of his sympathetic treatment of Jews in *Belshazzar's Feast*, that he must have Jewish blood. It amused William to tell that she had once played the *Sinfonia Concertante*, and then invited him back to her home for a drink. While William was sipping a glass of whisky, she had changed into a chiffon garment and asked William to hold on to a corner of the material. She then glided away, turning while walking until the chiffon had unwound and she stood stark naked. William couldn't stop laughing; la Cohen was very cross. Whenever she saw us at Covent Garden, she would rush up and say to me in a loud voice: 'O, you poor, poor thing. How I feel for you.'

I should add that those first performances at Covent Garden were made very much more acceptable to us by the personality of David Webster. He seemed to us to be a very able administrator, which was surprising because he always showed great reluctance to make decisions, leaving everything to the last possible minute. He had been what William termed 'a shop walker'—actually, general manager of the Bon Marché general stores in Liverpool—rather different from being in charge of the fortunes of the nation's opera-house. He had very white skin and very blue eyes and was portly. The good life would later affect his health badly. He always wore a trilby hat at a rakish angle, smoked a cigar, and liked to think of himself as a latter-day Diaghilev. Above all, he was a most generous host to his artists, who, after the performance, were always asked to dine at his house in Weymouth Street, instead of being left to their own devices. There was very little space, so usually everyone sat on the floor. The buffet table would be a pictorial wonder of lobsters and pâtés. Wine and champagne would flow and the artists would feel cared for and could unwind after the anxiety of the performance.

We invited our German composer friend Hans Werner Henze to come to London for the première of *Troilus and Cressida*. At first the immigration authorities would not let him in. He had come without money, and the official simply did not believe that he had been invited by William, and was planning to stay with us at Lowndes Cottage. They held him until they had checked the story with us. We were much relieved when he finally arrived. But what amazed us was that, despite this being his first visit to London, Hans was already very popular; there were endless messages for him to ring people who wanted to meet him.

Indeed, his sudden popularity at that time was often his undoing. While William and I were in the United States at the end of 1955 for the new productions of *Troilus* in San Francisco and New York, we lent Hans our house on Ischia. We thought he would enjoy a few months having the place all to himself. However, Luigi Nono and his bride, Schoenberg's daughter, who were on their honeymoon, neither of whom I have ever met, came to keep him company, and when we returned to Ischia in late January 1956, with Larry as a guest, we were shocked by the state of the house. The front door was stuck and could not be forced open; our sturdy double bed had collapsed; and the fridge and the lavatory had been smashed. Fortunately the piano hadn't been damaged. We had to stay at the house of a friend, Mimosa Parodi Delfino, until Casa Cirillo was put to rights.

Our friendship with Hans was unaffected. In 1958 Fred asked William to write the score for *Ondine*, a ballet on the subject of the water-nymph, for Margot Fonteyn and the Royal Ballet. William was too busy to accept, so, unbeknown to Hans, he suggested to Fred Ashton that he ask Hans to write the music. Fred was sceptical but we managed to get him to stay with us in Ischia and talk it over with Hans. Eventually Hans wrote the music. We were in London for the opening night, and felt proud of the brilliant result.

At Covent Garden we often met Garrett Moore, now Lord Drogheda, whom I regarded as the most handsome of William's friends. Tall, thin, and elegant, with an air of nonchalance, he had a way of arranging his long limbs as gracefully as a young colt when it lies down. I discovered that he had also been a great friend of Alice Wimborne, and had been very jealous when William became Alice's favourite. Garrett and his tiresome wife Joan later came to stay in Ischia, not really to see us, but to meet an elderly Italian, the Principe di Sangro, who was to take her off on a cruise. Garrett had planned to return to London on his own. When the Prince finally arrived, Joan refused to board the yacht which she declared was compromisingly small. Before leaving, Garrett asked us to dine in Porto d'Ischia at a night-club under the pine woods by the beach. We were delighted to be asked out. While dancing with me, he said, 'How tiresome women are!' I exploded with rage. 'What do you mean, *women*! The only pain in the neck here is your wife, who for ten days has enslaved me with her "Susana, I must go to the village to weigh myself," "Susana, please take me to try on my new shorts," or "Susana, please go to the village to telephone the Prince," or "Susana, where are you?" It has been "Susana!" "Susana!" "Susana!" from the moment she wakes up!' Garrett, who loves gossip, immediately told Joan what I had said. She in turn complained to William, who by now was thoroughly fed up with both of them. Garrett found he hadn't brought enough money to pay for supper and William refused to sign the bill so in the end the Prince paid.

We were soon to be embarrassed again. Following this visit Garrett asked us to dinner in London for the sole purpose of getting me to tell the story that he had heard on Ischia of Arthur Koestler's brief stay on the island. Among the other guests were the pianist Franz Osborne and his wife June, who, unknown to me, was much enamoured of Koestler. On cue, I told of how Arthur Koestler had created much ill feeling on the island by buying land, building a house, furnishing it, and living in it for a couple of months, all on credit, and then leaving without paying any of his debts. We heard that he had been upset by the death of his estranged wife, and by the two deaf brothers who were his neighbours on the lower terrace beneath his house who screamed at the tops of their voices in an effort to communicate; this, added to the church bells clanging every half-hour, made his house untenable. What had irritated us about Koestler's behaviour was the reaction it evoked in the islanders, who had exclaimed, 'Yet again, the English are behaving badly.' (Ischia had suffered during the War when it was used as a rest camp by the British troops.) But Koestler, we were at pains to explain, is not British!

Koestler soon heard from June Osborne about my description of his stay on Ischia. He was furious and asked his lawyer, Anthony Lousada, to telephone William to stop us from repeating the story; otherwise he would sue us. I was indignant with rage, so I told Lousada, who had been on a yacht staying in Ischia at the time with his wife Jocelyn, that, if we ended up in court, I would assert that he himself had fed us all the information—I called it 'dirt'—that I had repeated about Koestler. We never heard from him again.

One night, dining with Griselda and Louis Kentner, we were told another sickening Koestler story. Griselda had been at a recent dinner at Koestler's with our mutual friend Robin Maugham.* Robin, who wanted an heir, had been undergoing psychological treatment to change his sexual orientation. His specialist had urged him to look out for a woman, and not to hold back when he encountered an attractive female. Apparently, at that dinner Robin was seated next to a lovely girl, who

---

* 2nd Viscount Maugham, nephew of Somerset Maugham, and himself a successful author.

enchanted him. When, after dinner, he began innocently whispering in her ear and gently putting an arm around her shoulder, he found himself attacked and thrown down the front steps out on to the street. It so happened that this lovely girl was Koestler's present girl-friend. Incensed at hearing of this ill-mannered, brutal attack on Robin, William telephoned Arthur Koestler even though it was late at night, and told him exactly what he thought of him. But Koestler's only reaction to William's scolding was a grunt as he hung up the receiver.

Troilus was next produced in San Francisco on 7 February 1955. William flew over to attend the première. Cressida was sung by Dorothy Kirsten, and William thought that the production was imaginative. Then I joined him in New York for the City Center production. We were the guests of Mrs Lytle Hull, a kind patron of the New York Symphony Orchestra. The shop-windows on Fifth Avenue all took up the Cressida theme, with evening dresses in a colour the 'rag trade' called 'crimson Cressida'. They did us proud, and made a dress especially for me with a red chiffon scarf. It was fun to be photographed in it to help give the work prominence.

While staying in New York we visited Samuel Barber for a weekend in a house that he and Gian Carlo Menotti shared in Mount Kisco; we woke in the morning to find the roads had been washed away overnight by a violent storm. Another weekend was spent in Mrs Hull's house on the Hudson river near Poughkeepsie, the place I had visited as a nineteen-year-old when I addressed my contemporaries at Vassar College. We arrived after a delightful lunch with Dimitri Mitropoulous, who was not only an excellent conductor, but a considerable gourmet. He had ordered a special meal for us, a chicken cooked according to his own recipe. It was baked under a layer of what I first took to be almonds, but which turned out to be garlic. We feared that Mrs Hull would object. Luckily she made no comment.

If only we had been treated half as well when *Troilus* went to La Scala, Milan! The text had been translated into Italian by Eugenio Montale, a great poet and, later, a Nobel prize-winner. To hear the opera sung in Italian should have been a joy. It was a mistake. William had jumped at the opportunity of having the opera produced at the most famous opera-house in the world. Even today I cannot understand why La Scala was such chaos. The musical director, Victor de Sabata, was a marvellous conductor, and we thought he would see that the work was performed properly. The problem was that it was over-produced. In fact, they made a complete shambles of the first act. They must have thought that they had to do something to make it exciting. Productions at La Scala were famous for being lavish, so they constructed a great wall; and, as the curtain went up on this great wall of Troy, it slowly opened, and there was the chorus behind, singing. Unfortunately, because of this wall, the audience couldn't hear a note that the chorus was singing. The producer, Guenther Rennert, could not be persuaded that the plot of the opera was straightforward and dramatic. He kept looking for hidden meanings in the action: 'Couldn't Cressida actually be in love with Calkas, her father?' he asked. Dorothy Dow was Cressida, and David Poleri, Troilus. Miss Dow was a great disappointment; Nino Sanzogno, who was to conduct, was rehearsing at La Piccola Scala, so was absent during many of the rehearsals. William again found himself conducting the sessions with the singers. The staff of the opera-house pretended William wasn't there, though they knew he was directing the rehearsals. After all, no one had invited us. We were there only because William was vitally interested in seeing the work prepared properly. Apparently, the year before, Darius Milhaud had been invited to supervise the production of his opera *David*, and he had arrived with his whole family who were put up in a very good hotel. La Scala had had to pay for the lot. They were worried in case the same thing should happen again, so they refused to acknowledge our existence. They hardly said 'Buon giorno'. Only after the Christmas holiday, when they saw on their TV screens that we were spending some days on Lake Garda with Larry and Vivien, did they begin to recognize us.

William felt that La Scala had not bothered to employ first-class singers. They had spent their money on things like the wall, which had cost them over a million lire, at the time a fortune. Even Callas did not get a million lire when she sang then, and yet that was the amount of money they spent for one minute of this ridiculous wall of Troy.

William often complained of how he was hauled on to the stage at the interval to take a bow. He was received on the first night with boos, a few cheers, and hisses. That wasn't really surprising as the singers had been such a disappointment but had he had a whistle he would have liked to whistle back. A further annoyance for him was to sit in a box between Callas and Schwarzkopf, who crowed like two silly peacocks, damning Dorothy Dow, saying, 'Ah, she won't last an Act,' 'Ah, she can't sing; she can't be heard.' William was distraught, since either of these divas would have made a glorious Cressida, had she wanted to sing the part. Then, when during the last act the audience finally stopped whistling, William thought, 'My God! the music has at last reached them. They're listening. The exciting sextet in the third act has finally gripped them.' But before the searing aria 'Turn Troilus, turn', after which the soprano is supposed to kill herself with Troilus's sword, the audience again burst into laughter and more whistling, seeing Dorothy Dow rush round the stage like a hen in search of corn, with her head close to her toes, looking for the sword, which had inadvertently been removed.

Larry came to hear the second performance, which was better received by the audience. The owner of the *Corriere della sera*, Contessa Crespi, gave a splendid party; and Arturo Toscanini asked us to lunch at the house of his daughter, Contessa Castelbarco. We took Larry to have tea with Maria Callas, but none of these diversions could compensate William for seeing his work performed so badly. We had spent a miserable month, despite being the guests of the Casatis in their palace on Via Soncino. We drove down to Ischia, with Larry to console us.

14

Second Symphony

In November 1955, less than a year after the *Troilus* première, William was commissioned to write a new symphony for the Royal Liverpool Philharmonic Society. The three-movement work was first performed by this orchestra during the fourteenth Edinburgh Festival, in 1960 in the Usher Hall, conducted by John Pritchard. Although Frank Howes wrote in *The Times* that, 'Here at last was something by which to remember the Festival,' William thought it had all been a disaster.

The rehearsals had been held in a schoolroom, so Pritchard could not balance the orchestra properly. No one could make head or tail of what was going on. EMI, which had scheduled recording sessions for the new work, now wrote to William saying that they wished to wait until the work was better known before making a record. After the bad press the work had had, they said, William could not expect them to go ahead with the recording. 'The same old mixture,' one critic had written.

William was both furious and miserable. So when he heard that George Szell was to conduct the Second Symphony in New York, he decided to go over. Because of the expense, and I suppose to enjoy a bit of freedom away from me, William often travelled alone on his short trips abroad. But on this occasion, seeing how nervous he was about the reception of his symphony, I decided he needed his wife with him. I bought some new clothes, some chunky jewellery, and dyed my hair ash blonde. It almost gave him a heart attack when he saw what I had done. He would wake up at night and roar with rage at the strange creature in his bed. Alas, having dyed my hair once, I now found that I had to continue to do so, otherwise any new growth would look most peculiar mixed in with the ash blonde. In fact it went green.

This visit to New York was altogether extraordinary. The morning after we landed it snowed heavily and people were coming down Madison Avenue on skis. The mayor of New York had even prohibited private cars on the streets, in case the snowploughs picked up abandoned cars under the snow. The city was paralyzed, making it difficult for the orchestra to reach Carnegie Hall. Despite this the hall was full.

The Cleveland Orchestra conducted by Szell received an ovation. William's relief and happiness were immense. At supper following the première Szell celebrated by knocking off four glasses of champagne one after another. But, except for the twinkle in his eye, one could not tell how bursting with joy William was. He had felt that Edinburgh had almost killed his new work, and now Szell had caused it to be reborn. William was so grateful that he amended the original dedication to the Royal Liverpool Philharmonic to include Szell. And when Szell's subsequent recording, released in 1962, made some English critics reconsider their original negative assessment, William wrote to him:

This morning I received the recording of my Second Symphony, and have already played it several times. Words fail me. It is quite a fantastic and stupendous performance from every point of view. Firstly, it is absolutely right musically speaking, and the virtuosity of the performance is quite staggering, especially the *fugato*. But everything is phrased and balanced in an unbelievable way, for which I must congratulate you and your magnificent orchestra.

William remained sensitive to allegations that the Second Symphony was not as good as the First. He hated them being compared, because they were so different. He never got over the hurt of the initial lack of success, despite its acceptance by a younger generation of composers, such as Oliver Knussen, who wrote, 'It set standards of concision and craftsmanship for us all.' William would say, 'I've got ideas for a third, but I doubt if I'll ever write it.' Alas, he never did.

After New York William was supposed to deliver a lecture at the Institute of Contemporary Arts in Washington, since the Institute had made the whole trip possible by giving him a grant of $1,500. The night before the lecture we dined with Ambassador Bliss and his wife, who had made a gift to the nation of their mansion Dumbarton Oaks; they had been great friends of my parents when Ambassador Bliss had been posted to Buenos Aires before the War. I was delighted to have on my right President Kennedy's great friend who was also called Willie Walton. He told me that, during the War, he and William used to stay at the Grosvenor House Hotel in London. But when he discovered that all his post and his telephone calls were being diverted to William, he had given up the unequal contest and left the hotel. Joan Sutherland sang some Handel songs after dinner, which William assured me he had sung in his Oxford days as a choirboy, but much more beautifully.

The snow caught up with us in Washington and was so deep that life in the capital virtually ceased; so the lecture was cancelled, and we took the next train back to New York and the first flight back to England. When I returned to Ischia, I asked my mother to cut off all my hair so that I need never dye it again. Slowly it began to grow, but by now it was turning white—probably through the shock of having been dyed, William said. I assured William that this was a family characteristic.

Because Argentina was so far off, my mother tended to outstay her welcome when she visited us. One of her visits lasted a couple of years. She was good company and a great help, but, understandably, William became exasperated by her constant presence. One evening in a *trattoria* in Forio, where we were dining with friends, Mamita told them how fond she was of William. William retorted that he was not fond of her at all, and, to prove his point, cracked her on the head with a long wooden pepper-grinder. My mother smiled bravely and said that she loved William, nevertheless. She then stayed for a third year. Mama was known as Mamita to all our friends.

When William was busy composing the Second Symphony, I resolved to find a place of our own on Ischia. Forio seemed an ideal place for William to work. Behind Casa Cirillo a road had been cut through the vineyards, allowing access to the hill beyond. The evergreen ilex covered the steep slope, and enormous boulders made the area quite dramatic. Our friends the Casatis had already bought one part, and I fell in love with the adjoining land. Both Larry and William were of the opinion that I was crazy, because the land was nothing but a stone quarry and buying it would mean spending the rest of our lives breaking stones. However, William came round to admiring the immense lava boulders which loomed over the long valley, well defended from the sea-winds. After inspecting it several times, he agreed to buy it.

But, like doing most things on Ischia, actually buying the land was far from easy. The mayor of Forio, who knew all the families concerned, helped gather together all those who claimed rights. There were four families to contend with, and the complications were so horrendous that William got a violent headache and departed for London while the mayor, who luckily happened to be a lawyer, tried to find an amicable solution. It took several months to settle on a price. At least they were all willing to sell, as the islanders were still very poor and that land was a liability which produced no income. The papers for buying the plots were eventually signed in June 1956. We called the property 'La Mortella', as on old maps of the area this was the name of our part of the hill. Mama disliked the name, and assured us that it would be known as 'La Mortadella' (a large sausage made of horse-flesh). She would not accept my explanation that in Forian dialect it refers to the wild myrtle bush that covers the higher terraces of the hill.

A favourite game of the islanders is to denounce a neighbour anonymously to the authorities. This was called the *denunzia*. It had been bad enough having to deal with the impertinent owner of the building yard, who said one day, 'How am I to treat you? Are you a lady to whom we owe respect, or are you a what?' My icy reply was: 'From your point of view, I am a client buying a bag of cement. I am paying for it, so just put it into the back of the car, and that is the end of our relationship.' It irritated me to realize that they felt I needed a man to back me up on such occasions, as a woman alone was suspect.

But now I had to contend with the authorities. We were summoned one day to report to the local police station. I went alone. Our neighbours, it seemed, had 'denounced' us for breaking stones to build underground water cisterns. We had asked the mayor for a permit. He had told us to go ahead, without giving us a special permission. When I arrived at the office of the chief of police, he opened a little book and began reading out in a booming voice the article of the law we had supposedly broken. After ten minutes I politely interrupted to say that I had no doubt that, in his little book, there was some law we had infringed, albeit unwittingly as we had been led to believe by the mayor that we were allowed to build our water cisterns. But, I went on to say, the article he had just read out was not that which we had infringed. He knit his brows, said I didn't understand the language properly, and started to read it all over again. But, half-way through, he realized that he was making a fool of himself. He shut the book, and tried to bully me into signing various declarations. I was ready to sign these declarations, I told him, on condition that he also write that, for the first time in my life, I had been in a room with two men seated, he and his attendant, while I, a woman, had been left standing. He jumped up in a fury, yelling, 'What stopped you from being seated?' To which I replied, 'The lack of a third chair.' He advanced towards me, as if belching fire, ready to strike me, screaming, 'Get out! Get out before I lose my temper and lock you up.'

I was so shaken that I sent a message to the British consul-general in Naples. I was informed that I should never go into a police station alone, because a witness was always useful. The wild police chief was removed. But the denunciations did not stop. William told me that he was sick of these interruptions to his work routine and that something had to be done. So I thought that, if the local authorities liked melodrama, they could certainly have it. I walked to the mayor's office, a dilapidated building with a rickety door with loose glass panels. I gave the door an almighty kick that sent it flying. To the astounded faces of the employees, I said, 'If you want war, please say so now. But keep in mind that I have Spanish blood, and that, if you persist in waving a red rag in front of me, I shall get *all* of you flying out of your jobs in this office by complaining to the ministry. We are the only foreigners who are investing in your area, and we are being obstructed by these stupid anonymous denunciations!' Whereupon I kicked what was left of the door shut, and left. They were stupefied. We never again received a visit from the police. William rather enjoyed this element of theatre invading everyday life, as long as he wasn't involved personally. I took the brunt of these encounters.

15

Cello Concerto

WILLIAM'S attitude towards money was coloured by the fact that for years, when he was at the peak of his creativity, he had had none. He never ceased to feel resentful about this in later life, and when the great Russian cellist Gregor Piatigorsky first entreated William to write a cello concerto for him, William's way of accepting was to say, 'Well, I'm a professional composer. I write anything for anybody, if they pay me. Naturally, I write much better if I am paid in American dollars.' None the less, in his heart, William was much honoured that as great an instrumentalist as Piatigorsky should have asked him to write a concerto. Perhaps stung by the criticism that, since settling on Ischia, he had produced little music of any consequence, he poured all of himself into the work.

When the score was finished, he sent it off to Piatigorsky, very apprehensively. He need not have worried; Piatigorsky cabled his delighted acceptance of the concerto. William wrote back, on 4 November 1956:

Dear Grisha

I am so happy to receive your cable and . . . that you should think the whole work wonderful. It is to my mind the best of my, now, three concertos. But don't say so to Jascha. I must thank you in the first place for having commissioned the work, but more so for the patience with me in my darker moments, and some were very dark indeed. And I can assure you that without the confidence and urge with which you inspired me, I very much doubt if I should have finished, at any rate in time. . . . I only hope it will come up to your expectations when you come to play it with the orchestra. If anything in the orchestration—that vibraphone, for instance—should irk you, just cut it out, because it's not absolutely essential (though I might miss it).

It had been the pianist Ivor Newton who had suggested to Piatigorsky that he ask William to write a cello concerto for him. As usual, it had taken William a long time to do, about eighteen months. Again, the whole thing had had to be discussed by letter. The Cello Concerto followed more or less the pattern of his Viola and Violin Concertos. All three are melancholy pieces. William thought of the cello as a melancholy instrument, full of soul; accordingly he wrote a rather sad tune for the opening, a sort of variation of it for the second movement. To get out of having to write a cadenza, which he always said was a nightmare, he finished with a melody with variations. Some people believe they can hear the Italian seashore in the opening of the concerto, rather like waves lapping against the pebbles. William found this very irritating nonsense. I have often been asked which of the three concertos was William's favourite; I believe this depended on who performed the particular work. He certainly had a special affection for the cello concerto as it had come very spontaneously, and he felt it was the closest to his personality. He considered his concertos were more like chamber music, quite intimate works where he was not trying to show off the instruments. Not one of the three concertos is really a virtuoso work, in the sense, say, that a Paganini concerto is. The instrument that he was writing for always became a real personality to him.

The first performance of the Cello Concerto was to be on 7 December, with the Boston Symphony Orchestra conducted by Charles Munch. William wrote to Piatigorsky again:

This is to bring you all my good wishes and blessings for next week's so-to-speak trial by fire. For my part, I am absolutely certain that you will come through the ordeal triumphantly, and that you will give a most wonderful performance. Once again, thank you for everything; your patience, help, kindness, during my writing this work for you, and I only pray it will come up to your high opinion of it.

Again, every good wish. You will be constantly in my thoughts. In fact I am sure that I am more nervous than you about it. Please let me know how it goes.

In fact, the first performance had to be postponed because

Piatigorsky suffered what seemed like a nervous breakdown. William was distraught, but wrote:

I was terribly sorry to hear of your breakdown. With your prolonged and exacting tour, it is perhaps not surprising, but I only hope that you do not feel that my being behind-hand with the concerto has been a contributing factor.

Anyhow, now, after an adequate rest, you will be able to take the first performance in your stride.

The première eventually took place at the end of the following January, but it was not until a year later that it was presented in London. Although it was scheduled for the middle of winter, when we would normally be on Ischia, William felt he must attend, especially as Piatigorsky was crossing the Atlantic especially for the performance.

We had sold our old Bentley and replaced it with a Mercedes 300. It was handsome enough, but heavy to drive, and we were not looking forward to the long drive from Naples to London; we planned to see friends in Rome and stop briefly in Florence. We had not progressed much further than Rome, when, without warning, a cement lorry drove straight across our path. Instead of stopping in its tracks when I braked, as our Bentley would have done, the Mercedes slithered into the truck. What followed was horrible. It was January, cold and drizzly. The lorry driver lost his head, and frantically tried to pull me out of the crashed car. I had fainted when my head hit the metal rim within the driving wheel so I was covered in blood from a wound in my head. I came to, briefly, only to see William's head (he had also fainted) covered in blood where he had hit the windscreen, which had splintered. I remember the dread of thinking I had killed him. I soon regained consciousness, but found myself now trying to fight off the lorry driver as he lifted me in his arms, causing my skirt to ride up to my neck. He then ran wildly with me over his shoulder, from side to side of the road, followed by William crying, 'Lascia mia moglie.'

Eventually an army car stopped, and the lorry driver ran away. William hobbled over to the rescuers, clutching a hot-water bottle, his woollen dressing-gown and my basket in which we carried out documents and money. These he had retrieved from the crashed Mercedes. The nearest hospital was in Civitavecchia, but, although it had excellent young doctors, it was bereft of facilities. All the bones in my wrist were broken, and my hand was hanging on its side like an empty glove. The doctors set my wrist, without the aid of X-rays, by two men simply pulling it apart and putting it back in its correct position. Then they proceeded to try and stitch my forehead together, without an anaesthetic. This produced blood-curdling cries from me. The doctor declared that he could not stitch my forehead together if I continued to struggle; I replied that I had not asked him to stitch it, so would he please not do so. Instead, I asked him to give me a telephone, so that we could arrange to leave the hospital forthwith. I was desperate to get out.

All the while William tried to stop the doctors from torturing me, but they told him to shut up as there was nothing wrong with him. Without an X-ray machine they could not tell that his hip was broken. So, although he was in great pain, they paid no attention to him. A nun opened my basket and exclaimed, 'Why, it's full of money!' I retorted, 'Don't touch it! How do you expect us to travel back to London without money?'

After more anguish I contacted a dear friend in Rome, Mimosa Parodi Delfino,* who ordered an ambulance to transfer us to a hospital in Rome on Monte Mario. Villa Stuart had once been the Roman home in exile of Bonnie Prince Charlie's family. There we were fully X-rayed. I had quite a few broken ribs and a broken ankle. The previous hospital had made William walk up the stairs to the room I had been put in, but the doctor at the Monte Mario clinic immediately placed William on a board, with sandbags on either side, and would not allow him to move until his broken hip had set. We were hospitalized for almost three months. Mimosa came to see us every single day, bringing a flower, chocolates, or a magazine. For the first three days we were put to sleep to get over the effects of shock. But for days after we came round I could not stop crying, reliving the wretched accident. I had been cross with William that fatal

* Marina (Mimosa) Parodi Delfino, youngest daughter of Senator Leopoldo Parodi Delfino, a leading Italian industrialist. She first married Francisco (Baby) Pignatari, Brazilian magnate and international playboy, and secondly Prince Ferdinando del Drago.

morning, because we had left Rome later than I had wished. We had got over the not-speaking-to-each-other phase and had been looking for a side road in which to park and eat our picnic lunch when we crashed into the lorry. I kept on going over the whole awful incident. Eventually William declared that he would ask for another room in the hospital if I did not stop moaning.

It took seven years of litigation to obtain seven million lire in damages from Italcemento, the wealthy owners of the cement lorry, and I was outraged to listen to their lawyer say in court that I shouldn't receive compensation for my scarred forehead, since married women did not need beautiful faces to survive.

The accident meant that we never got to London to hear Piatigorsky play the concerto. William agonized over a small radio, trying to hear the performance over the air from London, conducted by Malcolm Sargent. Later, tapes were sent him of both the American première and the London performance. After listening to them, William wrote to Piatigorsky, offering several suggestions regarding his interpretation:

I do so hate asking you to do this, and I know you won't think it is because I don't appreciate your playing of the work as a whole; but it is just in these parts that the performance could be tightened up. While I, of course, don't expect you to adhere rigidly to my tempi, I do feel the discrepancy of your timings and mine is a little too much. . . . [Make it] altogether more tough and rhythmical . . .

When Piatigorsky recorded the work for RCA Victor, William wrote and thanked 'My dear friend Grisha' for 'an absolutely superb interpretation and performance. Everything about it is just as it should be, and your playing magnificent!'

Not long after the accident we decided to change our residence definitively from England to Italy. By so doing, we were able to transfer funds to Italy legally. Our liquid assets were the £16,000 Courtauld fund which William had given me as a wedding present. This paid for the new land.

While abroad we had let Lowndes Cottage, successfully, to Larry and Vivien for two years. Another tenant, the film producer Harry Saltzman, however, was most unsatisfactory. When we returned to London it was disheartening, to put it mildly, to find that two of our set of delicate Hepplewhite chairs had been broken and bundled into the garage. Apparently Saltzman liked to sit with his feet on the table, the chair tilted on its two back legs. We also found that the transformer was missing from the fridge, that there wasn't a light bulb in the house, and that the feather pillows from our bed had disappeared. On top of all this we had a struggle to get Saltzman to pay the enormous telephone bill he had run up. This experience encouraged us to sell Lowndes Cottage and take its contents to Ischia; the proceeds of the sale went into the improvement of our new property.

My first task was to clear the valley of dead vines and fruit trees, and, of course, Larry was right: it was a stone quarry. This only sharpened the excitement of landscaping the valley to make it into a garden. From friends we had heard of Russell Page, already well known, but soon to become the most respected British landscape architect of our time. We were lucky; when we asked him, he agreed to come. He and his diminutive Russian wife came to stay at Casa Cirillo for three days. In this time he drew up a plan for the wild rock garden to be. Russell was later to say that he had never worked so hard or met anyone as eager, and he predicted that this work would keep me busy for years. He also gave me valuable advice. A golden rule was never to plant one of anything, instead I should plant a hundred. He advised me to make dry stone walls, to hold the earth in place on the hill, and to make them straight, not curvy, so as to avoid pockets; also to free the great boulders of creepers, to show up their dramatic impact; and to plant very young trees, which were cheap to buy and would not be blown down by the first gales. It took us seven years to landscape the hill. Born under the earth sign of Virgo, I was really happy planning and working in the garden; it promised to be my lifetime's task. William was closeted with his piano for months at a time, and now I felt I had a really important job. I stopped leaping about the terrace of Casa Cirillo, and started to grow trees and bushes from seeds imported from the oldest nursery in the world, Vilmorin in Paris.

My father had never allowed me to interfere with the layout of the park that surrounded our house on the *estancia*, but now I had land of our own to develop. While digging in compost, I would be reminded of the history of the island. The Greeks had landed on Ischia before settling on the mainland. Who knows? Perhaps they had cultivated the ground in this very valley before me. I began to plant seeds of the trees I had known and loved in Argentina, the jacaranda, the judas tree (*Cercis*), magnolia, yucca, the Argentine native chorisia, and red-flowered eucalyptus. I took cuttings and bulbs that grew spontaneously on the island. It was a struggle to get any new plants to grow because, bereft of vegetation, the new stone walls, which looked just like those of a medieval fortress, reflected the heat of the sun. Worse, the rain-water which collected in the underground water cisterns was not nearly enough to keep the plants watered, so every summer we had to buy water by the truckful to prevent the garden from simply disappearing. The lava stream, which formed our cliff, had pushed all the natural humus aside into the valley. To enrich the soil, I had a brilliant idea. I convinced the local refuse-man to deposit all his rubbish in our valley; he thought I was crazy. But, after a few months, we had a mountain of compost, and several more *denunzias*.

Everything involved a gigantic effort of persistence and expenditure. We had to bring electricity to the area, as well as water. We had to pave the road and import truckloads of peat to stop the rain washing away our newly rejuvenated earth. All the young trees had to be secured to stout chestnut poles to avoid the sirocco wind from blowing them down; and we had to build huge boundary hedges in an attempt to keep wind damage to a minimum. Our first cypress hedges died of a mysterious virus that had no cure, so I replaced them with silver-grey cypresses, having been told that these were immune. They were not, and they also died. Eventually, we planted hundreds of bay trees, which grow wild on the island. These live and prosper.

A garden is an act of constant creation and renewal; it is never really finished. La Mortella now has plants from the Azores, such as hedychium (the ginger flower) which has an extraordinary scent, tulip trees from North America, ferns from the Canary Islands, anemone japonica from Japan, and, of course, lemon trees amid the shrubs and the flowers. They are part decoration, because they look so beautiful, but we also pick and eat the ripe lemons. There are bushes with red puff-balls called

Calliandra pulcherrima, from Chile, and papyrus from Egypt. When William went to Australia, he sent back some tree-ferns, which Customs seized and almost let die before I could rescue them. Mexican plants mix with Australian flora, and camellias furnish the garden with flowers from October to April. In the early days we used to scramble up the great boulders of lava, and dream of the house which we wanted to build on the hill. 'On these rocks we must build,' William had decreed! Before building our house, we converted the old derelict wine-cellar and the peasant cottage that were on the land, and added another three small houses to rent to summer visitors. We hoped these would produce income to help run the property. Our houses were very popular as at the time it was impossible for visitors to find a house with a minimum of comfort to rent on the island. But when we saw how comfortable they were, we couldn't resist moving into two of them ourselves. We named the largest house Cristabella, after dear Christabel Aberconway; another was called Drina, after my mother whose name is Alejandrina; a friend named the peasant cottage San Felice and the wine-cellar that we found in ruins we called Rudere (ruin); the fifth house we named Quartara. In local dialect that means a double-handed Terracotta water jug; one had been given to us full of wine to celebrate the laying of the roof. We were moving another step up the hill, leaving Casa Cirillo after eight years, and settling in San Felice. William used Rudere, which was next door, as his music room; there he was sufficiently isolated from the clatter of everyday life.

16

La Mortella

MY FATHER had, in 1958, finally come round to admire and like William; he even carried newspaper cuttings of his son-in-law's concerts to show his friends. In that year, after a visit to us, he died, run over by a speeding motorcyclist in Rome. He left me a small sum of money, and I followed William's suggestion that we should spend it on antiques for the house we planned to build on the hillside. We heard that Sicily was the place to find reasonably priced antiques, but we were also aware of the banditry that was rife there. William wanted me to meet the notorious Mafia boss 'Lucky' Luciano in Naples, and get a safe conduct from him. I was much too terrified to approach such a man, and preferred the risk of visiting Sicily without the boss's recommendations.

'Lucky' Luciano was then living in Naples, ostensibly to manage his household appliance business. An American citizen, he was able to avoid imprisonment for tax evasion and after the Second World War was instead sent back to Naples, his birthplace. This was a reward for the assistance he, through his local contacts, had afforded American troops when they landed in Sicily. He knew that the Italian authorities were keeping him under close watch, so when, a few years later, while waiting for a courier to arrive on a flight landing at Capodichino Airport in Naples, he noticed that the arrival hall was full of plain-clothes policemen; rather than give his contact away, he went up to the bar, asked for a strong black coffee, and fell down dead. It was presumed that he had taken poison.

Sicily remains a feast of baroque architecture, from the Villa Palagonia at Bagheria with its grotesque garden statues and mirrored ballroom ceiling, to the skilled Serpotta stucco decoration in oratories, frustrating to see, since the man with the keys was never on the spot. The many palaces, such as Palazzo Gangi, later used for filming the ball scene in the Visconti film *Il gattopardo* (The Leopard), and especially our visit to the Hotel des Palmes where Wagner completed *Parsifal*, were all new experiences.

We found a puppet theatre in a wretched run-down quarter of Palermo, where, on a small and dusty stage, a crusader on a very armorial horse continued to defeat the infidel Saracens night after night. Despite its fascination, the marionette theatre was empty except for a few urchins, and we soon left, unable to stand any longer the flea-bites on our ankles and bare necks, or the Sicilian dialect in which the historic drama of Tasso and Ariosto was declaimed.

The 'Norman–Byzantine' monuments are Palermo's chief attraction. A mosaic in Santa Maria dell'Ammiraglio depicting the coronation of Roger II shows him almost lifelike in remarkable embroidered robes, and his blond, bearded, northern face seems incongruous beneath a Byzantine crown, hung with jewel-and-pearl-strung tassels. He introduced from Greece the exquisite art of silk weaving, and also established in his palace a factory of mosaic workers. The tomb of Frederick II in the cathedral of Palermo, a huge sarcophagus of dark porphyry supported on the backs of four ferocious-looking lions under a canopy held by six antique columns, reminded us of how terrifying the military prowess of the crusaders must have been. We learned that, when the tomb was opened in 1781, the body of the emperor was found to be almost intact. Wrapped in splendid robes woven with Arabic inscriptions, Frederick wore an emerald ring; his sword and silken belt were fastened by a silver clasp, and his boots of embroidered silk were mounted with a pair of golden spurs. The imperial orb was still by his side, and the crown was on a leather cushion. Even dead he impressed the onlookers with wonder as much as when he had lived. I was not surprised to hear he was known in his day as *stupor mundi*.

The drive to visit the cathedral of Monreale allowed us to admire the garden of Sicily, La Conca d'oro, full of orange trees, in the midst of which the Muslims had built enormous pleasure palaces, set among vineyards and fish-ponds. Another delight was the gardens and kiosks of La Favorita, where their Sicilian majesties Ferdinand IV and his wife Maria Carolina, the oldest sister of Marie Antoinette, gave a Chinese fête for their guests of honour, Sir William and Lady Hamilton and Admiral Nelson. The pavilions are still latticed pink and green, with oriental eaves adorned with temple bells. Maria Carolina's bedroom amused William no end, with its medallion portraits of numerous family members covering the walls, each subtitled 'My treasure', or 'My jewel', or 'My only hope and consolation'. 'Sentimental nonsense,' William scoffed.

The Roman and Greek remains were more to William's taste. At Erice we inspected what was once a temple of Aphrodite, but became a medieval fortress. I remember the stone-paved alleyways which were impeccably clean. We went to the Doric temple of Segesta, the large archaeological site of Selinunte, the Greek temples at Agrigento, the town of Enna, built like a horseshoe on top of a hill. We loved Piazza Armerina, a picturesque town with an imposing cathedral. We saw the old Roman villa, now a popular site because of the well-preserved mosaic floors, which depict dramatically realistic scenes of fishing and hunting, of tilling the earth and collecting grapes, of animals being taken on board ship from Africa for use in the Roman circuses, all of which look as fresh as the day they were originally laid. (William found the much admired 'bikini' girls at their gymnastics very interesting.)

At Taormina we found an antique shop run by a Florentine beauty and her husband, the Pannarellos. This was, after all, the main purpose of our visit to Sicily, to buy antiques for our future house on Ischia. We made friends with the owners of the shop, went out dancing with them in the local night-club, and bought what seemed like the entire contents of their shop for a very modest sum. We returned to Ischia happily waiting for the loot to follow. I had even managed to collect some autumn crocus bulbs (saffron is made from the stamens) for our garden, but, alas, William left them in a taxi. Worse, the crossing from Catania back to Naples on the ferry was so rough that I spent the night on my knees being sick, while William sweetly held my head.

The next spring we went to Oldham, where William was presented with the freedom of the borough. He returned to Ischia proudly carrying the beautiful silver tray and the illuminated resolution in a book with a finely tooled white leather binding. William intended these mementoes to have a place of honour in our new house; but on our return, busy once again in his music room, he simply didn't want to know about the problems of constructing our house on the side of the rocky hill. After three architects had been and gone, however, he said that we had wasted enough money on useless architects, and that we had better design it ourselves. Mama was staying with us, and, as she could draw, with the help of a local engineer, Cesare Longo, we worked on the plan.

It took all summer to finish the details. William's wish to build the house on the hill created technical problems. Cesare Longo had to design the house from the top down as he had to select the right terrace on the hill where our sitting-room, terrace, dining-room and kitchen could all fit on one level. He embraced the terrace with two wings, one of which is the music room. The terrace between serves as a very cosy and sheltered open-air sitting-room and dining area, shaded by a double awning, which we enjoy during the six warm months of the year.

On different descending levels, linked by a staircase, Cesare designed the bedrooms, my work-room, laundry, and on the ground floor, the entrance hall. He followed the pattern of local houses, built around a central court open to the sky, much like the old Roman atrium; the main staircase, rising from floor to floor, skirts the four walls, allowing access to all the rooms of the house. Because of lack of space, we had to roof our entrance hall, but the principal is the same. A deep archway under the ramp of the stairs houses a terracotta figure of Pulcinella who greets arriving guests. Such a figure is considered to be good luck in Naples. William had always been attracted by this character from the *commedia dell'arte*. Indeed, his comic overture, *Scapino*, written as long ago as 1940, was inspired by one of the four main 'masks' in the *commedia dell'arte*. Scapino is Harlequin's companion and sometimes his servant. He is generally depicted as holding a lute as he serenades Spinetta; as a character, he appears to be an astute intriguer, a clever inventer of plots and stratagems, maybe a cynic but never a vicious one. He is one of Italian comedy's most appealing characters. 'Honour is like a snake,' he says, 'you catch it by the head and it escapes you by the tail.' William's Scapino was inspired by the well-known engravings by Callot from the *Balli di Sfessania* (Neapolitan dances); therefore he is more of a carnivalesque figure. We searched the antique shops in Naples for eight years for our Pulcinella until we saw him in the window of a shop as we were driving in a taxi to the National Museum. He is the portrait of Antonio Petito, the most famous actor and playwright of the nineteenth century. We stopped the taxi, we bargained, and we acquired Pulcinella and stood him on the front seat next to the driver. We proudly returned to Ischia with our lucky mascot who ever since welcomes all our friends from his pedestal.

William asked Cesare to design a door in his music room leading out on to a private terrace accessible only from the hill. I'm sure he had in mind the plight of Puccini, whose wife used to lock him up in his music room, and who, in order to escape to go out to shoot duck, would have to climb out of the window. William's escape route was seldom used by him alone as he always called for me before going out for walks. I was luckier than Puccini's wife.

Our house was built like an old peasant house, with eighty-centimetre-thick walls of light grey granite hewn from the site; thus it would be cool in summer, but easy to heat in winter. The only problem, we soon discovered, was damp plaster. We had made the stone walls so thick that despite the heat of the summer months, they took at least two years to dry out. We faced the doorways and windows on the façade with darker lava stone from more recent eruptions brought from Porto d'Ischia, and we plastered the outside walls with a mixture of cement and *ferrugine*, an iron-coloured earth quarried locally. This was to make the house blend in with the rocks and olive trees; when finished, our house was to look part of the landscape.

I admit that, newly built and without surrounding greenery, the house looked rather severe, so much so that the village called it 'la caserma' (the barracks). We knew it would take time for the creepers and trees to grow, but we were disappointed that no one seemed to understand our vision of the house as part of the landscape. The villagers felt that, when a new house was built, the owner should show it off by painting it white, to make it stand out. This was the opposite of what we wanted.

Work on the building started in November 1961, and by July 1962 it was completed. In August we moved in. William and I had been preparing for this great event for years. We had had carpets woven in Sardinia, and had bought wrought-iron door handles and locks in England. My mother had been busy painting doors, copying designs we had found in the bishop's palace in Forio. From Bolzano we had ordered handmade majolica stoves to heat the house and dry the salt-laden air that winter storms enveloped us in; in Vietri we had bought stone steps and the stone floor of our entrance hall. From Taormina came inlaid marble tables, majolica sconces, pelmets, and antique pillars.

Seen from below, the mountain seemed to grow out of the house. To reach the area above our cliff house, we carved out of the rocks a track for a mini-funicular. This soon proved to be a most amusing toy for grown-ups; when it was first installed, William frequently had to drag me away from it, as I could not stop going up and down the hill in it, to prove that it worked.

The next big problem—and not just because we had built a swimming-pool on the top of the hill—was the water-supply. The very existence of a subtropical garden depended on a constant supply of water for the sprinklers, but the whole island had hardly sufficient water during July and August, especially with the steady growth of tourism; so we were forced to build two mammoth underground tanks at the top of the hill, which we filled in winter when the water-supply from Naples was not needed for the hotels and holiday homes. This ensured that we had a constant supply of water throughout the year. When no one else had water, we could continue to water the garden, regardless. Needless to say, we were immediately 'denounced' for having installed what was suspected to be a pump that sucked the island's aqueduct dry! We were furious when the Water Board engineers appeared, accompanied by the police. To bring a police escort in order to check our water meter appeared to me to be 'Fascist' behaviour. But the Water Board officials calmed down when shown the great sunken reservoirs.

We were lucky to find an expert electrician. Signor Barr devised an elaborate system to switch on or off from five different places in the house the lights in the garden, the jets of water for the fountains, the road lights, and the electrical mechanism which opens and closes the gate in the gatehouse at the entrance to the property. We also installed a telephone link to the gatehouse. I can now screen anyone who calls on a closed-circuit TV. These devices are now commonplace; but when Mr Barr put in the electrically controlled gate, it was thought revolutionary by many of the islanders. William was delighted to be able to protect his privacy, as well as to keep at bay the many German tourists who previously had just wandered round the garden, taking group photographs by the fountains, and even coming up to the house saying 'Allo, Allo', or 'Schön', and registering surprise when told this was a private house.

Now that the house and its garden had become a reality, the property acquired great importance for both of us. At last we had a home, a house facing south and full of light. William had discovered the quality of light on his first trip south with the Sitwells. Born in Argentina, light is part of my life. To live without it would be a considerable deprivation. I still remember running to open the curtains of Lowndes Cottage every morning and complaining, 'O God, grey again!' A beautiful clear day puts me in a festive mood. For William it was even more important, because to write black notes on white paper was a strain on his eyes. The delight William felt made me see how the boy from Oldham marvelled at having achieved the goal to live and work surrounded by grounds full of flowering bushes and lemon trees. It had been fun to create, and the peace, privacy, and beauty of it made us very proud. The only slight blot on our idyll was our debts, which grew to be portentous. Our accountant and friend Nino Mattera negotiated gradual repayments with the aid of those ingenious bits of paper called *cambiali*, which in Italy one buys in the tobacco shop, and which our builders seemed delighted to accept, as they could immediately discount them in a bank. As long as our credit held good, the moment of handing over real money was delayed.

Our bank manager then started to enquire anxiously if William was about. 'Il Maestro c'é?' he would ask. The legendary composer whom the locals had hardly ever set eyes on, was, he hoped, in good health. But, despite the debts, we were free of worry and happy to have accomplished what we had set out to do, against tremendous odds.

Russell Page returned ten years after that first visit when he had designed the garden. Since then it had, of course, changed. In the original plan he had not included any fountains because the island had no water, but we had built a small pond with several thin jets of water that disgusted Russell. He called them 'pipi de chat'. He liked the house which he thought looked like a Minoan palace, and he wanted the garden to reflect its quiet dignity. Russell decided to develop the garden's features and designed several more fountains. William groaned at the cost of it all; but, undeterred, Russell proceeded to stake out the perimeter of an egg-shaped pool, with a high centre jet of water where the L-shaped garden rises opposite the house, and with steps leading up to a smaller replica fountain. I placed a lead putto in the centre of one of the new fountains, but Russell explained patiently that ours was not an eighteenth-century garden, and please to remove it. He was not quite so successful with a pair of sphinxes which I had had carved in stone by a Florentine sculptor. When visiting the gardens of Bodnant, Christabel Aberconway had told me that sphinxes were Egyptian gods who protected gardens, so I was determined to keep them. Russell frowned, and insisted that they be covered up somehow. They now look like green ivy poodles, each with only its face and one claw visible. I hope they like their overcoats, and have not taken offence. William laughingly thought that the gods would never forget this insult! He really knew very little about plants and got bored hearing me rattle off Latin names to visitors.

One friend recalls coming on me unexpectedly, gleefully applauding the first performance of the new giant jet spraying majestically towards the sky from Russell's new pool. It seems that I was clad in a bathing suit, and was jumping up and down in the pool, while William scrambled over the rocks to adjust the jet, and an electrician in his underpants was in the pool fitting underwater lights. Beside the fountain some of William's smartly dressed London friends, among them Sonia Cubitt,* were contemplating the scene with supercilious amazement. I'm sure they thought that their darling William and his 'native' wife had gone to seed.

On Ischia William wore suits he designed himself. The jackets were unlined and were loose-fitting, with special breast pockets to hold two pairs of spectacles. I expect that was how he was dressed that day. Until comparatively late in life he never wore a wrist-watch, because of the need to feel that his arms were free.

The general opinion of friends in England continued to be that it was 'not done' to live abroad. William had not wished to live in England since our marriage and never changed his mind. We were happy to visit England, but after a few weeks he would ache to get back to the sun, the quiet of his music room, and the garden. A fact, often forgotten, is that to live in England would not have helped William, as most of his major orchestral compositions written since 1940 had been the result of commissions from American orchestras, in Cleveland, New York, Washington, San Francisco, and Chicago.

William often explained that living abroad emphasized one's Englishness. One doesn't become Italian simply because one lives in Italy. The only problem with living abroad was that he increasingly had the feeling that people in England had forgotten that he existed. When, unexpectedly, in 1967, the Queen's private secretary wrote to him to enquire whether he would accept the Order of Merit, he burst into tears when he opened the letter, which was brought to the front door. 'To think that the Queen actually knows I am alive!' he exclaimed.

The award of the OM, the most coveted honour in British public life—there are only twenty-four recipients at any one time—filled William with joy. Commenting on William's OM,

* A daughter of King Edward VII's mistress, the Hon. Mrs George Keppel, and first wife of the Hon. Roland Cubitt, later 3rd Baron Ashcombe.

Both of us photographed by Cecil Beaton at his house, 1970

The garden and house of La Morrella

Two old friends, William and Sachie, entering the Garrick Club, March 1981

Mstislav (Slava) Rostropovich and William with the score of *Prologo and Fantasia*, his last work and composed specially for Slava

The memorial stone, Musicians' Corner, Westminster Abbey, donated by the Performing Right Society and unveiled by me at the Thanksgiving Service, 20 July 1983

one critic wrote that William had paid dearly for his success. 'I don't think I've paid at all,' William told me. 'Sure, it's better to have success than to be an absolutely miserable failure. But it's just as difficult to overcome success as it is to overcome failure,' he added.

William followed a regular work routine: he used to get up early, start work after breakfast, work until lunch and again in the evening. As he grew older, I gradually changed his routine, so as not to tire him; we got up later and he worked fewer hours. He listened to a lot of music on records and tapes. Apart from this there was little else to entertain him on the island. He was never a prolific composer, though he made a habit of writing at least something every day, even if only a couple of bars, almost like an exercise. I knew he had always found writing difficult and that he would continue to destroy most of it, so I did not worry unduly when he complained. The debts on the building of the property were an incentive to encourage him to accept commissions but in his later years even these obligations lost their appeal.

William resented being accused of writing in an archaic language, of being musically backward and so on. Critics like Colin Mason have written that the Violin Concerto is a 'retrogression'. William's opinion was that critics talk a great deal of nonsense and that, anyhow, far too much is written about music; but when they wrote about his music he felt they were often prejudiced beforehand and were trying to be as disagreeable as they could manage, which some certainly were. He became philosophical about getting old, hoping that if he lived long enough his work would experience a revival. In a bantering spirit he would advise all sensitive composers to die at the age of thirty-seven. After writing his Violin Concerto he thought his halcyon days were over and coined the expression: 'Today's white hope becomes tomorrow's black sheep.' When depressed he used to say that the critics might well be right about his works, but still he was never ashamed of them himself. He felt akin to someone like Dave Brubeck, who worked within a clearly defined musical tradition, expanding and enriching that tradition. Alan Frank sent him records of the Beatles and William would listen to them and try to understand.

He did not like pretentious, imitative tunes like the ones that made *West Side Story* famous; these did not develop the tradition from which they stemmed. His view was that Bernstein is a marvellous musician, but as a composer doesn't begin to compare with Gershwin, whom he very much admired. He did not mind people saying that his Violin Concerto had an extraordinary affinity with Gershwin's *Summertime*, although he did not agree (the concerto is in the same key and had a similar drooping phrase). In any case, William was proud of the comparison, saying that both belonged to the same tradition.

As to the future, he hoped both traditions would continue, atonal music coexisting with the tonal. Music, he would say, is bound to modulation, a simple thing, but essential. In the eighteenth century it was easier for composers, because modulations were planned; they worked within a formula and could just churn it out. He thought the future of music depended principally on what kind of instruments everybody would use in the next twenty or thirty years. We once heard a piece by Stockhausen which bored him to extinction in ten minutes. He found it monotonous with no new sounds revealed. He said with a chuckle that he found it rather old-fashioned, not unlike what he was doing in the mid-1920s, pretty barbarous with too many high notes for the clarinet. His brother Noel, who had retired, had taken to writing serial music, as he had nothing better to do. William thought it was no worse than anybody else's.

In fact, William flirted with atonality for the sake of experiment. The third movement of the Second Symphony has vague implications of serialism. He wanted to get the hang of it, as he had already attempted in his Violin Sonata where he cheated by ending the coda of the variations tonally. So I suppose one could say that the last movement of the Second Symphony, although designated 'Passacaglia', is in fact a twelve-note tone-row. He admitted pinching a bit of it from Alban Berg who'd been so kind to him in Salzburg all those years back. William had a notion that twelve-tone composition developed a bit like Communist cells. He maintained that in every country of the world there were fanatics for Communism, as there were fanatics for twelve-tone music, but he found it very difficult to tell apart a twelve-tone piece by a Brazilian from a twelve-tone piece by, say, an Englishman.

A pessimist, William was wont to see the darker side of everything, be it politics or the weather, yet this did not stop him from enjoying the sun when it came out. He was sure that the end of the world was alarmingly near, so he was an avid reader of newspapers and, having lived through two world conflicts, he dreaded the thought of a third war. His favourite books were about buildings and painting; he introduced me to biographies and novels, to Balzac, Flaubert, Proust, Swift, Trollope, Virgil, Suetonius, Dostoevsky, Chekhov, and anything else we could manage to get out to Ischia. I was aware that the life of an artist is sometimes sad, though we never dwelt on this as he was not self-pitying. On one hand, he had been lucky to meet the right people at the right time; on the other hand, he knew he had to battle with himself every day, to create, to express the essence of his thought, to discipline himself to work without cease.

He moaned that he deserved to have been awarded one of the glittering money prizes for what is known as 'services to music'. Yet he had received quite enough public recognition. Apart from his knighthood and the prestigious Order of Merit, he received the gold medals of the Royal Philharmonic Society and of the Worshipful Company of Musicians, the Benjamin Franklin medal, the Incorporated Society of Musicians' nomination as 'Musician of the Year', and the Ivor Novello award for services to British music. He also received honorary degrees from the Universities of Oxford, Cambridge, London, Durham, Manchester, Trinity College, Dublin, and University College, Cork. He was an honorary student of Christ Church, Oxford, an honorary fellow of the Royal College of Music and the Royal Academy of Music, and an honorary member of the Accademico di Santa Cecilia, Rome, the American Academy and Institute of Arts and Letters, the Royal Northern College of Music and the Swedish Academy.

William liked to boast that his greatest achievement in life had been to force OUP, his publishers, to join the Performing Right Society, by joining himself as a composer. Until he joined, they had thought it below their dignity to do so. He would cynically quip that, if the PRS had existed earlier, composers such as Webern would have written much longer pieces than they did to collect more royalties. He would say 'Think of Schubert. Penniless and dead at thirty-one, with over a thousand works to his credit. What the PRS and a decent Health Service could have done for him!' William had a great fondness for Schubert, especially the B flat trio, and admitted that he had found Schubert an inspiration—quite different, of course from the novelist's idea of inspiration, 'looking at the beautiful blue Mediterranean', etc.

He was particularly pleased about his success with women all his life. He declared that he might easily not have married had he not met me. That is probably untrue as he had, at the time, many lady friends and he continued to have a susceptible heart whenever a lovely woman crossed his path. On the other hand, I felt unjustly admonished when people like Leslie Boosey, at the PRS luncheon to welcome us soon after we reached London, stressed my responsibility—the creation of future works depending, so to speak, on my influence on William—or when Malcolm Sargent used to say it was my duty to lock William up in the music room to force him to work harder. I knew I had a delicate job to do, but surely new works were William's burden, not mine. Of course the pleasure of looking after William became my job, but what more could I do than make him happy and provide the environment best suited for his work? My main concern, especially when his health failed, was to keep him as well as possible. I believe that what Leslie Boosey feared was that a younger wife would lead the serious composer astray with her exuberance and love of life, instead of which William accused me of putting an end to what he termed 'La Dolce Vita'. It was he who loved night-clubs, to dance and to flirt. I found those places ghastly, noisy, and full of smoke. It was, of course, his decision to live on Ischia that stopped him dissipating time in pleasant pursuits like seeing friends and going to concerts.

I did sometimes resent living through long periods during which he concentrated entirely on his work. Seeing what a hard struggle each new composition entailed and how time-consuming it was, I came to accept this as necessary for his survival as an artist; he had to be entirely self-centred. He cut off from his surroundings to envelop himself with the right atmosphere, and to be undisturbed. When he worked, we met at mealtimes, took an afternoon walk, and slept in the same bed, but rarely communicated. In his absent gaze I could imagine the relentless repetition of a musical phrase, or a note, hammering away. When he was orchestrating, or between works, we had happy and hilarious times and we travelled. Therefore I had to become fairly independent. Caring for a home, plus the five other houses in the garden, provided me with constant pleasure. I was also lucky to have been taught by my mother to embroider in *petit point*. When I was a child, she had allowed me to finish the background of her embroidery. While this had bored me at the time, it was good training and enabled me to amuse myself over the years with large wall hangings, which the Royal School of Needlework in London prepared for me to embroider. Whenever William felt like a chat or wanted to break away from work, he knew I would be either embroidering or in the garden, and a whistle from the terrace would bring me out from under a bush.

17

Guests, Tenants, and Friends

FRIENDS would come to stay to recover from the strains of life. One of our earliest guests, before the house was even built, was guitarist Julian Bream. He arrived immediately after a long tour in Germany, as a result of which he was suffering from depression, and had decided that he would never play again. His guitar was stuffed full of German marks. We put him in Cristabella. Although this house was at the opposite end of the garden, he could easily walk over for meals.

He was short, stubby, pugnacious, and funny, with a sense of humour as obstreperous as William's. When William asked him what Aldeburgh was like these days, he replied, 'Oh, it's olrite, as long as you keep your back to the sea!' I found that he didn't conform to any pattern of what I considered normal behaviour. He would usually talk while eating, and when he had had enough food, would just get up and leave. I never knew if something had upset him or if he would return. But he did, to satisfy his need for 'a nice cuppa char', several times during the day. The lack of tension and the peace of our house gradually seeped into his bones, and he began, visibly, to cheer up. One day he accompanied William to the barber in the Porto d'Ischia. Most barbers in Italy either paint or play the guitar. This one did both. It was such agony for Julian to hear the guitar played badly, that he eventually took over. That cured him of his depression; he found he could play again.

Other old friends of William's came, and most of them were enchanted by what we were doing. Joan Zuckerman, who enjoyed sketching the garden, gave us one of her water-colours. Lilias Sheepshanks came to recuperate from back trouble. William's godson, Colin Clark, came to recover after a grave illness, stayed on, and bought a house. He then married a French ballerina who did not find Ischia to her liking. He sold the house and eventually they divorced.

Friends, like Harold Acton, rented one of our holiday houses. Some of the tenants whom we didn't know previously became our friends—not, I may say, the Nazi war criminal, Baldur von Schirach, once head of Hitler's Youth and Gauleiter of Vienna, who arrived immediately after his release from Spandau prison. We were horrified when we learned who our tenant was; Hans Werner Henze who was a guest in our house at the time took to his bed, and another guest, John Peyton* spat with rage. When I finally caught sight of the unwelcome tenant, I found it hard to believe that this meek-looking, almost blind old man had such an awful past.

Elsa Schiaparelli was one eccentric tenant. On arriving she insisted in no uncertain terms that nobody, but nobody, not even the gardener, must approach her rented house or disturb her in any way, as she needed absolute tranquillity. The next morning we discovered that she had moved to the fashionable Regina Isabella hotel because she found the house too isolated and too quiet.

Vaughan Williams and his wife Ursula, the pianist John Ogdon and his wife Brenda, the ballerina Nadia Nerina, and her husband Charles Gordon were tenants. Charles Gordon brought George Weidenfeld, and Walter Legge sent us Sidney Beer, who, when he was wealthy, had employed Herbert von Karajan to teach him to conduct and had subsequently rented famous orchestras so that he could exercise his questionable skill. The leader of one orchestra told Sidney that, if he stopped the orchestra during a rehearsal just one more time, they would retaliate by following his beat. It was also said that Sidney practised conducting a piece to a gramophone recording. At the point where the record had to be turned over, he would always miss a beat or two when conducting the piece live.

Sidney's glamorous wife Heidi caused a furore on the island. Born an Austrian baroness, she had spent her pubescent years living on a houseboat on the Nile with her worldly mother. In Egypt Lord Carnavon, the son of the Tutankhamen Lord

---

* Lord Peyton of Yeovil, created Baron in 1983 (life peer); MP, Yeovil, 1951–83; POW Germany 1940–5.

Carnavon, became the first of Heidi's ardent admirers. By the time the Beers came to one of our houses, most of Sidney's money had been spent on his passion for conducting orchestras. William, enchanted by her golden locks and accomplished flirtation, fell victim to her charm, but I read the riot act, and the Beers moved to another house.

The journalist Alistair Forbes, who occupied the house next door to the Beers, brought the amusing Iris Tree to stay. Tenants from the theatre world were great fun. Terence Rattigan, who stayed for several seasons, invited Margaret Leighton and Moura Budberg among other delightful people. Robin Maugham, who also took a house several years in a row, invited Hermione Baddeley. We have her portrait, painted in Forio by Gino Coppa. John Perry and Binkie Beaumont came for several summers, and also invited charming guests—among them Kay Kendall, Peter Shaffer, and Mollie Keane. Sviatoslav Richter wanted to rent one of our houses, but, as they were all booked, we found him the house of a German neighbour.

Hans Werner Henze was a frequent guest. In 1961 we went to Schwetzingen to hear the latest collaboration between Auden, Kallman, and Henze: *Elegy For Young Lovers*. It was a bizarre journey. We flew to Frankfurt with my young Argentine cousin Patricia Conway, who had been staying with us on Ischia. There were few tourists in Germany, and we noticed a distinct coldness when they heard us speak English. A cashier at the airport closed the shutter of his till when William came to change money. It was only when William declared in loud tones that behaviour such as this was what had lost them the War that the man opened up his till. Patricia and William ended up hooting with laughter at the airport: we had to go through different doors, one clearly marked 'Damen', the other 'Herren', but met on the other side in the same room. In Heidelberg our hotel bookings mysteriously did not exist; Patricia was sent to sleep in a bathroom on the top floor!

The Prince and Princess Ludwig of Hesse and the Rhine asked us to lunch at their castle in Wolfsgarten, but the main hall could not be shown to us, as it had been damaged by fire over Christmas, when Ben Britten and Peter Pears had been house guests.

At Bamberg William insisted on trying as many different beers as he could find, and then on racing from bridge to bridge, putting coins into the machines that caused a stretch of the façade of the building along the river to be illuminated. He found that, if he was quick enough, he could light up the whole town. Finally, still *en route* to Henze's new opera, William insisted on visiting Bayreuth. We stayed in what was then a small inn by the side of the Eremitage, the castle where King Ludwig had stayed when he had gone to see Wagner and the festival. The garden, with its secret grottoes, gave us many ideas of how to improve our own garden on Ischia. William declared that the right time to visit Bayreuth was when the festival was not on.

The performance at Schwetzingen, when we eventually got there, was curiously disappointing. William said that Hans no longer needed a libretto to write music for a new opera. If the text did not reach him in time, he would simply set the telephone book; the libretto by Auden and Kallman was immoderately long and the librettists had refused to shorten it. Hans was already putting on weight, which William put down to the fact that, as an indirect result of William's earlier efforts at Bologna and elsewhere, Hans had discovered how pleasant it was to drink wine!

William, always mindful of how much he owed his own early success to the Sitwells, was determined to help young composers whenever he could. This was particularly necessary, he felt, when they were confronted by institutions such as Covent Garden. On a visit to Salzburg to attend the first night of Hans's opera *The Bassarids*, we were astounded to overhear Garrett Drogheda, then chairman of the board at Covent Garden, vow that, as long as he was in charge, such a work would never be heard there. Worse, he expressed this view, for all to hear, in the middle of a party organized to celebrate a successful opening night, meant to congratulate Hans, as well as the librettists Auden and Kallman.

The following evening we went out to dine with Hans. For no apparent reason a matchbox was brought to him by a waiter. Hans thought nothing of it, and stuffed it into his pocket. Next morning, as we left together on the train back to Rome, he brought out the matchbox, and, instead of matches, found a message from Peter Heyworth, music critic of the *Observer*. Seemingly, he had been dining at another table, but was afraid to approach Hans directly, because of a bad notice he had given him for an earlier work. Peter Heyworth was trying to patch up what he imagined was a discord with Hans. The effect of the matchbox message, however, was to make Hans even more disgruntled. William had himself suffered from Heyworth's viperish pen. In 1955 Heyworth had written that he found 'little ... of interest in either the Violin Concerto or the First Symphony. As for the Cello Concerto and *Troilus*,' he had added, 'Walton's later works are deeply embedded in the stagnant waters of the past.' 'You see,' said Hans, referring to the matchbox message, 'critics are not worth the paper they write on, except as tapers to light a cigarette.'

When we returned to London after the serious accident which had prevented us from hearing the first performance of the Cello Concerto, William had seen Peter Heyworth at a concert, sitting two rows ahead of us. William was still walking with the aid of crutches; he got to his feet and, leaning forward, gleefully thumped Peter in the back with one of his crutches, daring him ever to write such rude notices again. William knew that Heyworth was keen on a reconciliation with Hans, so, despite Heyworth's dislike of his own works, William asked both Hans and Heyworth to stay with us on Ischia. Hans was not mollified, and William remarked, 'Some people don't know when they are lucky!'

In 1971, after the first performance in Rome of Hans's work *The Footpath to the House of Natasha Ungeheuer*, William met Peter Heyworth in the foyer of the theatre. This time William strode over to him before he could beat a hasty retreat, and said, 'Well, that's splendid, isn't it?' 'Do you really think so?' Peter retorted. 'Yes,' William said, his eyes twinkling, 'but if I had written it, of course, you would have said I had gone stark raving mad.'

When Hans built his impressive house at Marino, near Rome, we were surprised to see how spoilt he had become. His friend and secretary Fausto Moroni would jump up to light a cigarette for him. Even his clothes had to be ordered from a tailor in Rome without bothering the busy artist. Fausto had a dummy made, and the maestro's suits were finished without a fitting.

Hans ran into financial trouble in building the house, just as we had, so we suggested he should use the splendid *cambiale* system which had delayed payment of our debts, but he managed without it. What we could not stomach, though, was that, amidst all this comfort and affluence, he expounded Communist ideals. On one of our visits to him I asked if living like a nabob was not against his principles. Would it not be more consistent to sell his sumptuous mansion and distribute the proceeds? He became very, very cross, and said, 'How dare you insult me in my own house?' To which I replied, 'This is not an insult but common sense. Where else, Hans, can I draw your attention to the inconsistencies in your life, which contrasts with your ideals?'

He then began to boast that, as a good Communist, he loved to go to Cuba. But, when the Cuban authorities would not renew his visa any longer, Hans decided that the Americans must have insinuated God knows what to stop his pleasant excursions. It never occurred to him, said William, to think that his sort of music might have disturbed the traditionally minded Cubans. How the Americans could have influenced the decision of the Cuban authorities was beyond us. I asked Hans whether, on his visits to Cuba, he had also done his quota of building roads and cutting sugar-cane, or whether Fausto had done the work for both of them? William collapsed in laughter. Of course that made Hans rather cross. He said I was the worst type of Spanish colonialist he had ever met. He had obviously not met many.

Ingeborg Bachmann, a German poetess whom Hans admired and dearly loved, came to dine one evening while we were staying with him. Hans had set some of her poems to music, and she wanted to hear the result. After dinner he played a tape of the music. Inge started to cry. Hans was irritated, and asked why she was blubbing. She said, 'Because you hate me so much that you have destroyed my words with your music.' All hell broke loose. William and I went to bed, and Fausto spent the night running from Hans's bedroom to Inge's, trying to pacify the offended artists. We left next morning without seeing either. What a different life from ours!

The contemporary composer with whom William struck up the closest relationship in his early musical career was Paul Hindemith. William never forgot Hindemith's kindness when at the last moment he had stepped in to play the first performance of the Viola Concerto. It took William thirty-five years to repay the debt. He then composed a set of variations based on a theme from Hindemith's Cello Concerto, including a reference to *Mathis der Maler* (the opera, not the symphony). It was first played by the Royal Philharmonic Orchestra conducted by William at the Royal Festival Hall for the one-hundred-and-fiftieth anniversary of the Royal Philharmonic Society in March 1963. William was overjoyed to receive the following letter from Hindemith from his Swiss home in Blonay:

You wrote a beautiful score and we're extremely honoured to find the red carpet rolled out, even on the steps of the back door of fame. I'm particularly fond of the honest solidity of workmanship in this score; something that seems completely lost nowadays. Let us thank you for your kindness and for the wonderfully touching and artistically convincing manifestation of this kindness. (Even old Mathis is allowed to peep through the fence, which for a spectre seems to be some kind of resurrection after artificial respiration!) I am glad that George Szell had a great (and well-deserved) success with the piece in the States. I also shall put it on my programmes as soon as possible.

Less than six months later Hindemith died, so William repaid his debt only just in time.

The two of them were of one mind, moreover, when it came to the question of musical education, especially in relation to composers. Craftsmanship was one thing, and that was essential. But craftsmanship alone did not make a composer. By the time William came to live with the Sitwells, for instance, he had tried in vain to take an Oxford degree. A lack of academic qualification, however, was flung in William's face on many occasions. With the Sitwells' encouragement, it was believed, William had simply refused to continue a conventional music education. William liked to quote Hindemith's Harvard lecture of 1949:

The most conspicuous misconception in our educational method is that composers can be fabricated by training. If you go through two years of harmony, one of counterpoint, fulfil your requirements in Composition One and Composition Two, have some courses in orchestration and form, throw in some minor courses for credits, and do some so-called 'free work' in a post-graduate course, you are inevitably a composer, because you [have paid] for your courses. . . . [But] composing cannot be taught the democratic way. If there is anything remaining in this world that is, on the one side basically aristocratic and individualistic, and on the other as brutal as the fights of wild animals, it is artistic creation. It is aristocratic because it is the privilege of a very restricted number of people. [It] is individualistic because it is as private as your dreams. . . . Finally, artistic creation is excessively brutal, because works that have no strength are eliminated and forgotten like living beings that [do not] survive the struggle of life.

William was absolutely of the same opinion. It irritated him (and Hindemith) that UNESCO had a policy of spending money on unknown composers. Both he and Hindemith maintained that agencies like UNESCO should concentrate all their resources on making as widely known as possible the creations of artists who had been recognized, rather than frittering away all their money on total unknowns. I remember that they both used to laugh at the ability of some young 'composers' to survive, year after year, on scholarships and grants from agencies like UNESCO, without ever having written a single note of worthwhile music.

In 1963 we were invited to visit Israel during the July music festival. William was asked to conduct *Belshazzar's Feast* in Hebrew. The rehearsals were to be in Tel Aviv, with three concerts, one each in Jerusalem, Haifa, and Tel Aviv. Jerusalem was especially fascinating for us. We saw the Dead Sea Scrolls, and visited Nazareth and the Sea of Galilee, where we saw fishermen mending nets. Later we swam in the Dead Sea, and saw the ruins of Caesarea.

What especially pleased William was to meet again Helga Keller, who had worked with him as an editor on Olivier's Shakespeare films. It was she who took us to a kibbutz. A friend of Helga's, a ballet dancer, had married a young man who was in charge of a small factory attached to a kibbutz. They were only allowed to see their children in the late afternoon, as the children lived separately in various nurseries, according to their age. In the room allotted to them, nothing belonged to the couple. The one concession was a small entrance porch where they could brew a cup of tea, and once a week they were allowed a cake with which to entertain friends. The communal dining-room was drab and noisy, and the food very ordinary. William marvelled at the dedication to an ideal which made it possible for people to live in such an apparently restrictive community. The husband of Helga's friend, for instance, had recently been sent to work in the fields, because the elders of the kibbutz thought he had become too independent-minded working in the factory. I found the lack of provision for anyone to leave the community the most unacceptable aspect.

Whenever people were on their best behaviour, William felt a compulsion to upset the *status quo* by some irreverent observation. After conducting *Belshazzar's Feast* with the Israel Philharmonic Orchestra during this summer festival, William astonished his fellow guests at the final dinner in Tel Aviv, offered to thank the artists who had taken part, by saying, 'I have something that no one here has.' When everyone turned to him expectantly, he smiled beatifically and said, 'A foreskin!' I alone found this outrageous statement funny.

On the night after I returned from Israel to Ischia, I unwittingly did something which caused even more consternation. I was invited to the house of Prince and Princess Said ibn Hussein in Forio, to a party celebrating the wedding of their only son, Prince Raad, who had become a close adviser to his cousin, King Hussein of Jordan. Full of my trip to Israel, I expounded on the progress and advantages of that country until I noticed that my host and hostess wore frozen expressions. My gaffe dawned on me, and I fled.

When on his return from conducting in Ravinia and New York, I told William about my indiscreet remarks, he laughed. Perhaps composers have a special sense of humour. I remember Arthur Bliss coming to Lowndes Cottage to meet me when I was a new bride. Over dinner, glaring at William, he said, 'This is too much. His having married you is the last stroke of luck that will come his way.' I was rather indignant at this statement, and

replied, 'On the contrary, from now on he will be even luckier.'
Bliss then invited me to appear at Covent Garden as one of the
goddesses who come down from heaven in his new opera, which
was then in rehearsal. I thought this rather a compliment until I
saw *The Olympians* and realized that the goddesses were naked
ladies!

Another eccentric composer was the Australian Percy
Grainger, who came to lunch at Lowndes Cottage to photograph William's blue eyes, for a museum of eyes he was setting
up. He had a notion that composers worth their salt all had blue
eyes. It was a sunny day, and William sat on a wicker chair on
the roof garden. Grainger stood a few paces away. We thought
he was deciding on the best angle from which to photograph,
when, with one leap, he landed on William's lap. Luckily
William had a stout heart, or he would have suffered a stroke.
Grainger then took a close-up of the famous blue eyes. He was
very agile. With a few more leaps and jumps, he was downstairs
and out on the pavement.

Following the visit to Israel, William flew directly on to the
United States to conduct the Chicago Symphony Orchestra at
Ravinia. John Ward, OUP's music editor in New York, insists
that William arrived in sandals and shorts. William would never
have travelled in anything but a suit. What actually happened
was that his suitcases were lost, and days went by before they
were returned, so he had no choice but to arrive at parties in one
of the casual Ischian leisure suits which he designed himself.
Surprisingly, the smart Chicago set took the unconventional
attire in their stride. William never enjoyed conducting an
orchestra so much; he established an immediate rapport with the
Chicago Symphony. His white dinner-jacket arrived in time for
the opening concert, so all was well. On his way back, he
conducted at the Lewisohn Stadium in New York.

William particularly disliked the endless press and television
interviews. In New York he told John Ward that the BBC at
least paid an artist a pittance for his time. He was informed that
in the States an interview was considered a favour to the artist
and therefore was gratis. William was not mollified. It exercised
him that the journalists went on incessantly about *Façade*.
Eventually he perplexed all of them by saying: 'Façade is my

first name.' As *Façade* was not the work he most wanted to be remembered for, it is perhaps ironic that the last time he conducted was in Aeolian Hall, London, on 12 June 1973, for the fiftieth anniversary of *Façade*.

In 1964 I was working on our garden in Ischia, hurrying the stone-breakers to finish the landscaping in the valley at the foot of our new house, when, over Christmas, I slipped on a large stone and broke the socket of the bone below the knee. I heard it snap with a resounding crack, and I ended up in plaster up to my thigh for five months. Our doctor maintained that, with such a long period of inactivity, my bones would deteriorate, and he suggested that I go to London to see an English surgeon in case the leg could be operated on. But by the time I got to London, the crushed bits had grown together, and no operation could be performed.

William had agreed to conduct a three-month tour of Australia, Tasmania, and New Zealand, in order that we should both be given round-the-world tickets to visit India and Hong Kong on the way out and Japan, Hawaii, and Vancouver on the return journey. However, because of my accident, he had to travel alone, and resented being away for such a long time. I cried myself to sleep for nights after he left. Mama was kind enough to come from Buenos Aires to keep me company. During those long months I became desperate, because I received not one letter from William.

Our friend Terence Rattigan, who was staying as a tenant in one of our holiday houses, explained to me that hotels in Australia usually kept the stamp money of letters destined for Europe and threw their clients' letters away. Had it not been for Terry and a number of other friends—including Robin Maugham, Binkie Beaumont, and Nadia Nerina—who occupied our houses, I would have become even more miserable. One of Terry's friends in particular, the novelist and playwright Paul Dehn, was delightful company.

William visited his sister Nora, who lived in New Zealand, and enjoyed conducting the New Zealand Choir very much. Surprisingly, he had not been informed that he was a guest of honour at the Adelaide Festival, where he was conducting

Troilus and Cressida, with Marie Collier as Cressida. It was to
be the main event. When asked as he landed what he thought
about the festival, he simply replied that he disliked festivals.
This remark was widely quoted, and caused great offence. I
know he meant only that festivals did not usually allow
sufficient time for rehearsals, and that, as a consequence, the
resulting performances were disappointing, as had happened in
1960 at the Edinburgh Festival when the Second Symphony was
first performed.

Another tremendous rumpus in the Press was caused by
William trying to stop a truncated version of the national
anthem from being played before each concert. The rule was
that, if no one of any importance was present, a few bars were
enough. Only when the governor-general was present was the
whole anthem played. William thought it undignified to cut the
national anthem, and suggested that it should not be played at
all unless it was an important occasion. He was berated and
accused of having accepted a knighthood only to try to stop the
national anthem from being played!

In May I finally received a telegram to say that he was on his
way back. What a relief to have him return. I had felt deprived of
his company and had become increasingly anxious when long
months went by without news from him reaching me. When he
arrived home he was amazed to learn that I had not had a letter
from him, as he had written regularly. We had to believe that
Terry Rattigan's explanation was true. William told me that he
had consoled himself while away, not with Australian beauties
but by visiting as many botanical gardens as he could find. With
his sister, Nora, he arranged to send back to Ischia some shrubs
known as 'Christmas bushes', so called because at Christmas
they are covered in red flowers. Their Latin name is *Metrosider-
os*, and on Ischia they flower in July. They formed the begin-
nings of the tropical garden that we were building around the
house. William also sent some tree-ferns, which became a
distinctive feature of our new garden.

We now experimented with a series of tall thin sprayers to
water these New Zealand tree-ferns from the air; in this way we
created a rain-forest effect that cooled the air in the long summer
evenings. The New Zealand Christmas bushes were massed in a

large grouping by Russell, who wanted them surrounded by yuccas, aloes, agaves, blue palms, beschorneria, and Australian cordellines. He wanted the terraces beneath the house to be completely covered with Mexican plants, and suggested planting the creeping fern *Woodwardia radicans*, which fastens its new growths into crevices in the dry stone walls, eventually carpeting the area beneath the tree-ferns. How simple, we thought naïvely. It took us another three years of levelling, rebuilding, and transplanting to finish the work he mapped out! On a later stay Russell finally declared that the garden was becoming 'rather distinguished'.

The director of the Naples Botanical Garden, who had helped us get our tree-ferns through Italian customs, came to visit the garden, and was particularly fascinated by the *Woodwardia* fern. He looked very relieved when I told him that I had been given it by Viscount Chaplin,* a friend and contemporary of William's. He feared that I had found it on Ischia. He knew of one cleft in the hill of Mount Epomeo, he said, where this fern grew naturally and, as far as he was aware, this was the only place in Europe where it could be found in a natural habitat, so he did not want people to find out about it, lest it be stolen and lost from Ischia. We reassured him, and he paid us the greatest possible compliment by declaring that he could quite understand how such a garden and such a house could become a haven from the world, a truly life-giving environment, as much for people as for plants. This pleased William, who had become increasingly fond of the garden.

* 3rd Viscount, born 1906.

18

The Bear

WILLIAM claimed that *Troilus* had put him off writing opera. It was not until fifteen years later, after repeated urging from Peter Pears, that William wrote his one-act comic opera *The Bear*, which was first performed at Aldeburgh in June 1967. Peter had suggested something short, about three-quarters of an hour, with a small cast and a small orchestra, and had proposed several Chekhov stories. William chose *The Bear* because, after singing a few lines, he realized at once that it could work.

It was not the first time William's work was heard at Aldeburgh. His cycle of six songs *Anon in Love*, written for Peter Pears and Julian Bream, had been performed there at the 1960 festival; but with *The Bear* William felt he was really taking on Benjamin Britten in his own field of endeavour and on his own ground. To William's relief, Ben seemed pleased with the result.

Christopher Hassall had died of a heart attack while running to catch a train from Canterbury to London to attend a performance of *Troilus and Cressida*. So at first William toyed with the idea of doing his own libretto for *The Bear*; but he soon came to the conclusion that he needed a professional librettist, because libretto writing is a specialized art. Someone suggested Paul Dehn, whom we had met and liked when he had been Terry Rattigan's guest on Ischia. Paul and William got on famously, and Paul wrote an excellent libretto. Sadly, Paul died of lung cancer before he and William had an opportunity to collaborate again.

In the autumn of 1965 William seemed to be suffering from the remains of a bout of influenza which he just couldn't shake off. We met Lord Harewood in Rome and he told William that he thought he had bronchitis, and should go to London for a

197

check-up. In December William travelled to London to conduct the first performance of the orchestral version of *The Twelve*, to celebrate the nine-hundredth anniversary of the founding of Westminster Abbey. Before the concert, he went for a drink with an old friend, Dr Jean Shanks, at the flat of my gynaecologist, Dr Michael Hemans. When she noticed that, after coming up a long flight of steps, William was puffing in an unnatural way, she became alarmed. After the concert she arranged for William to see a heart specialist. The specialist examined William, found that his heart was all right, but noticed a shadow. A second opinion confirmed that William should be operated on at once. William told me later that he knew immediately what the problem was. He had cancer.

He telephoned from London to say that he could not return and must go into hospital. He would not say what was wrong, so I got it into my head that he had been run over by a car. But the next day he rang again to say that perhaps I should come over at once, as the operation had been set to take place in three days' time, and that it was cancer of the left lung. I was quite relieved. At least, I thought, he was not maimed. He couldn't resist being witty at his own expense saying, 'I am in the middle of writing *The Bear*. I haven't got very far, so it would not be a great loss if I popped off at this moment, musically speaking.'

He also asked me to throw away his collection of pipes and tobacco, as he would never smoke again. William had smoked like a chimney; he had been a non-stop pipe-smoker, at the rate of twenty pipes a day. It was a pleasure for me to jettison the tobacco and the pipes.

My relief over William not having been injured was short-lived. Our local doctor told me that operating on the left lung was very difficult, it being so close to the heart, and that survival over a long period was doubtful. Arriving in London full of apprehension, I discovered that, although William had originally been scheduled to be operated on at the Middlesex Hospital, his surgeon had agreed to perform the operation in the London Clinic, because new lifts were being installed at the Middlesex, making it an inferno of electric drills. Sir Thomas Holmes Sellars was concerned, however, that the after-care at the London Clinic might not prove as good as that which would be provided by his own team at the Middlesex. He asked the sister at the London Clinic to engage special nurses to sit with William twenty-four hours a day.

The hours of waiting for the operation to be over were agony. Eventually Sir Thomas appeared, looking grey and drawn. My heart gave a nasty turn. He said that, though the operation had been long, it had been entirely successful. He asked me to disappear for at least three days, as he did not want William to make the effort to be polite, even to me. The special nurses and the physiotherapist would take excellent care of him, he said. William was kept sedated, as the surgeon had left a tube to drain fluid from the scar on the left lung.

When Malcolm Sargent had been at Casa Cirillo, one of his guests had been Lilias Sheepshanks, and she became a dear friend of ours. Now she kindly took me with her to the country, and Michael Hemans followed to console me and give me fortitude. It seemed like years, instead of days, before I was allowed to return to London. To my surprise, William seemed quite cheerful; he obviously adored his nurses, especially the physiotherapist, who had to hold him in her arms to thump his back to free the lungs of phlegm. William took advantage of this embrace and hugged the physiotherapist gleefully. She came several times a day, and he fell quite in love with her, and said he would like to take her back to Ischia with him. I explained that, if he thought he would need a nurse, it meant he was not well enough to leave the London Clinic. No more was said about taking her with him.

David Webster convinced us that while William was recuperating, we should treat ourselves regally until he was allowed to return to Ischia. We booked ourselves into a river room at the Savoy Hotel, which had a clear view of the Festival Hall. The view across the river with the bridges and the boats steaming up and down was a source of constant pleasure to William. While he was in the clinic, many visitors, including, irony of ironies, Peter Heyworth, came to see him. Peter arrived at the same time as Malcolm Arnold, who had come equipped with several bottles of champagne. Poor Malcolm was outraged to think that Peter, who had been consistently uncomplimentary about William's music in the *Observer*, should be allowed in before him, and in no time every nurse and visitor who passed our corner of the corridor was being offered a glass of champagne. Eventually Malcolm burst in, carrying a huge bunch of flowers and what was left of a magnum of champagne, attempting at the same time to lift me off the floor in an embrace. We both fell on the carpet, crushing the flowers, but saving the bottle. Malcolm exclaimed, 'Who would have married a woman like this?' as if his clowning was my fault.

The operation on the lung had stopped William working on *The Bear*, and this worried him. As soon as he arrived back in Ischia, he decided that work was the best cure. After a few months, however, a pain suddenly gripped his left shoulder. Another check-up revealed that the cancer was back. During the operation Sir Thomas had tried to scrape the pleura clean of the growth, since he could not cut it out, as he had with the lung; presumably he had failed, so now the only solution was cobalt ray treatment. We returned to London to stay with Michael Hemans, himself an able surgeon.

What followed was eleven weeks of torture. Every morning William would walk to the Middlesex Hospital for the ray treatment, which exhausted him. By the tenth week it became clear that the rays were not improving his condition. He became so weak that he could hardly walk. The treatment also upset his stomach, so he could hardly eat. When I asked the surgeon what good the cobalt rays were doing, he said, 'We can do anything! We can simply burn a hole straight through him.' I dared not ask any more details of this treatment. All those burnt tissues had to be eliminated from his body; this caused him to feel like death, as the body struggled to recover each day from this poisoning of the system.

Finally the specialist, Sir Brian Wyndere, decided to double the dose. In despair, William made Michael Hemans promise that, if this were not successful, he would save him from a long and painful death. William was haunted by memories of the agony Alice Wimborne had suffered at the end of her life. He would tell me how she had gone literally black from lack of oxygen. She had had cancer of the bronchial tubes and the manner of her death had been a ghastly shock to him.

However, doubling the strength of the rays cured William.

The treatment finished and, after a short recovery period, we returned to Ischia where he settled down to finish *The Bear*. The ray treatment had burned the skin on William's chest; this, coupled with the scar from the operation (the surgeon had had to cut William almost in half, to lift the rib cage clear away so he could get at the lung), meant I could no longer hug him; his skin was too sensitive. He remained very delicate and in cold weather would easily catch a cold or fall ill with bronchitis. The rays had also burnt his oesophagus, which meant he had to eat small quantities of finely cut up food and gradually he even had to give up drinking wine, which he resented very much. In spite of a highly successful trip to the United States for the first performance of his overture *Capriccio Burlesco* in New York, it took William at least three years to recover from this treatment.

Work on *The Bear* was completed a few weeks before its scheduled first performance in the Jubilee Hall, Aldeburgh, part of a double bill with the première of Lennox Berkeley's *The Castaways*, also with a libretto by Paul Dehn. In May William wrote to Paul: 'Finished with B. B. [Bloody Bear], not what you think. I don't know what to think of it. It has taken far longer than necessary. It is I think sufficiently in time.'

It has been said that the rehearsals started before the score was actually finished; but this is untrue. The producer was Colin Graham, and Monica Sinclair and John Shaw were the protagonists. James Lockhart conducted the English Chamber Orchestra, and for once the critics were polite. William wrote later to his friends Dario and Dorle Soria: 'I have become so used to being slated by those critics, that I felt there must be something wrong when the worms turned on some praise. However, you will hear the record soon; pretty good.'

In fact, William didn't like the record. He thought that Monica Sinclair did not have the right type of voice; it was too heavy. He continued:

The music is light and humorous. Of course *Façade* crops up frequently in the critics' notices, but it has no real connection except that I happen to have composed both. The so-called jokes are not in quotations, but *à la manière* of Russian music. In fact by now I would be hard put to tell you which they are. The odd thing is that it has all, so to speak, sunk into the landscape and all sounds as if it were me, which in fact it is.

The only incident to cloud the first night was when Ben and Peter shocked us by ignoring the conductor, James Lockhart, who had done very well. But the Aldeburgh duo disapproved of him, so they strutted through his dressing-room without acknowledging his existence.

Unfortunately, a later television performance of *The Bear*, although conducted at the BBC studios by William, was a painful experience. Never having conducted for television before, William was distressed to be told not to stop when the orchestra and the singers got out of sync as it would all come right in the processing. The singers were conducted by James Lockhart while William dealt with the orchestra who were crowded in a corner just off the set. Naturally, William stopped the performance whenever the singers got a few bars behind the music, and the television producer was soon spitting with rage, shouting that only he was allowed to stop the filming. The result was chaos. Relations with the BBC were not improved with the making of a documentary profile. At a preview, William was so bored that he fell asleep; but I was furious to hear the commentator say, 'We think that what he has written since the War is negligible, so let us return to 1920 and *Façade*.' We sent the BBC a telegram saying we would sue if the programme went out. To me it seemed unnecessarily insulting and even libellous. The programme was recut before being shown.

In 1976 *The Bear* was performed at the Barga Festival by young students, or rather, I should say, by young professionals who were learning how to play, to produce, and to perform on stage. We spent a magical week in this medieval town with these eager, talented young people helping London Weekend Television to film their successful efforts to rehearse and put on stage William's *opera buffa*. It was sung in Italian; the translation was by Professor Bruno Rigacci who was in charge of the training scheme.

In 1967, returning to Ischia after the first performance of *The Bear*, we were met by our cook, who told us excitedly that she was getting married. Then, seeing our distress, she quickly added, 'But I am leaving you in much more competent hands; my seventeen-year-old sister, Reale, would like to take my place.' Reale became an immediate favourite with William. She was a very serious little girl who quietly took over the entire management of the house and became very attached to us. Reale eventually married our electrician, Peppino, and they came to live in the gatehouse. Their two daughters, Ella and Francesca, are my godchildren. Reale's cooking, inspired by William's desire for new and exciting dishes and stimulated by my research, is a great attraction for friends staying at La Mortella.

My family's tradition of cooking had come in handy; for the first eight years on Ischia, I cooked. Then I taught several young girls how to cook, and wrote a cookery book for each in Italian, with our favourite recipes. Reale has been my star pupil, as she loves experimenting with new dishes, and also cooks delicious local food. William was always very interested in his food, and he kept us on our toes. For years we drank demijohns of the local white wine, but gradually we replenished the wine-cellar with more sophisticated wines from other wine-growing areas of Italy.

Discovering new wines to taste and trying out different regional dishes of Italy has been great fun. Many of these succulent recipes are neglected now that 'fast food' *cotoletta alla milanese* has become universal from the toe of Sicily to the Alps. Naples had a fine old culinary tradition, with its roots in Bourbon times. In fact, Neapolitan chefs are still called 'Monsu', a derivation of 'Monsieur', and a reminder of the days when every important Neapolitan family employed a French chef. My own favourite Italian regional specialities, not necessarily for the weight-conscious, are *Zitti Ritti* (cheese soufflé poured over upright pipes of macaroni with mozzarella and ham), *Crespolini* (crêpes filled with ricotta, salami, and herbs) and *Triglie all'Anconetana* (red mullet with raw ham and bay-leaves), a dish from the Adriatic coast. William's favourite was delicious *Gnocchi di spinaccia* (noodle-balls of ricotta and spinach). What I really like are the southern Italian ways of serving pasta with vegetables instead of the better-known meat-based sauces of northern Italy. But William never lost his longing for Lancashire hot-pot and English sausages. I even bought pigs, and made our own sausages with a bread, pork, and veal content, as prescribed by Mrs Beaton, to keep him content. Of course, I did not forget to import from Fortnum's plum pudding and mincemeat for pies for Christmas.

William loved travelling and we continued to do so for as long as his health allowed. Whenever an invitation to conduct his music in any part of the world arrived, William was tempted to accept. He disliked long tours so we never accepted to go on a marathon conducting visit to the United States, despite enticing offers. He liked receiving invitations to conduct because, he said, they proved that people knew he was still alive and well. In his early days he felt he had a duty to conduct his own works, especially when a work was new, so that the orchestras and the public would be in no doubt as to what he intended; but he found the physical effort a strain. In his words: 'I really got into this conducting lark because of *Portsmouth Point*.'

Unlike some other composers who can hardly be kept off the platform, William never liked public occasions, and did not enjoy applause. He was so self-critical and shy that it embarrassed him. I remember how uncomfortable he felt when the excited audience indulged in wild applause, as happened after the concerts for his seventieth and eightieth birthdays, or after a prom. He was always full of misgivings and doubts, and the critics exacerbated his insecurity. They would say that he was not *modern* enough, while he believed that he was far too modern for many countries and many orchestras who still, to this day, cannot play his music properly.

In addition to necessary travel for William's work, we managed some delightful sightseeing excursions on the Italian mainland, a yacht trip through the Greek islands as guests of a friend Erni Jurgens, and a visit to Tunisia, where we found inspiration for decorating the door to our gatehouse in the work of local artisans at Hammamet.

In 1969 William was invited to Houston, Texas, as guest conductor of the Houston Symphony Orchestra, whose principal conductor was André Previn, by then a great supporter. William was delighted to accept, because it was half-way to

Mexico, which he had long wanted to visit. While we were in Houston, Columbia Artists' Management rang to say that there were two concerts at the Carnegie Hall in New York which William could conduct if he wished. 'Ah,' said William, 'more filthy lucre.' The American Symphony Orchestra's Carnegie Hall programme included the Viola Concerto, as well as the *Johannesburg Festival Overture* and *Façade*. William amused the orchestra by his remarks during rehearsals: 'It's a nice programme, much more varied than a programme of Bach. Not so good perhaps, but more varied.' He liked the orchestra, and in particular admired the knees of some of the women fiddlers; he made the orchestra laugh by telling them so. By the time we got to Mexico City William had caught flu, and, because of the altitude and his health, which had become so delicate after the pneumonectomy, we had to beat a retreat and fly back to London.

Determined to put himself to work 'before it was too late', as he kept telling me, William produced a steady stream of enchanting miniatures, including the Benjamin Britten Improvisations and the Five Bagatelles for Julian Bream. 'Never having thought of writing for the guitar,' William said, 'I asked Julian for a chart which would explain what the guitar could do. I managed to write some rather pretty pieces for him, except that the first six notes of the first piece all need to be played on open strings. So when he begins to play, the audience will probably think he's tuning the bloody thing up.'

In 1971 the London Symphony Orchestra and André Previn invited us to the Soviet Union as their guests. They had scheduled a tour there with Benjamin Britten and Peter Pears. William disliked what Soviet officialdom had done in the name of freedom, which he valued so highly. But we couldn't resist the temptation to see with our own eyes what life there was like.

Things began badly; first we lost William at London airport. William dutifully followed a young man carrying a violin case, believing him to be a member of the orchestra. Alas, the young man was on his way to Spain, so Previn had to sprint after William to rescue him. On our first night in Leningrad, where the orchestra was being entertained by the Soviet Ministry of

Culture at Friendship House, it became evident that the Russians did not know that William was a guest of the orchestra. Although they had given us visas, they probably could not believe that a well-known composer was merely a guest of an orchestra; in Russia, this would not happen.

At the reception a Leningrad chamber group played Benjamin Britten's Simple Symphony, and William's voice was heard, loud and clear above the music, saying, 'Oh, not that piece!' to the great amusement of the LSO members.

The speech of welcome was fulsome about Ben, with many references to 'The Great Britten', while never mentioning William. We could see how uncomfortable Nina, our kind interpreter, looked, since Ben, who was a guest of the British Embassy, had not yet come to Leningrad. The general manager of the orchestra, Harold Laurence, and his wife were relieved to see William enjoying the situation; they feared he would be offended.

Though it was April, we found Leningrad very cold and drab. The pavements on the Nevsky Prospekt were full of people in heavy overcoats with blank expressions, wandering listlessly. They appeared to be in no hurry to reach their destinations. We concluded that, though in the Soviet Union everyone is said to be employed, the many people in the streets on a working day could not all have been night workers off duty. Perhaps they had part-time jobs and were passing the time of day. We felt in a strange land, not because the people themselves were unfriendly, quite the contrary, but one couldn't but object to the endless queues. Queues to buy food, queues to pay, queues to collect, and this waste of time for a meagre sausage or an egg. We found great difficulty in buying mineral water that was palatable. We were saddened by the dirty windows of the shops, and could not bear to see the ubiquitous drunks pushed off the sidewalk into the street. No wonder that fifteen years later Mr Gorbachov waged war on alcoholism. We were surprised by the vast room allotted to us in the hotel, which contained only the beds and a large mirror. We heartily disliked the stolid tea- or key-ladies who constantly watched our door, and even forbade us to leave the room with a tooth-glass to have a drink next door. That all seemed to us to be signs of a tyrannical oppression. Even the dining-room, set aside especially for the orchestra, had a guard at the door, 'to stop us stealing the cutlery,' William said. I organized a contest with the orchestra during every meal to discover what exactly it was that we had been given to eat; it was often impossible to taste the difference between the meat, the vegetables, and the fish. My contest made one of our interpreters very cross. 'Curly', as I called him (because of his frizzy hair), objected to Soviet food being made a subject of fun. He told me sternly not to ask for a double vodka as this meant nothing to the waiter; in the Soviet Union drinks were ordered by the gram. The enjoyable part of this visit was to be able to admire the beautiful buildings and visit the Hermitage, and to know we were among friends in the company of the LSO.

The first concert was not a success, but we could not tell whether the poor reception was because the audience was uncertain of the propriety of applauding a foreign orchestra's efforts, or because Vaughan Williams's Fourth Symphony did not appeal to it. There were very few printed programmes on sale, and what there were had been printed on rubbishy paper. The orchestra was depressed by the indifferent reception. The hall was magnificent, however, and after the concert people stayed in their seats, chatting away, delighted to be in such a grand marble hall illuminated by magnificent crystal chandeliers.

The second concert was received with more warmth. It included a Rachmaninov symphony, and met with an immediate response from the packed audience, many of whom wept openly. Still, the applause was perfunctory. It was not until the third concert, with William's First Symphony in the second half, that the audience was won over. The orchestra pulled out all the stops. William was their guest, and they were determined to show a Russian audience what a marvellous work they were being given the chance to hear. The performance was stunning, and at the end Previn turned around and gestured to William to stand and acknowledge the applause.

The audience, as far as we knew, had been quite unaware that the composer was present, and immediately started cheering. William walked slowly, but in a determined way, to the front, and shook Previn's hand and thanked the orchestra. Then he was mobbed. He was surrounded by a mass of young people, all trying to get his autograph. Some preferred the miserable bits of programme paper; some could offer only a matchbox. William disappeared into the crowd as the young people climbed on to each other's shoulders to get a glimpse of him. The orchestra was proud that William was its guest, and not the official guest of the British Embassy, as Ben was. The British Ambassador greeted William after the performance of the symphony in Moscow, where it was an even greater success with the public, by patting him on the back and saying, 'Not bad this. Have you written anything else?'

William and I had decided to give a party after the concert in Leningrad for Previn and some of the orchestra members and their wives, to thank them. When we arrived at the hotel room reserved for the party, we found our way barred by the redoubtable tea-ladies. They said we could not enter until we had paid for the vodka and caviar we had ordered. As we had no idea that this would happen, and did not carry large sums of cash in our pockets, the party almost didn't happen. Luckily, a young diplomat from the British Embassy was able to lend us some dollars.

The insidious bureaucracy pursued us everywhere. Rostropovich had been given permission to play Britten's Cello Symphony, which had been written specially for him. Ben himself was to conduct. This was in itself extraordinary, since it was the first time that the authorities had allowed Rostropovich to play with a foreign orchestra since his disgrace following his support for the banned novelist Solzhenitsyn who had lived for years in the garage of the Rostropovichs' *dacha*. Rostropovich came to the door of the hotel dining-room to say hello to the orchestra, but was not permitted to join us. Nor was he allowed to come to a lunch party in Moscow given by the British Embassy. Ben and William made an enormous fuss, and Rostropovich was finally allowed to appear, with his wife Galina Vishnevskaya, at an evening reception offered by the British Embassy for the whole orchestra. The wife of the ambassador, Lady Wilson, and Mme Furtseva, the Soviet Minister of Culture, both came in simple brown dresses, but the wives and ladies of the orchestra were dressed to kill, and we were delighted to see Rostropovich's wife arrive in a stunning, full-length evening dress, and covered in jewellery. Our interpreter, Nina, was immediately sent home by Mme Furtseva to smarten herself up. Normally, she had a long trip home with two changes of bus. This time she was back quickly, looking very glamorous and chic. Mme Furtseva had given her an official car for the journey! I wondered if the stunning clothes were also provided by some mysterious government department nearby.

In Moscow William and I met the secretary-general of the Composers' Union, Tikhon Khrennikov. I asked him if he had liked William's First Symphony. 'What is good, is good,' he replied. He explained proudly that the Composers' Union had three million rubles in the bank. I interrupted to ask whether it would not be preferable to have less money and more composers. He replied that to produce and publish a symphony was very expensive; surely it was better to be certain of the quality of the music before publishing it? This was the man, William reminded me, who had masterminded the denunciation of Shostakovich, Prokofiev, and Stravinsky during Stalin's rule.

Mme Furtseva invited us to the Kremlin for a reception. Sadly, I told her that, as the bus in which together with the orchestra we were usually transported was not allowed into the Kremlin, we should have to refuse, since William was not able to walk the distance from the front gate to the reception hall. She was horrified to find that we were being treated like the orchestra. She immediately ordered a Chaika limousine and a driver to take us to the reception. William noticed that the buffet table had towering dishes of oranges as centre-pieces, and we both realized that even the simplest food was an enormous luxury in Russia. So when a member of the audience brought André Previn an orange as a thank-you gift after the concert, we realized that this must have been a truly heartfelt sacrifice. Ischia seemed more and more like a paradise at the centre of a mad, mad world.

19

Celebrations

LUCKILY, William was in good health for his seventieth-birthday celebrations. We spent six months of 1972 travelling through England, Scotland, and Ireland for concerts in his honour, many of which he partly conducted himself. It seemed at the time like one long party, the gold seal of which was a dinner given at 10 Downing Street by the Prime Minister, Edward Heath, for seventy-five guests, including the Queen Mother.

The idea for the dinner had come originally from John and Mary Peyton, two friends from our earliest days on Ischia. John Peyton had become Minister of Transport in Mr Heath's government. The Prime Minister insisted on taking responsibility for all the arrangements. As he is a good pianist and an enthusiastic amateur conductor, he took enormous trouble with the after-dinner musical entertainment. Herbert Howells contributed a grace, and Arthur Bliss, then Master of the Queen's Musick, an ode with words by Paul Dehn. Ten numbers from *Façade* were even recited by BBC announcer Alvar Liddell, with David Atherton conducting the London Sinfonietta.

William had put on our guest list for the occasion Dr Jean Shanks, who had first advised him to see a heart specialist and thereby initiated the discovery of his cancer in time to save his life; the surgeon Sir Thomas Holmes Sellars, whose skill had actually saved his life; and our general practitioner in London, John Hunt.* Mr Heath remarked that, apart from the President of the United States, he could not recollect having entertained any other guest who had three doctors in attendance.

* Lord Hunt of Fawley, created Baron in 1973 (life peer), CBE 1970, MA, DM, Oxon, FRCP, FRCS, FRCGP, President, Royal College of Gen. Practitioners 1967–70, Hon. Fellow Green College, Oxford, since 1980.

No. 10 Downing Street had not fêted a musician for over 150 years. Musicians usually came in through the side door to entertain the guests, but not this time. The Prime Minister was an excellent host. Over cocktails he told us how he had watched William's public appearances and admired William's laconic replies to interviewers. He arranged for William to be presented with the original manuscript of the *Battle of Britain* music, salvaged from the archives of United Artists. The 'Battle in the Air' music was not included in the presentation, the company having claimed ownership because it was used in its film. In reply to enquiries later, it said that the manuscript of this piece could not be found, so up to now it is missing from the collection of William's work.

William's reply to the Prime Minister's speech of welcome was typical. Knowing that he would have to make such a speech, William had consulted Laurence Olivier. Larry had sent a telegram to Ischia with a few suggestions. I remembered to bring the telegram with me to Downing Street, just in case. As William stood up and looked around in wild alarm, I took the yellow Italian telegram form out of my bag and asked the Prime Minister to pass it to the Queen Mother to pass on to William. William, looking at Larry, who was next but one to him, said, 'You sent me this. Why don't you do the reply speech?' 'No, no!' said Larry. 'You were supposed to learn it, old boy!' Much laughter. William then read out Larry's telegram just as it was sent to him, preceded only by 'Your Majesty, Prime Minister, Lords, Ladies, and friends':

Dear Boy

This, no joking, is your speech, and is sent you herewith to give you chance to learn it absolutely by heart with no worries stop. Edit it of course, do anything you want with it or don't use it at all, but I promised to do this for you and here it is:

Ladies and Gentlemen you will understand I hope that it is extremely difficult for me to speak on this occasion for the very simple reason that it is beyond the conduct of this medium of speech or the control of human emotion that true expression can be found for my feelings. I beg you to forgive me and to understand that I am made happy beyond words by your extraordinary kindness and generosity with which being matchless it is not possible for me to compete. I thank God for making me seventy so that you could make me so happy. Stop.

Mr Heath's party was almost a reunion of those I had first met at that 'Welcome to London' party in 1949. Apart from Larry, there was our solicitor and old friend Arnold Goodman,* the great comforter, who always pours oil on troubled waters. When we had consulted him originally in the offices of Rubinstein and Nash, I remember, Arnold had had such a small office that he and his desk occupied most of it, and William and I were made to sit partly in the corridor. We were then trying to buy a garage on the back mews which had once belonged to Lowndes Cottage, and was situated immediately under the kitchen. Arnold had handled this little transaction with consummate skill. William used to say that Arnold's bushy eyebrows allowed him to scrutinize his clients without revealing what he was thinking. To me, his eyes seemed like lenses of a great brain ticking away like a computer. Arnold is certainly never inconspicuous, and not just because of his size. He is the greatest champion of musicians, and a great ally to his clients, dissuading many from useless litigation, preferring compromise to confrontation. He told us once that the best way to deal with your opponent was to write his or her name on a slip of paper, and put it away in a drawer. Years later, you would come across this same slip of paper, forget completely what it was that had annoyed you, and realize that God had taken care of the enemy!

Lionel Tertis, then over ninety, was also present, but André Previn, who had brilliantly conducted the birthday concert the night before, was recording *Belshazzar's Feast* and could not come. Henry Moore was there, a man who seemed increasingly to have the same strength as his sculpture. He was short and stocky, with the most engaging smile when his grey eyes lit up. William had hoped he would design the sets for the original production of *Troilus* at Covent Garden because he believed Henry would have been uniquely able to convey the mysterious and overriding power of the gods who control the destinies of

* Lord Goodman of the City of Westminster, created Baron in 1965 (life peer), CH 1972, MA, LLM.

their poor human puppets, allowing them to enjoy their passions, only to be struck down in the end. Alas, he had declined. David Webster had then invited Hugh Casson, whom we had first met as the architect of the Festival of Britain. William had not been impressed with Casson's sets. They were elegant, he said, but slight, and in William's view did not convey the majesty and power that he had hoped Henry Moore would have translated on to the stage.

One of William's treasures was a maquette for a large piece of sculpture of Henry's called *Madonna and Child*. He was proud of having been able to buy it at a sale to collect funds for the War effort. It is only the height of an open hand; but one is impressed with the strength of the powerful seated figure, clad in a gown, with a small, stiff child on her knees, the embodiment of Mother Earth rather than a sentimental notion of a mother and child. William was very pleased to see Henry Moore again.

Kenneth Clark was another guest. For some years Kenneth had been the greatest personality of the art world in Britain. He had been director of the National Gallery during the War, when only twenty-seven, and later Keeper of the Royal Pictures, and had served on the boards of many important museums throughout the world, including the Louvre and the Metropolitan in New York. His eyes always lit up when he was asked to show pictures, and his love and knowledge of painting made him a most unassuming, yet brilliant guide and instructor. He would take infinite trouble to explain why he thought a particular picture was interesting, usually adding some little anecdote about how and where he had found it. He was also very generous with advice to friends (such as William) as to what to collect, although the advice was usually given with such diffidence that most people took no notice, and only afterwards regretted not having followed his suggestions.

William was always on his guard with Kenneth, not least because of his earlier affair with his wife Jane. Jane was very materialistic and not a little bored with the élite of the art world. She had always had an ambition to become a great society hostess in London, and Kenneth had made that possible. He, however, was essentially contemplative and studious. William believed that he had allowed Jane to push him into positions of power, often against his better judgement. William told me that Kenneth knew full well of Jane's affair with him, and had once offered to send him and Jane off together. Knowing that William could not afford to keep Jane in the luxurious life-style to which she had become accustomed, Kenneth had even offered to finance the operation. Apparently he himself was keen on someone else, and thought it would be ideal if William were to take Jane off his hands. But Alice Wimborne was then still alive, and this made living with Jane impossible, even had he wanted to. Luckily Jane then transferred her attentions to the French ambassador—'Froggie,' as William used to call him— and William soon fell from favour.

Although Kenneth was unfailingly kind and polite to me, I did resent him saying, when we met in 1949, that William had not been educated properly. 'If only he had had the benefit of studying with Nadia Boulanger in Paris,' he had said, 'it would have made all the difference to his talent.' William was quite cross when I repeated this to him, and even more so when I told him that Jane found our wish to live abroad ridiculous, since she had decided that William would then not write any more music! None the less, William was godfather to Colin, their second son. Colin came to Ischia to stay, as well as his twin Colette whom William also liked. Kenneth and Jane also came to visit, although having them to stay on Ischia filled William with apprehension; he feared that they would ask us to return the gifts they had bestowed on him when he was in favour, which included our dining-room table.

They did not ask for anything back, but, as I strolled through the garden with them, Jane asked in a patronizing manner, 'How ever has dear William managed to build such a lovely place?' I suppose the Clarks thought that artists ought to keep to their garrets. A lot of water had gone under the bridge since, as a young bride, I had been relieved when they voiced approval of the William Morris wallpaper I had chosen for Lowndes Cottage. Jane seemed surprised that an ignorant Argentine should have known about William Morris. In fact, I didn't. I had not selected it because it was the 'in' fashion but because I liked it more than any of the other wallpapers I was shown. I told Jane that wallpaper was a novelty for me, because in Buenos Aires walls are plastered and painted; she wrinkled her nose in distaste. I did not tell her that William was shocked when he discovered that my redecorating of Lowndes Cottage had cost almost £2,000! I knew that the Clarks spent much greater sums on improving one room. For example, they would commission an artist to design a fabric especially for them.

At Mr Heath's party, all that seemed long ago. Kenneth looked older than I had expected, and Jane's drinking had got out of hand. Twice during dinner she fell off her chair, and immediately after supper Kenneth had to take her home. I wrote to him later that evening, before William could stop me, to say that, even if he believed himself superior to the rest of mankind since his Civilization series had been shown with such success on television, this was hardly a good enough excuse for snubbing Sir Thomas Holmes Sellars who sat on Jane's right and had been kind enough to keep an eye on her. I had introduced them before the dinner carefully explaining to Kenneth that this was the surgeon who had saved William's life and he would be Jane's dinner companion, only to hear Kenneth reply how useful that would be as she was suffering from bronchitis and he might have a suggestion to make to ease her condition. I found his offhand behaviour insufferable.

As the evening came to an end, we were entertained by part of Schubert's B-flat Trio, the piece which William said he would have most liked to compose himself. The music continued until very late, or rather until very early in the morning, by which time our driver had left, thinking he had missed us. The Prime Minister, William, and I walked up and down a deserted Downing Street and Whitehall, looking for transport. The security personnel would never allow such a thing today.

On the evening before, at the main birthday concert at the Royal Festival Hall, William conducted Yehudi Menuhin in his Viola Concerto, and Previn conducted the Benjamin Britten Improvisations and, after the interval, *Belshazzar's Feast*. As a surprise encore, six friends, including Nicholas Maw, Richard Rodney Bennett, and Peter Maxwell Davies, performed six miniature 'Happy Birthday' pieces they had composed. 'A real tribute', quipped William, 'from the avant-garde to the almost dead and buried.' William sent the orchestra over a hundred half-bottles of champagne, delivered backstage while the concert was in progress, each in an individual carton with a card reading: 'Quaff the health of William Walton on the 29th of March.'

A surprise telephone call the evening after Mr Heath's party interrupted dinner with William's brother Alec. William was called to the telephone, to discover that it was André Kostelanetz and the strings of the Vancouver Symphony Orchestra playing a transatlantic *Happy Birthday* overture! William was too overcome to speak; Kostelanetz continued with the *Capriccio Burlesco*, which he had first conducted in 1968 and which was dedicated to him. As Kostelanetz finished the piece, William heard a wag in the orchestra ask whether they had reversed the charges. William walked back to our table, shaking his head and saying, 'I will never be seventy again.'

There were concerts at Bath and King's Lynn. Here Lady Fermoy, the chairman of the festival, asked us to be her guests. An eleven-year-old, Diana Spencer, now the Princess of Wales, was staying with her grandmother; she and her brother and sister kept us all entertained.

At Christ Church, Oxford, the choir with Simon Preston gave the first performance of Jubilate Deo; and at Edinburgh, Alexander Gibson and the Scottish National Orchestra performed the Violin Concerto with Christian Ferras as soloist. Most touching of all, perhaps, was a concert given by the Leicestershire Schools Symphony Orchestra, who performed *Belshazzar's Feast* and presented William with a chiselled silver box.

At Aldeburgh, Benjamin Britten had arranged two special performances of *The Bear*. Mme Popova was sung by Patricia Kern, and Smirnov by Thomas Hemsley. Both gave delightfully subtle and witty performances, a great contrast to their predecessors. Members of the Royal Ballet danced *Façade*, choreographed by Frederick Ashton with Peter Pears reciting the words. This was the first time ever that *Façade* was danced to the spoken text. It was not entirely satisfactory, though, because one could not decide whether to listen to Peter recite or to watch the ballet. When Lindsay Kemp produced it later, in 1983, the characters in the ballet spoke the text themselves, and, as a result, it was integrated.

Prince Charles flew to Aldeburgh in his helicopter for the performance, and at the party afterwards, given by Lilias and Robin Sheepshanks, he said, trying to make me feel not left out: 'Now we must prepare an equally lovely party for *your* seventieth birthday.' He flushed pink when I told him that he would have to wait more than twenty years for that to happen!

William's publishers gave a great party at their premises, Ely House, in London, and presented William with a de luxe edition of *Façade*. Their American representative, John Ward, sent William an electric eraser. William quipped, 'Now I can rub out all my work.'

On 14 September William was given the enormous pleasure of a promenade concert dedicated to his music. André Previn conducted the London Symphony Orchestra in *Scapino* and Act II of *Troilus and Cressida*, with Richard Lewis and Jill Gomez, and *Belshazzar's Feast* was heard after the interval. William could hardly hold back his tears on at last hearing some of *Troilus* properly played and beautifully sung. The applause was like a tornado. Even Peter Heyworth sent a congratulatory telegram. William thanked him for his good wishes adding, 'I will need them, especially from you.' William's closest friends banded together to give him a stereo tape-recorder and record-player with good loudspeakers. Until then he had listened to records on a rather primitive machine. Back in Italy, Jack Buckley, arts officer of the British Council, organized a concert in William's honour with Maestro Francesco Siciliani, the head of the Radio Audizioni Italiana orchestra. When Jack telephoned originally about this, my reply was, 'We have lived here thirty years without the Italians finding out that William writes music. Let's leave it at that.' Jack, however, convinced us to go to Rome. Maestro Siciliani offered to perform whatever William fancied. William suggested that André Previn conduct the RAI orchestra with Kyung-Wha Chung in the Violin Concerto and John Shirley Quirk in *Belshazzar's Feast*. Ninety members of the London Symphony Orchestra choir were flown over specially. This concert took place in January 1974. The Italian audience was amazed to learn that the chorus was an amateur one, which sang for the pure joy of singing; every word was crisp, fierce, and dramatic; the critics admired their precision and intensity.

The choir had a dramatic return journey. They were embarking for their flight at Ciampino airport when a terrorist bomb exploded. Ninety throats responded with the mighty word, 'Slain!'

The Italian EMI made the grand gesture of producing a box of William's records, for sale in Italy. Earlier, in November 1973, William had written an *Anniversary Fanfare* for EMI's seventy-fifth birthday concert at the Royal Festival Hall, London. He had used six notes of 'Happy Birthday' and arranged it so that it would leap without a break into his coronation march *Orb and Sceptre.*

In the spring of 1974 Derek Bailey, Russell Harty, and his colleagues came to Ischia to interview and film part of *Sir William and Our Gracie.* Then we went to Capri, where the rest of the film was shot. Russell's idea was to immortalize the first meeting of two Lancashire expatriates living on neighbouring Mediterranean islands. We had been longing to meet Gracie Fields, and were far from disappointed when we did. She was ebullient, vivacious, and apparently ageless. She told us that she had been shy at the prospect of meeting a star of classical music, and had hurriedly bought William's records. William reassured her that he had long been a fan of hers.

A quite different reminder of Lancashire was the unexpected appearance one sunny afternoon of a tall, rough-looking young man with long hair, barefoot, with heavy boots slung round his neck by the laces. He climbed over the hill and surprised us basking by the swimming-pool. I was at first frightened, and thought that this intruder was up to no good. I could not imagine how he had got into the property, and expected him to pull a gun on us at any moment. He seemed to be addressing us in some unknown tongue, until it dawned on me that he was saying, 'Are you my Uncle Willie?'

Since the death of William's mother communication with the family in Oldham had been sporadic, and William took some minutes to realize that the lad must be a grandson of his brother Noel. When William, who was not feeling avuncular, gathered that he had hitch-hiked to Naples and had no further plans beyond staying with us, he panicked and vanished to his music room, after telling me to cope with the situation. I hit upon the idea of providing the nephew with sufficient money to explore Sicily and urged him to enrich his education by going to the south. We found him a hotel for the night, and after a friendly lunch on the terrace he went on his way, which relieved William.

Over Christmas of 1974 William worked out a new ending to the Cello Concerto to encourage Piatigorsky to return to the concert platform after a long illness. As before, they had a long exchange of letters. Grisha wanted a 'less melancholy ending'. 'It was very difficult to know quite what he wanted,' said William. But anyhow he tried to do a new ending for him, and by the end of the following February Piatigorsky cabled that the new version met with his approval. William wrote to him with evident relief:

I don't know why it [the new ending] bothered me so much. I'm losing confidence in my powers and find composing increasingly difficult. I never found it easy, but now it is the very devil. . . . I cannot tell you how much we are looking forward to hearing you do the concerto in the flesh.

Alas, Piatigorsky never performed the concerto again, as he died of cancer in August. It was a sad blow for William, and the new ending has never been performed to this day.

One of the first of his fellow composers to congratulate William on his Cello Concerto was the much younger Malcolm Arnold. He had first come across William's music, he told us, when he played first trumpet in the London Philharmonic at a concert performance of the Violin Concerto. The printed score, he said, had so many mistakes in it that it deserved to be 'junked'. Arnold, however, had kept his copy; it was, he felt, 'a curiosity to be prized'. As he came into our lives, we quickly discovered that he was always great fun to be with, although he would embarrass William with his constant eulogies, which were certainly well meant. Malcolm would always take us to places we had never been before; he took us one evening to Danny La Rue's club, where the band played the first movement of William's Violin Concerto as a bossa nova. William thought it worked very well, and so did all the clients.

William and Malcolm were at opposite ends of the political

spectrum: Malcolm was an admirer of Communist ideals, and William was not, so they avoided the subject. Malcolm is tall and heavily built, with wide shoulders that are in striking contrast to his delicate, small hands. He had enormous success writing music for films, especially with *Bridge over the River Kwai*. This produced larger and larger amounts of royalties, which allowed him, he said, the luxury to write serious music. Soon after, William and he almost collaborated. They were asked to write together the score for David Lean's film *Lawrence of Arabia*. But, after seeing the rushes and drinking a fair amount over lunch, they decided that it was a travelogue needing hours of music, and declined. This deeply offended David Lean, an old friend of William's, and provoked an irate phone call from Paris from Sam Spiegel, the producer, who berated William for his failure to understand commercial cinema. In early 1969 Malcolm and William did work on a film together: Malcolm was an enormous help to William, orchestrating and generally encouraging him to work on the music for *The Battle of Britain*.

I felt Malcolm resented my being so close to William, whom he hero-worshipped. Once, he came to stay in one of our holiday houses to work on a new symphony. He and William always met at midday to have a chat and a beer, and once a week we all dined together. Malcolm, who thought I was wildly extravagant, determined to save William from my bad influence; so, on our next evening out, in a quixotic mood and emboldened by a lot of wine, he started to lecture us. I thought it was a joke, but William got cross and put an end to the conversation by saying that Malcolm had stayed with us often enough to have seen how I had built up the property and to know how well run it was, and that he should apologize. Malcolm packed and left early the next morning without even saying goodbye; but he left a note for me, saying that he loved William too much to allow me to force him to have a fight with him! The friendship cooled, but it survived this misunderstanding. Malcolm has generously given me the manuscript of William's Five Bagatelles and William's letters to him, beautifully bound, for the Walton Museum. For my part, I was really happy to be able to attend

Malcolm's sixty-fifth birthday concert in the Queen Elizabeth Hall in 1986, and to see him looking so well.

As Larry's health declined in later years, he came to Ischia more and more frequently. In 1975, after being in hospital for months suffering from dermatomyositis, a most treacherous disease kept at bay only by massive cortisone treatment, he came to Ischia looking as if he was at death's door. His fingers were still wound up in plaster bandages; as the finger tips were constantly breaking into new sores, I suggested taking the bandages off to let the skin breathe. I spent hours each morning changing the dressings on his bleeding fingers, and I bought white cotton waiter's gloves to keep the light bandages in place.

Larry was also on an intensive course of injections, and already looked like a pincushion; there was not an inch of his skin left that had not had a jab. It became a great joke as I patted him with cotton wool soaked in alcohol in one place, while my housekeeper Reale injected in another. Gradually, however, the sores healed, and at last he could dress without pain when his clothing touched his skin. He even became interested in cooking. Before long, he and William were holding hymn-singing contests to see which of them could remember his choirboy days the best. I do believe William was a little jealous, complaining that more of my attention was being lavished on Larry than on himself. William used to knit his brows and tease me, saying he knew I was secretly in love with Laurence Olivier. The truth is that I have always adored Larry.

It was not until almost twenty years after the first performance of *Troilus* that William became enamoured of the tonal quality of Janet Baker's voice; and when she expressed an interest in the part of Cressida, he responded immediately by cutting and revising the work, trying to adapt it to her contralto voice. I know William would have preferred the work to be produced by the English National Opera under Lord Harewood at the Coliseum, especially after his unhappy experiences at Covent Garden; but Harewood insisted that Covent Garden had first priority to it, and said the two opera-houses never poached on each other's work. In addition, the then general manager of Covent Garden, Sir John Tooley, who had become a friend of

William's, made a special plea that *Troilus* should return to its rightful home.

After much persuasion, EMI agreed to record *Troilus* from the stage production. The tenor Alberto Remedios had decided to sing in Paris, so we were bereft of a tenor. Colin Graham, the producer, had been to Sweden to audition Gösta Winbergh for the tenor part and had returned enthusiastic, but the Swede was turned down by EMI as not having the reputation the recording company expected. We were lucky that Colin had agreed to direct the new version. To William's indignation, the board of directors at Covent Garden would authorize spending only the equivalent amount of what it would have taken to renovate the old production. So much for the offer of a 'new' production! Colin told us that the old production was in tatters and would be impossible to use, and that £15,000 was the miserable sum allotted for the production. Only a friend would have accepted to direct under these conditions. Most of this small sum went immediately on the 180 costumes necessary for the double chorus; the remaining £5,000 or so was, of course, insufficient for three new settings. As a result, pieces of scenery had to be borrowed from other productions, and bits of furniture came from the old one. The extremely sparse production was saved by the lighting of William Bundy, the ingenuity of designers Christopher Morley and Ann Curtis, and, not least, by the poetic and imaginative direction of Colin. His gallant attempt to stage a major lyric opera on such a meagre budget was attacked by the critics, who had no way of knowing the true situation.

At the same time Covent Garden was budgeting for a fashionable new production of Puccini's *La Fanciulla del West* that eventually cost £150,000. I think the Board of Directors performed a disservice to the cause of English opera, but above all to William. I trust they were gratified by the standing ovation given to *Troilus and Cressida* every night by a theatre 92 per cent full during the five repeats, which must have handsomely repaid their measly £15,000

A week before the rehearsals were due to start, the conductor, André Previn, had bursitis. He had asked William to be in London for the rehearsals, as he would need his advice; we would never have come to London for such a long period otherwise. William's health was becoming increasingly delicate, and he needed the relaxed life of Ischia, which really suited him; but we had agreed, and travelled to London.

To stay a month at the Savoy was more than we could afford, so we decided on a cheap hotel in the Aldwych, because it was close to Covent Garden. But we had not realized that the hotel was accustomed to groups of travellers. The entire establishment stank of cooking cabbage. Janet Baker was our one comfort; she seemed to be in constant good spirits, and the rehearsals were enormously helped by her identification with the role of Cressida and by the way she lifted the morale generally. Meanwhile Lawrence Foster, the new conductor, battled nobly to learn the score. The tenor, Richard Cassilly, who was acceptable to EMI, appeared to William unsuitable, although an excellent singer. Gerald English made Pandarus into a sensitive study of mercurial behaviour, and Benjamin Luxon was a strong Diomede.

During that month William seemed to get weaker by the day. He retired more and more from the world around us. At the end he could hardly stand on his feet, and twice lost his balance and fell on the floor of the hotel. After the final performance, greeted as usual with a triumphant ovation, we invited the cast and a few friends to supper at the Garrick Club. William looked miserable, and collapsed before the end of the meal. He was unable to stand or walk and only with difficulty did we get him back to the hotel.

Our doctor recommended that William have a brainscan, fearing he might have suffered a slight stroke. The scan showed that this was not so, but that his blood circulation had become severely restricted. The doctor told me William was so ill that I should consider institutionalizing him. I could hardly believe my ears. Next morning we set off back to Italy.

The sea was too rough to cross over to Ischia. For three whole days, while we waited in a hotel in Naples for the weather to clear, William slept. Back on Ischia, our local doctor prescribed a glucose drip. By telephone, Michael Kremer, the well-known London neurosurgeon, prescribed ritalin. Alas, it was banned in Italy, because young people had discovered that in liquid form the drug was a powerful narcotic. I was in despair. Then a friend suddenly arrived from Switzerland with a large supply. It was some time before we discovered that this friend had been sent to Ischia with the medicine by Walter Legge.

Alas, the agonizing nightmare was not yet over. Reale, our housekeeper, gave William daily injections of vitamin B_{12}, but William's mind had withdrawn from the world. He recognized me, Reale, and our accountant and friend Nino Mattera, but that was all. The doctor in London had given William sleeping-pills, which were having a terrible effect. He began having hallucinations of being burned alive in an aeroplane he was being forced to pilot, or of being eaten alive by insects. It would take quite a time to wake him and convince him that he was in his own bed and not in a burning plane. Only by massaging his legs could I prove to him that he was not being attacked by insects. One night he almost choked to death; only by violently pounding him on the back did I manage to wake him and prevent him from choking. I threw the sleeping-pills out. Our local doctor prescribed, instead, a gentle draught used for children.

We lived for weeks in our bedroom. William slept most of the time, and I sat by the window and embroidered. He refused to go near his music room, and told friends who visited how sad it was that he had been unable to see the revival of *Troilus* in London, as he had fallen on the stage and hit his head and had thus been prevented from attending. Even as he began to recover, I dared not leave him alone. If he tried to get up from a chair without help, he was liable to fall.

It took him three months to recover. Nature had protected him from the disappointment of recalling the treatment meted out to his beautiful work with what I believe was a serious nervous breakdown. But he did recover. Probably Ischia speeded that recovery, because of both the mild climate and the comforts of the house we had built, as well as all the loving care with which Reale and I cushioned him.

20

Final Tributes

WILLIAM became increasingly delicate. A hazardous visit to London planned to celebrate the success of a second biographical film, this time by London Weekend Television, was, in fact, spent mostly in bed with sciatica and bronchitis. He began to lose weight because a hiatus hernia made it difficult and painful for him to swallow food. His weight dropped to only 62 kilograms, less than 10 stone. None the less, he continued to compose. With the aid of a powerful magnifying glass, after months and months of torture, he managed to finish a piece he had promised Rostropovich, *Prologo and Fantasia*. Rostropovich had asked all his composer friends to write something for the National Symphony Orchestra, of which he was now principal conductor. William felt great distress that an artist like Rostropovich should have been deprived of his nationality when he was expelled from the Soviet Union; he felt that to be an unwilling exile was an unnecessary strain on the life of any artist. For this reason he was determined to finish the composition, despite the physical hardship that writing caused him. In fact, it made him miserable. The cataracts in his eyes grew worse, and his blue eyes no longer shone with glee. But we were always together, and he loved being taken out for drives up little-known paths on the island. He continued to walk down our drive every day to collect the post from the gatehouse, and leisurely walks on our paths on the hill still attracted him on sunny days.

In William's eightieth year the Queen asked us to lunch for a gathering of all holders of the Order of Merit. The eminent twenty-four now incredibly included five of William's close friends: Henry Moore, Kenneth Clark, Solly Zuckerman, Fred Ashton, and Larry Olivier. William kept telling me that he did not want to travel; his birthday could be celebrated without him, he said. But he did want to lunch with the Queen, and when he discovered that Slava Rostropovich and his National Symphony Orchestra were on a European tour at the same time and would première the Prologo and Fantasia at their concert in the Royal Festival Hall, he was tempted to go.

He was apprehensive about the new work, and kept wondering what it would sound like, so I took the plunge and booked our old room at the Savoy. We flew to London for the weekend of 20 February, and William was pleased to be able to hear the piece he had suffered so much to produce and was reassured by Slava saying that it was exciting and full of vigour and sounded as if it had been written by a young man.

Three weeks later, on 14 March, we flew back to London. Slava had decided to perform the Passacaglia for Solo Cello which William had written for him in 1980, but which he had never played. This work was the belated result of an exchange between them at the Aldeburgh Festival some years before. William had asked Slava when he would play his Cello Concerto, and the reply had been: 'You write me new work, and I will play new work and old work.' William was relieved that Rostropovich was now playing 'new work', and hoped that 'old work' would follow soon. At the concert, with the London Philharmonic, the whole orchestra sat in their places in silence while Rostropovich brought on his cello and played the Passacaglia, not once, but twice, as a birthday greeting. This produced an enormous ovation. William dropped to his knees in his box, and crept out on all fours so as to get to his wheelchair without being noticed and to be taken down to hug Slava. Rostropovich was meanwhile running up the back stairs to save William from coming down. When they finally met, there was much laughter and tears. Even at that time the wheelchair was used only in concert halls and airports; at home he managed happily on his feet with the aid of a walking-stick.

To avoid William becoming exhausted by his fans and friends in London before the great events, we decided to rest quietly in the country, and spent a week with Brian and Ulli de Breffny at Castletown Cox, their house in Ireland. There William seemed very well and in excellent spirits. He reminisced to friends abut a previous visit to Ireland in 1974, when his *Cantico del Sole* had been performed at the Cork Music Festival, and how on that occasion we had met the ninety-year-old veteran Irish statesman Éamon de Valera, and visited many beautiful gardens in the south-west.

While we were at Castletown Cox William was very touched by the visit of young musicians from the North-east Ulster Schools Symphony Orchestra. Their leader, David Little, had been a student of William's brother Noel, and is a fervent admirer of William's work. He drove from the extreme north of Ireland to the south with three young performers so that they could see and greet the maestro. They presented William with a crystal carafe.

On the evening of 29 March both the Philharmonia and the London Symphony Orchestra had arranged to celebrate William's birthday with a concert, the former at the Royal Festival Hall with Princess Alexandra in attendance, the latter at the Barbican. As it was impossible to be present at both concerts we attended a rehearsal of the London Symphony Orchestra's concert, with Nabuco Imai playing the Viola Concerto, after which William blew out the candles of a huge cake that was presented to him, and we went to the actual performance of the Philharmonia at the Festival Hall with André Previn conducting the Violin Concerto played by Kyung-Wha Chung, and *Belshazzar's Feast*, with Thomas Allen as soloist. The ovation was overwhelming.

William was in tears, and begged me to make the audience stop. 'They have gone mad,' he said. He simply could not believe that all those people had bought tickets just to see him and let him know how much they loved him and his music. Eventually he stood to acknowledge the applause. Princess Alexandra helped me to keep William standing, as his legs had started to tremble. After the concert there was a lovely reception and supper at the Festival Hall, hosted by both the *Observer* and the OUP.

It was a very busy week. On 1 April we drove to Windsor Castle with Larry Olivier for the OM luncheon given by the Queen and the Duke of Edinburgh. At Westminster Abbey Simon Preston and the Abbey choir performed William's *Te*

Deum. William declared that this was his favourite birthday concert. On Sunday, 28 March, Edward Heath gave us dinner and after held a reception for William. The Royal Society of Arts gave a luncheon. Sir John Tooley for Covent Garden asked us to dine at the Garrick Club. At the end of the week we went to stay with old friends in Suffolk to recover.

On our return to London — we were flying to Ischia the next day—I went to see my own doctor for a quick check-up. When I arrived back in our hotel room, I found that William had been sick and, too weak to sit up in bed, had choked on his vomit. He was rushed to St Thomas's Hospital, almost opposite the Savoy—just in time, as his heart had stopped.

They kept him in the intensive care unit for a whole week. My darling was full of tubes and drips and was wired permanently into all sorts of machines and a respirator. A pump was installed to feed a milky substance into his stomach, the equivalent of 2,000 calories every twelve hours.

At first the doctors thought that his hiatus hernia had haemorrhaged, and that that was why he had been sick. But no sign of a haemorrhage could be found. I was only allowed to see him for a few minutes twice a day; I noticed that his heart machine would flutter wildly the moment he heard my voice, despite the sedation. Great tears would stream from his eyes while he tried repeatedly to say a word, which I took to be 'horrible'. The expert treatment saved his life, but he was still distressed and weak. He believed that he had actually got back to Ischia and had fallen ill there, so he was astonished, as he told me, how well the nurses spoke English!

He hated the hospital food, so I fed him with delicacies from Fortnum's, or what I could cook myself. Strawberries and asparagus were his favourites. When the time came for me to leave in the evening, he would start having nightmares and become confused. He would try desperately to leave with me, furious to be left behind, and absurdly suspicious of what mischief I might get up to on my own.

Mercifully, he recovered enough to permit us to return to Italy. Dr Still, our neighbour on Ischia, sent us his private jet for the journey as a birthday offering. This was an enormous boon. We had never been transported in a private jet before. A car drove us right on to the tarmac, skirting the tails of the jumbos parked nearby. The pilot and his wife, the co-pilot, were expecting us, so we just settled into our seats and relaxed. William was amused to see this tiny plane in the take-off queue behind the huge 747s, and once airborne, the co-pilot, 'a delightful young woman,' William noticed, brought us a tray of delicate patés and smoked-turkey sandwiches with a bottle of wine. In only two and a half hours we landed in Naples, where our driver came to collect us in his limousine and took us home. What luxury!

We reached Ischia in time for a local tribute. The authorities had organized a concert in the castle of Ischia. *Façade* was performed by the Koenig Ensemble conducted by Jan Latham-Koenig, with Marghanita Laski and Jack Buckley as the speakers. The Tony Palmer film of William's life was shown, and an exhibition of photographs lined the walls. This was to be the last time William heard his music live.

William was well enough on 22 July to accept Tony Palmer's invitation for us to play the parts of the king and queen of Bavaria in his television film *Wagner*. Tony brought his crew to Ischia, and, in front of a backdrop set up on our terrace, William, in a military jacket, was filmed, doing a splendid impersonation of himself falling asleep while listening to Wagner's music. I stood at his side in regal attire. Having Tony and his crew at the house reminded us of the happy days when he had made the eloquent film *At the Haunted End of the Day*, a panorama of William's life.

William was still determined to improve his sight. His health improved greatly, and he decided to risk returning to London for a cataract operation. The operation on the first eye was a complete success; but after the second one, he was brought from the operating theatre blue and hardly breathing. It took me an hour to persuade the clinic to take William into intensive care. I feel sure that otherwise he would have died. Again, we were very lucky.

I was beginning to feel ill with nerves after all these horrible experiences. William would never let me out of his sight. If I went into the garden to talk to the gardener, Reale would come out minutes later to tell me that William was calling for me: 'Il Maestro la vuole.' While I sat embroidering, close to his armchair, he used to surprise me by calling out 'Darling' unexpectedly, and for no other reason, he said, than to see me smile. His sight returned to both eyes.

As Christmas 1982 approached, William and I rejoiced in the thought that, with the eightieth-birthday celebrations and the cataract operations over, we need never again make the effort to travel far from home. It was now time to allow the music to speak for itself, he said. We felt safe, rejoiced over being together, able to enjoy our joint creation, La Mortella.

I arranged to spend the Christmas holidays in Ravello, on the mainland, because I thought William would be pleased to be surrounded by happy memories of his youth. I had also asked Prue,* William's current favourite, and her husband, 'the gentle Eric' as William called him, to join us. Knowing the pleasure that seeing Prue would have given William's susceptible heart, I was taken aback by his vigorous rejection of the plan. I realized too late that he felt exhausted, physically too weak to be sociable or even to enjoy leaving the island. I resolved never again to organize an outing unless he suggested it. He thought I might be hurt if we did not go to Ravello, so he agreed to come, provided I promised not to drive the car. So I asked the driver we often used, to take us to the Hotel Palumbo in Ravello in his comfortable limousine, while the Penns drove from Rome airport to meet us for a late supper. After that, William did not stir outside the hotel. He left our guests to admire the country-side alone. He seemed to enjoy his friends' company, but he was delighted when their visit was over, 'to be left alone at last,' he said. He became convinced that he had not long to live.

William, who had always slept in a darkened room, now insisted on my leaving the curtains open at night. He became obsessed with the need to have me close to him all the time, and could only go to sleep if I was hugging him.

For the last twenty years I had been embroidering a large wall panel, and William, seeing that I had only about two years' work left to complete it, told me that he intended to live to see it finished. I replied that I hoped *I* would live to finish it.

At the beginning of March we finally paid off our last debt for

* Wife of Sir Eric Penn, Comptroller, Lord Chamberlain's Office, née Prudence Stewart-Wilson.

the improvement of the property. This debt had weighed heavily on William during those last years. We were looking forward to constructing Russell Page's gift for William's eightieth birthday, a new fountain for the garden, octagonal in shape, placed within another octagon, the area to be paved in large blocks of granite from Mount Vesuvius. It was to be linked to the lower, existing fountain by a rivulet which William could already visualize cascading down the valley walk. He had been asking for this feature to be added, and on the very morning of his near-fatal collapse in London, Russell Page had brought the drawings to the Savoy.

On the morning of 8 March William awoke early, feeling unwell and breathing only with difficulty. This had happened once before, but he had recovered immediately when our local doctor had given him an injection. I telephoned the doctor; it was only 6.30 a.m., and I hoped he would not yet have left for his duties at the hospital. The doctor rushed over, and reassured us by giving William a gentle booster for his heart. He told him to lie back in comfort, and that in five minutes he would feel better. Reale and I propped William up on some pillows, and, while I held him tightly in my arms, he said, 'Don't leave me, please don't leave me.' The doctor was filling out a prescription for a cylinder of oxygen to be brought from the hospital to ease the breathing, when, suddenly, William was shaken by a slight tremor, and died.

Reale and I looked at each other, and up at the doctor, in blank amazement. He had only just told us not to worry, and had told William to lie back and relax. I was frozen in disbelief. Reale now took charge; she suggested that I got out of my night-gown, while she and Maria Esposito, who takes care of our holiday houses, dressed William in a pair of white pyjamas and shut his blue eyes. They then covered the bed with an eighteenth-century embroidered silk brocade bedspread which had belonged to Alice Wimborne. On Ischia the custom is to dress the dead in a suit, shoes, shirt, and tie; but Reale somehow knew that this would have irritated William. She made him look naturally asleep, with his head lifted slightly on a herb cushion.

Before leaving the doctor told us that he would return later to make out the death certificate. It was hard to take in. A flash of hope reawakened in my heart when I kissed William's eyelids, and found them still warm. Strange how swiftly the soul departs, and how long it takes for the body to cool. Don Pietro, priest of the church of Santa Restituta, came to bless William on his death-bed.

The village transmitted the news of William's death by affixing posters to the roadside walls, and I was amused to see that the official poster could not, even then, after all those years, deal with the musician to whom they had given hospitality for over thirty-five years. Could music really be a profession, they always asked? They now played safe by calling him 'an artist'. At my request, another poster asked the villagers not to send flowers or call at the house, as was the local custom. It was the habit on the island, however, to sit with the family of the departed until the next day; but I asked the few young neighbours who had come to hold my hand to leave in the evening. I sat at the foot of our bed, curled up on a Victorian settee, the one Osbert Sitwell had given us as a wedding present, which was covered in the *petit-point* embroidery designed for it at the Royal School of Needlework, my first winter's job on Ischia. The night passed in a flash; in my mind I chatted to William, reviewing our plans for the future of the property and what the William Walton Trust's future activities were to be. I turned my thoughts on the happy chance of our unlikely meeting in Buenos Aires, the several battles with the islanders, how we had cared for our love, and how it had grown more and more. I could see William frowning at the worries and difficulties we had overcome, and remembered how attentive he had always been in keeping me from steering a course of my own too far from his side. I knew he was smiling. We had been so fortunate. Now God had freed him from the obligation of putting his great talents to further use. Was he sad that he could not write the *Stabat Mater* he had decided would be his next effort?

Meanwhile our friends were arguing with the village authorities, who would not sign a permit allowing William's body to be moved to Florence, the nearest town that permitted cremation of a person who had died elsewhere. It took six hours of pestering the officials to cut through the red tape and get the permit signed. Next morning the driver with the hearse came to take the body to Florence, sealed in a metal container in a simple coffin, the car a bower of white magnolia blooms from our garden.

Two friends travelled at once to Ischia from Rome, Jack Buckley and George Mott, who photographed the sheet of music-paper left on the piano with a few notes sketched on it, together with William's rubber, pencil, and spectacles, left there the evening before he died. Today they are still just as William left them.

The cremation ceremony in Florence was gruesome. Our friend, Brian de Breffny, having just returned to his home in Ireland from a holiday in the United States heard the news of William's death over the radio, and telephoned immediately to organize the Hotel de la Ville in Florence, where he arranged for us to spend the night and join friends journeying from London: Tony Palmer, who two years before had made the enchanting film of William's life; Christopher Morris, representing Oxford University Press; Francis Sitwell, the younger son of Sachie, who had offered William hospitality all those years ago; Humphrey Burton, who had arranged the BBC television coverage of the glorious eightieth-birthday celebration; Gillian Widdicombe also came. She had caused William so much disappointment in his last years by not completing and publishing his biography. William had spent many precious hours with Gillian, helping her to write the book and had longed to see the result.

Brian, who was the first to arrive in Florence, coped with the consternation of the hotel staff and management when enormous wreaths were delivered to the foyer just as a wedding reception was about to begin. Not knowing exactly where the crematorium was, I had given the address of the hotel. I arrived by car from Ischia with Jack, George, and Cesare Longo, to join Brian and the others.

The crematorium is high on a hill overlooking Florence, in an area known as Trespiano, on the last and highest terrace above the huge cemetery. I had to sign a few papers, and, while we waited, the official in charge decided that some piped music ought to be played. We had quite a struggle to convince him that this was not necessary. He was even more baffled and offended when Gillian asked for a last look at William's face. Unfortunately, I was so distraught and confused that I agreed. It was now Friday, and the alabaster features that on Tuesday had been such a comfort to gaze upon during our last night together had become discoloured and distorted. William had always been particular about combing his hair very carefully, and I was shocked to see it falling untidily on his forehead. My heart gave a turn; I now faced the knowledge that what William had tried desperately to avoid, had now happened: we were apart for ever.

Finally the coffin was closed again. We strolled up and down the terrace, enveloped in a ghastly smoke. Steven Wikner, a young musician who had been at OUP promoting William's music, had travelled all night by train from London to pay his respects, and now joined us. Later, after a farewell champagne, we returned to collect the urn with William's ashes before driving back home.

Brian came back to Rome with me. Mama and my older brother Harry had come as quickly as they could from Argentina to comfort me. We collected them from the airport and drove to Ischia. Back at La Mortella we gathered in William's music room and listened to his music and to his voice talking on tape. It was agonizingly sad, but cathartic. Brian put me to work at once on all those thank-you letters in response to messages of condolence. He addressed hundreds of envelopes himself, before returning to Rome to attend the première of Lindsay Kemp's production of *Façade* with costumes and scenery by Luzzati. William and I had so looked forward to seeing it. He had been thrilled by Luzzati's witty costumes and scenery, with its cut-outs of Queen Victoria and Alice in Wonderland and the notion that the dancers themselves would recite the poems.

Brian telephoned to say that I must, somehow, get myself to Pisa for the second performance. So, with Mama, I decided to go, just as William and I had originally intended. The British ambassador Lord Bridges and his wife drove up from Rome, and afterwards organized a wonderful dinner at which Lindsay Kemp drew all our portraits on the table-cloth. I was very happy, as happy as William would have been. To begin and end with *Façade* would have seemed to him the most splendid irony. After all, that night would have been his eighty-first birthday. For me, thirty-five exceptional years had gone by.

21

Coda

THE first years of coping with a left-over life have not been easy. The poignant memories of the memorial service in Westminster Abbey, where I unveiled a black stone engraved with William's name in bold white lettering, for ever embedded in the floor of the musicians' corner of the Abbey, followed by Larry Olivier's tribute, the thrilling St Crispin speech from *Henry V*, declaimed in ringing tones from the pulpit, help me to exist without William.

> Wordsworth says:
> The music in my heart I bore
> Long after it was heard no more.

My consolation is to be fortunate enough to be able to continue to hear his music, which is often performed, disclaiming William's anxious assertion that he would be forgotten soon after his death. In Ischia he will never be forgotten: he asked to have his ashes kept in his 'stone', as he named the large natural pyramid, once a boundary stone, that towers high above our garden. I carved a space for the urn beneath its conical top, and composed an inscription which reads:

> Sing a song of praise beloved and revered Master
> This rock holds his ashes
> The garden he surveys
> Russell Page designed
> Together we happily brought it to life
> > Susana
>
> 'All Bliss consists in this:
> To do as Adam did.'

The Reverend Charles Cowley, acting chaplain to the British community in Naples, came over to the island to hold the ceremony of dedication, as did the British consul-general, John Church, and his wife, Marie Genevieve. A gay procession wove its way up the hillside, bearing large, coloured parasols to shield us from the July rays: Mama, Brian de Breffny and his daughter Sita-Maria, Colin Graham, Enrico D'Assia, together with other friends and neighbours, Reale, Maria, and the gardeners, headed by me and the consul and his wife, gathered around William's stone. The Reverend Charles Cowley said:

We few gather here to complete that which was begun in *William Turner Walton* in the year of our Lord 1902, and by consecration here to sanctify this place that it may be holy, and by these words to dedicate our love for him to God.

Then, before the final prayer, Colin Graham recited from *Cymbeline*:

> Fear no more the heat o' the sun
> Nor the furious winter's rages:
> Thou thy worldly task hast done,
> Home art gone and ta'en thy wages:
> Golden lads and girls all must,
> As chimney-sweepers, come to dust.

The short ceremony ended with me reading the words inscribed on the memorial stone, after which we all kissed, hugged, and wept, and returned for a cool glass of champagne on the terrace of the home William and I had created. I could sense William also raising his glass, with a chuckle.

I constantly call upon him in my mind, sometimes in a loud voice, to guide me in my efforts to make La Mortella into a handsome living memorial to him. It was always William's wish that after his death and mine the proceeds of the estate should go to promoting his own music and to helping young musicians; he always had in mind that the house could become a place for musicians to live and work. We—the William Walton Trust and its twin, La Fondazione William Walton—are building an Arts Centre beside his music room. A permanent exhibition of photographs to illustrate his life, letters, posters, and other personal memorabilia, as well as video films of his life and of him conducting and records of his music will be available to visitors, who will also be able to enjoy walking through our enchanted garden. Our plan is for part of the Arts Centre to be a recital room, where master classes for young professional musicians will be held. Our friend Yehudi Menuhin plans to play the Sonata for Violin and Piano in the new recital hall. Thus the first work William composed on Ischia will inaugurate the hall. Margaret Price, Rostropovich, and other artists have expressed enthusiasm about the project and their willingness to participate.

William wished his manuscripts to be kept together as a collection, and Mr Frederick Koch of New York has made this possible by buying them and loaning them to the Pierpont Morgan Library in New York. A number of original manuscripts have been lost over the years, and I shall continue to search for them indefatigably. Collecting his letters has become my obsession. To read his unmistakable handwriting brings him almost physically alive, and I can again smile at his turn of phrase. Writing this book has reminded me of endless happy and a few sad moments of our life together, all of which I cherish. As Terry Rattigan has said so well:

> What makes magic is genius,
> and what makes genius
> is the infinite capacity for taking pains!

And pains I shall continue to take in my endeavour to see a growing love of William and his music spread, and our creation La Mortella known and admired.

I am fortunate still to have Mama in Buenos Aires, a sustaining beacon, giving me unstinted love and good advice; her high spirits give mine added buoyancy and the determination to follow on. Being with her is a large part of my new life on my own, as is exploring the world, seeing places William and I had dreamed of visiting together, and which I now do in the company of friends. The affection of friends, old and new, and the execution of William's wishes are what will make the remaining years of my life worth enduring.

EX LIBRIS

WILLIAM T. WALTON

APPENDIX A

Desert Island Discs

WILLIAM appeared twice on the BBC radio programme 'Desert Island Discs', during which the 'castaway' is invited to choose the eight records he would most like to hear on his desert island. Walton's choice is not an absolute guide to his musical tastes, but it reveals some amusing (and predictable) quirks.

A. 22 JULY 1965

Stravinsky, *Pulcinella* (ballet after Pergolesi).

Mozart, Piano Concerto No. 19 in F major, K. 459.

Beethoven, Piano Sonata No. 29 in B flat major ('Hammerklavier').

Hans Werner Henze, 'A l'acqua de liffuntanelle' (No. 2 of Five Neapolitan Songs).

Bellini, 'Come per me sereno' (from *La sonnambula*).

Debussy, 'Pour invoquer Pan, dieu du vent d'été (No. 1 of *Six Epigraphes Antiques*).

Schoenberg, Variations for Orchestra.

Walton, Symphony No. 2.

B. 2 APRIL 1982

Samuel Wesley, 'The Wilderness'.

Mozart, Piano Concerto in A major, K. 488.

Walton, 'Old Sir Faulk' (from *Façade*).

Walton, Violin Concerto.

Sibelius, Symphony No. 5.

Puccini, *Tosca*.

Hans Werner Henze, Five Neapolitan Songs.

Walton, *Belshazzar's Feast*.

Walton Missing Manuscripts

(list compiled by Stewart R. Craggs)

		Thematic catalogue reference (1977)
The Winds: song for voice and piano (1918–21)	vocal score	SRC p. 44
Quartet for Piano and Strings (1918–21)	full score	SRC pp. 45–8
The Passionate Shepherd: song for tenor voice and 10 instruments (1918–21)	full/vocal score	SRC p. 49
Dr Syntax: pedagogic overture for full orchestra (1918–21)	full score	SRC p. 50
Façade: an entertainment for reciter and chamber ensemble: the following have not been traced: Tango Pasodoble: I do like to be	full score	
A Man from a Far Countree	full score	
Yodelling Song (1926 version)	full score	SRC pp. 51–71
Bucolic Comedies: five songs (1923)	vocal score	SRC p. 76
Fantasia Concertante: for two pianos, jazz band, and orchestra (1923)	full score	SRC p. 76
A Son of Heaven: incidental music to the play by Lytton Strachey (1925)	full score	SRC p. 78
Siesta: for small orchestra (1926)	full score	SRC p. 79
Belshazzar's Feast: cantata for baritone solo, mixed chorus, and orchestra (1931)	full score vocal score	SRC pp. 88–91
Make we joy now in this Fest: old English carol (1931)	vocal score	SRC p. 92

Walton Missing Manuscripts

		Thematic catalogue reference (1977)
Three Songs: for voice and piano (1932)	vocal score	SRC pp. 93–5
Escape me never: music for the film (1935)		
Church music	full score	
Ballet music (piano)	score	
Ballet music (orchestral + 6 sections)	full score	
Playout music	full score	SRC pp. 96–7
The First Shoot: ballet (1935)	piano score	
	full score	SRC pp. 102–3
As you Like It: music for the film (1936)		
Duke's march in	full score	
Fanfares Nos. 1 and 2	full score	
Fanfare No. 3	full score	
Fanfare No. 4	full score	
Duke's march out	full score	
2nd Rosalind theme	full score	
3rd Rosalind theme	full score	
Corridor background music	full score	
Weeping music	full score	
What shall he have?	vocal score	
Escape music	full score	
Flute solo behind Adam	score	
Dreams and Moonlight music	full score	
There was a lover	vocal score	
Tell me where is fancy bred	vocal score	
Choral ballet	full/vocal score	
Fanfare end of ballet	full score	SRC pp. 104–5
The Boy David: incidental music to the play by J. M. Barrie (1936)	full score	SRC pp. 105–6
Dreaming Lips: music for the film (1937)		
all items	full score	SRC p. 110
In Honour of the City of London: cantata for mixed chorus and orchestra (1937)	full score	
	vocal score (part)	SRC pp. 110–11

Appendix B

		Thematic catalogue reference (1977)
Set me as a Seal: anthem for unaccompanied mixed chorus (1938)	vocal score	SRC p. 112
A Stolen Life: music for the film (1939) all items	full score	SRC p. 113
Concerto for Violin and Orchestra, original version (1939)	full score	SRC pp. 113–16
The Wise Virgins: ballet in one act (1940)	piano score full score	SRC pp. 121–2
Scapino: comedy overture for full orchestra, original version (1940)	full score	SRC pp. 123–5
Major Barbara: music for the film (1940) all items	full/vocal score	SRC pp. 125–6
Next of Kin: music for the film (1941) all items	full score	SRC p. 126
The Foreman went to France: music for the film (1942) all items	full score	SRC pp. 128–9
The First of the Few: music for the film (1942) all items	full score	SRC p. 129
Went the Day well?: music for the film (1942) all items	full score	SRC p. 133
Red Army Fanfares (1943)	full score	SRC p. 134
Henry V: music for the film (1944) all items (full score) except: Titles 11B and 11C Charge and Battle The Sun doth gild Several fanfares		SRC pp. 140–1

242

		Thematic catalogue reference (1977)

Hamlet: music for the film (1948)
all items (full score) except:
  Funeral March
  Something is rotten
  Oh that this too too solid
  O cursed Sprite
  Hamlet and Ophelia
  To be or not to be
  Ophelia by the stream
  The Death of Ophelia
		SRC pp. 153–4

Sonata for Violin and Piano (1949)	score	SRC pp. 157–9
Two Pieces for Violin and Piano (1951)	score	SRC pp. 160–2
The Star-spangled Banner *God Save the Queen* (1955)	vocal score full score	 SRC p. 186

What Cheer? Christmas carol for
  unaccompanied mixed chorus
  (1961)
	vocal score	SRC p. 209

The Battle of Britain: music for the
  film (1969)
  Air Battle
	
	full score
		
		SRC p. 239

Three Sisters: music for the film
  (1970)
  Title music
  Dream sequence
  End titles
	
	full score
	full score
	full score
		
		SRC p. 242

Index

Index

Berlioz, Hector, 68;
  references to works: Harold in Italy, 68
Berne Convention on Copyright, 4
Berners, Gerald, 50, 50n, 52, 110
Bernstein, Leonard, 180;
  references to works: West Side Story, 180
Berthoud, Roger, 127
Beverley Hills Hotel (Los Angeles), 140
Bliss, Ambassador, 158
Bliss, Arthur, 65, 88, 192, 210;
  references to works: The Olympians, 193
Bloomer Girl, 26
Boccaccio, Giovanni, 135
Boldini, 110
Bologna (Italy), 119, 128
Bonaparte, Joseph, 19
Bonaparte, Napoleon, 19
Bonnie Prince Charlie, 165
Boosey, Leslie, 1, 2, 4, 6, 9, 182
Boosey and Hawkes Ltd., 36, 63, 126, 133, 146
Boston Symphony Orchestra, 163
Boulanger, Nadia, 214
Boulevard Solitude, 118
Boult, Adrian, 51
Bower, Dallas, 93, 94, 95
Brahms, Johannes, 84
Bream, Julian, 184, 197, 205
Breffny, Brian de, 226, 233, 234, 236
Breffny, Sita-Maria de, 236
Breffny, Ulli de, 226
Bridges, Thomas E., 234
Brindisi (Italy), 137
British Broadcasting Corporation (BBC), 68,
  71, 72, 94, 135, 193, 202, 233
British Council, The, 1, 9, 11, 14, 28, 29, 88,
  89, 90, 91, 97, 125, 217
Britten, Benjamin, 1, 2, 36, 37, 63, 122, 123–
  126, 131, 132, 133, 186, 197, 202, 205, 206,
  208, 216;
  references to works: Cello Symphony, 208;
  Concerto for Piano and Orchestra, 126;
  Gloriana, 131, 132; Peter Grimes, 122, 125,
  133; Simple Symphony, 206; Variations on
  a Theme by Frank Bridge, 124–125
Brown, Carlyle, 114
Brown, Marjorie, 114
Browning, Gareth, 116
Brubeck, Dave, 179
Buckingham Palace, 41, 132
Buckley, Jack, 60, 217, 229, 233
Budberg, Moura, 186
Buenos Aires (Argentina), 1, 3, 4, 6, 7, 9, 11,
  15, 16, 21, 26, 27, 28, 29, 32, 34, 38, 97, 101,
  158, 194, 214, 232, 237
Bundy, William, 222
Burton, Humphrey, 233

Busoni, Ferruccio, 48, 52

Caesarea (Israel), 191
Callas, Maria, 154, 155
Callot, Jacques, 174
Camargo Society, 132
Capodicchino Airport (Naples), 170
Capote, Truman, 113
Capri (Italy), 5, 16, 38, 101, 218
Carlyle Square (London), 46, 51, 52, 53, 56, 57,
  58, 62, 70, 82
Carnavon, Lord 185–186
Carnegie Hall (New York), 157, 205
Caruso, Enrico, 11
Casa Cirillo (Ischia), 107, 109, 112, 118, 119,
  136, 151, 158, 167, 169, 199
Casamicciola (Ischia), 111
Casa Rosada (Buenos Aires), 26
Casati, Anna Maria, 110
Casati, Camillo, 110, 116, 155, 158
Casati, Lidia, 110, 116, 155, 158
Casati, Luisa, 110
Cassilly, Richard, 223
Casson, Hugh, 213
Castaldi, Pasquale, 104, 105, 106, 107, 108,
  109, 112, 137
Castelbarco, Contessa, 155
Catania (Sicily), 172
Chandler, Miss, 98
Chaplin, Viscount, 196, 196n
Charles, Prince of Wales, 72, 217
Chaucer, Geoffrey, 135
Chekhov, Anton, 63, 181, 197;
  references to works: Three Sisters, 63
Chenil Galleries (Chelsea), 59, 64
Chicago Symphony Orchestra, 178, 193
Child, Amando, 37, 98
Chorlton-cum-Hardy (Lancs), 41
Christ Church (Oxford), 42, 43, 45, 64, 181,
  216
Chung, Kyung-Wha, 217, 227
Church, John, 236
Church, Marie Genevieve, 236
Church of San Martin de Tours (Buenos
  Aires), 13
Ciano, Galeazzo, 118
Civitavecchia (Italy), 165
Clanwilliam, Earl of, 120
Clark, Colette, 214
Clark, Colin, 184, 214
Clark, Edward, 68, 70
Clark, Jane, 32, 34, 35, 213–215
Clark, Kenneth, 32n, 34, 213–215, 225
Cleveland (Ohio), 91
Cleveland Orchestra, 157, 178

246

Index

Index

Index

Little, David, 227

Lockhart, James, 201, 202

Logroñe (Spain), 20

London Clinic, 87, 198–199

London Evening Standard, 82

London Philharmonic Orchestra, 219, 226

London Sinfonietta, 210

London Symphony Orchestra, 32, 69, 80, 84, 205, 206, 207, 217, 227

London Weekend Television, 202, 225

Longo, Cesare, 173, 174, 233

Lopokova, Lydia, 132

Loren, Sophia, 103

Louisville (Kentucky), 26

Lousada, Anthony, 152

Lousada, Jocelyn, 152

Lowndes Cottage (Belgravia), 32, 33, 38, 49, 55, 80, 97, 101, 132, 140, 150, 166, 167, 176, 192, 193, 212, 214, 215

Lucas, Brenda, 185

Lucia, 118

Luciano, Lucky, 170

Ludwig of Hesse, Prince, 186

Ludwig of Hesse, Princess, 186

Luigi, 102

Luxon, Benjamin, 223

Luzzati, Emanuele, 234

Lyceum Theatre (London), 55

McEacharn, Neil, 75, 79

Mackie, William, 130

MacPherson, Amy, 71

Mafalda, Princess, 112

Maltings, The (Snape), 123

Manaos (Brazil), 25

Manchester City News, 42

Mankiewicz, Joseph, 140

Mansion House (City of London), 126

Mappin, Constance, 117

Maraini, Dascia, 117

Marcello, Benedetto, 42;
references to works: O Lord, Our Governor, 42

Margarita, 11

Maria Carolina of Sicily, 172

Marie Antoinette, 172

Marino (Italy), 188

Markova, Alicia, 132

Marret, Mrs, 100, 105

Mary, Princess Royal, 37

Masefield, John, 52

Mason, Colin, 179

Massine, Leonid, 12

Mathias, Mrs Robert, 58

Mattera, Nino, 115, 176, 224

Maugham, Robin, 152, 152n, 153, 186, 194

Maugham, Somerset, 152n

Maw, Nicholas, 215

Melba, Nellie, 11

Mengelberg, W., 83

Mennella, Ella, 203

Mennella, Francesca, 203

Mennella, Peppino, 203

Mennella, Reale, 203, 221, 224, 229, 231, 236

Menotti, Gian Carlo, 153

Menuhin, Diana, 122–123

Menuhin, Yehudi, 122–123, 215, 237

Messel, Oliver, 128

Miami (USA), 25

Middlesex Hospital, 198–199, 200

Milhaud, Darius, 57, 154;
references to works: David, 154

Millington-Drake, Eugene, 12

Mills, Florence, 54

Mimi, Aunt, 20

Mitropoulous, Dimitri, 153

Modane (France), 48

Monreale (Sicily), 171

Montague, Arthur, 3, 28, 29

Montague Square (London), 58

Montale, Eugenio, 153

Monte Carlo, 101

Monte Mario (Rome), 165

Montegufoni (Italy), 61, 101, 102

Montevideo (Uruguay), 22

Moore, Garrett, 35, 35n, 79, 151–152, 187

Moore, Gerald, 123

Moore, Henry, 35, 212–213, 225;
references to works: Madonna and Child, 213

Moore, Joan, 151

Morante, Elsa, 117

Moravia, Alberto, 117

Morley, Christopher, 222

Moroni, Fausto, 188–189

Morris, Christopher, 233

Morrison, Angus, 53, 54, 57, 77, 78, 82

Mortimer, Raymond, 47

Moscow (USSR), 208, 209

Motion, Andrew, 55n

Mott, George, 233

Munch, Charles, 163

Museum of Modern Art (Buenos Aires), 6

Musical Times, The, 83

'Musician of the Year', 181

Mussolini, Anna Maria, 117

Mussolini, Benito, 60, 118

Mussolini, Edda, 118

Muzio, Claudia, 12

Nalda (Spain), 20

Naming of Wild Flowers, The, 116

Naples (Italy), 32, 101, 102, 103, 106, 108, 113,

250

Index

Index

Index

Index

Index